The Archaeology of the Medieval Cathedral and Priory of St Mary, Coventry

The Archaeology of the Medieval Cathedral and Priory of St Mary, Coventry

By Margaret Rylatt and Paul Mason

With contributions by Trevor Anderson, J Andrews, Philip Armitage,
Paul Blinkhorn, Wendy Carruthers, Vanessa Clarke, George Demidowicz,
Zenon Demidowicz, Miriam Gill, Tim Hallam, Richard K Morris
and Iain Soden

Published by
City Development Directorate
Coventry City Council

First published in the United Kingdom in 2003 by City Development Directorate,
Coventry City Council, Civic Centre 4, Much Park Street, Coventry CV1 2PY

ISBN 0-9546187-0-X

This book is available direct from

Oxbow Books, Park End Place, Oxford, OX1 1HN
(*Phone:* 01865 241249   *Fax:* 01865 794449)

Herbert Art Gallery & Museum, Jordan Well, Coventry, CV1 5QP
(*Phone:* 02476 832286   *Fax:* 02476 832410)

Cover illustration: Reconstruction of the west end of the cathedral nave
(*reproduced courtesy of MindWave Media*)

Designed, printed and bound in Great Britain by
Short Run Press
Exeter

Contents

List of Figures

(All illustrations and photographs by employees of Coventry City Council and Northamptonshire Archaeology unless otherwise stated)

List of Plates

Plate 1

(a) Architectural fragment from nave with stencilled *fleur-de-lys*

(b) Architectural fragment from refectory pulpit with polychromy

(c) Tiled floor from refectory – as excavated

(d) Tiled floor from refectory – re-assembled

Plate 2

(a) Carved head-stop/corbel from nave

(b) Carved head-stop from refectory undercroft

(c) Carved head-stop from refectory undercroft

(d) Carved head-stop from refectory undercroft

(e) Carved head-stop/corbel from refectory undercroft

(f) Carved head-stop/corbel from north-south undercroft

Plate 3

(a) Chapter house blind arcade stone with painting

(b) Detail of 'Apocalypse' panel
     (*photo Richard K Morris*)

(c) Chapter house blind arcade stone with painting

(d) Detail of 'Apocalypse' panel

Plate 4

(a) Reconstruction of exterior west front of cathedral
     (*reproduced courtesy of MindWave Media*)

(b) Reconstruction of interior east end of chapter house
     (*reproduced courtesy of MindWave Media*)

Foreword

This report details the astonishing findings of the archaeologists during their excavations on the site of the Phoenix Initiative. I don't think any of us, even in our wildest dreams, dared to anticipate the magnificence of what we were about to discover when we put our first spade in the ground.

As the Priory was slowly revealed, sometimes intact, sometimes in pieces, we began to realise the importance of the work to ourselves, to the project, to the city and to the country as a whole. Each revelation was a joy and a nightmare! Detailed designs were changed again and again to accommodate our findings. The cost increased two fold, then three fold and finally four times more than we first anticipated. Was it worth it? Of course it was.

To reveal the standing remains of the Priory for the public to appreciate and enjoy became one of the project's priorities. To construct a twenty-first century building on top of parts of the Priory Undercroft in such a way that the public can view and enjoy the splendour of the work of the thirteenth-century masons is a triumph. For this undercroft to return to its original position but beneath a building 800 years later than the original is a master-stroke.

To carefully record and to accommodate all the valuable stone in the site from which it was first excavated is a tribute to the respect of the archaeologists, the design team and the project team for history in the making.

The Priory Visitor Centre now displays an extensive range of artefacts, masonry, tiles and glass from the Priory. Carved heads, parts of statues, parts of a pulpit, painted glass, hand made floor tiles and the beautiful fragment of wall painting from the arcading in the Chapter House. Visitors to the centre can view the craft of masons from three ages in the rear wall. The thirteenth-century north nave wall, supporting the seventeenth-century boundary wall, in turn supporting the twenty-first century wall is now the rear wall of the visitor centre.

When this project started I was ignorant of the value of archaeology. I would never claim to be an expert but the little knowledge I have gained through the life of the project has been a fascinating glimpse into the past.

You can only truly know where you are going when you know where you came from.

Chris Beck
Project Director
The Phoenix Initiative

Introduction

The popular adage 'third time lucky' would have been an apt motto for the builders of Coventry's modern cathedral, St Michael's. Consecrated in 1962, it became the third cathedral to serve the city, replacing the ruined shell of its predecessor of only twenty years, infamously destroyed during the Blitz of 1940. Far less well known but subjected to an equally catastrophic fate was the City's first cathedral, St Mary's, whose size and magnificence would have cast both of its successors into the shade. Its origins are closely intertwined with Coventry's most famous citizens, Earl Leofric and Lady Godiva. They founded an abbey on the site which was consecrated in 1043. By the middle of the thirteenth century, if not earlier, the original foundation had been completely replaced by a great medieval cathedral and Benedictine priory. These were destroyed as a result of Henry VIII's Dissolution of the Monasteries in 1539 when Coventry became the only city in the realm to lose its cathedral. The ensuing centuries saw the ruined buildings disappear from the landscape as the city around it changed, resulting in its very existence slipping from popular memory, a sad fate for a religious institution which had dominated the spiritual and secular life of the city for some 500 years.

The 950th anniversary of its dedication was commemorated in September 1993 by a symposium which focused primarily on the medieval cathedral. The outcome of the symposium was the identification of a number of themes for research relating to both the cathedral and the conventual buildings. It was agreed that many of these could only be addressed through archaeological excavation. At the time, it could not have been envisaged that within four years Coventry's Millennium Project (The Phoenix Initiative) would present archaeologists with the opportunity and finance to address many of the academic priorities identified.

The Phoenix Initiative was conceived to link two of the major attractions in the city centre, the Cathedrals Quarter and the Museum of British Road Transport. Between these landmarks the restoration of two historic buildings, Blue Coat School and a nineteenth-century silk ribbon-weaving factory,

was planned. In addition, four new public spaces, a development of cafes, bars, retail outlets and housing and a visitor centre were to be built. These proposals involved cutting a great swathe through the site of St Mary's Priory including the nave of the cathedral, the cloister, chapter house and other conventual buildings.

From the outset, the preservation and recording of the archaeology of this important monastic site was recognised as being a major requirement of the scheme. This was particularly relevant for the Priory Gardens which were planned for the site of the cathedral nave. Here full-scale excavation was needed to determine the positions of surviving architectural features and thus inform the design of the garden. Elsewhere, the archaeological work would take the form of evaluation trenches and watching briefs in accordance with planning guidelines. The importance of establishing levels of survival was underlined by the desire to preserve remains *in situ*. With this in mind a number of evaluation trenches were excavated in 1997-9, initially focusing on the site of the nave of the cathedral, as this was where the initial phase of the development would commence.

An assessment of the cathedral remains was complicated by the fact that they were buried below a disused eighteenth/nineteenth-century graveyard belonging to Holy Trinity Church. An evaluation by Wessex Archaeology in 1997 was undertaken to establish the depth of the medieval archaeology and to locate one of the pier bases of the north aisle (Oakey & Andrews 1998). The second and third piers from the west end (piers 2 & 3) were found, thus allowing an estimate of the distance between each pier to be made. This evaluation also assisted in the calculation of the number of eighteenth/nineteenth-century burials likely to be encountered during the major excavation to follow. Further evaluations in 1997 were conducted in the area of the north-west tower to locate the foundations of the north wall of the nave (Rylatt & Thompson 1999). In 1999 an area of the cathedral forecourt against the exterior of the north-west tower was investigated in advance of the restoration and proposed extension to Blue Coat

School (Paul Thompson, forthcoming). The resulting archaeological evidence corroborated post-Dissolution documentary sources which recorded the presence of a sacristan's building in this area (Demidowicz 2000, 12).

The Phoenix Initiative's archaeological scheme was given national television exposure when Channel 4's 'Time Team' (1999 & 2001) and BBC2's 'Meet the Ancestors' (1999) were invited to film on the site. 'Meet the Ancestors' excavated a vault in the eighteenth/nineteenth-century graveyard, belonging to a local family (named Conroy) that had been found during the Wessex evaluation but not disturbed. The Time Team's first visit to the site coincided with the beginning of the large-scale excavations. Trenches were opened in the area of the chapter house and north transept of the cathedral. Almost two years later they returned to film the exceptional discoveries made by Phoenix Initiative archaeologists in the intervening period.

In the summer of 1999 the planned archaeological work began on a large scale under the remit of the Phoenix Initiative. In September 1999 the excavation of the cathedral nave and subsequently part of the claustral north range (2000) were contracted out to Northamptonshire Archaeology. Their first task was to record and remove the burials from the graveyard that overlay the medieval archaeology. Members of the Coventry and District Archaeological Society had previously recorded those gravestones which were to be moved. The excavations encountered thirty-seven brick lined vaults and 1706 articulated inhumations with disarticulated remains spread throughout the grave soils. Based on these figures it was estimated that at least 2500 individuals had been buried in the plot (which measured 47 x 32m/154 x 105ft). All but 100 of the skeletons were re-buried in London Road Cemetery, Coventry, with due ceremony conducted by the Rev David Urquart (formerly of Holy Trinity Church). Those retained were assigned for further study by Dr Jenny Wakely of the University of Leicester.

Phoenix Initiative archaeologists continued to undertake evaluations and watching briefs until the summer of 2003. During this period a significant area of the nave, north transept, cloister, conventual buildings, drainage system and mill were excavated (Fig 1). The complete archive has been deposited in the Herbert Art Gallery and Museum, Coventry.

Acknowledgements

The authors are indebted to Coventry City Council and the Millennium Commission for funding the archaeological programme. Utmost gratitude goes to George Demidowicz, the City Conservation Officer who was responsible for all heritage management matters throughout the project and for ensuring that the requirements of PPG16 were met. Thanks again to George and to Richard Morris and Iain Soden for their continuous support and advice throughout the project and for providing helpful comments on the manuscript. Thanks also to Zenon Demidowicz who undertook the Herculean task of proof reading the final draft. The authors reserve their special thanks to Chris Beck, Phoenix Initiative Project Director and Colin Dale, Phoenix Initiative Project Manager for their continued enthusiasm for the archaeology even when we had to do some hard negotiation for more time and money. We are equally indebted to Suzanne Smith, Phoenix Initiative Office Manager for her helpfulness and camaraderie. Mention must also be made of the following people who gave their expert advice freely on various finds from the excavation: Sally Badham, John Cherry, Miriam Gill, Michael Hinman, David Keen and Jenny Wakely.

For much of the project the archaeological work was undertaken alongside the building contractors. For their co-operation our thanks are extended to Try Construction, Balfour Beatty and Harrabin Construction. Similarly our thanks go to the Cathedral Fabric Committee and the staff from both Coventry Cathedral and Holy Trinity Church. Thanks are also due to the staff of the Herbert Art Gallery and Museum of whom Paul Thompson in particular is thanked for his hard work during the initial phase of the project.

For their role in the archaeological programme the authors are grateful to the management and employees of Northamptonshire Archaeology and Wessex Archaeology.

Thanks to the following staff for their hard work in the field: Adrian Adams, Robert Atkins, Simon Carlyle-Lancaster, Peter Cinquini, Vanessa Clarke, Andrew Crabbe, Sophie Edwards, Jonathan Elston, Rolf Engels, Helen Finnegan, Taleyna Fletcher, Rhiannon Gaskell, Fred Harris, Sam Hemsley, Tim Hallam (supervisor), Erlend Hindmarch (supervisor), Mark Holmes (project officer, Northamptonshire

Archaeology), Marc Hudson, Barry Lewis (supervisor), Mark Lewis, Rowena Lloyd, Sinclair Manson, Jason Marchant, Lisa Marlow, Joe Nikel, David Priestly, John Roberts, Nigel Rowe, Mark Sanderson, Iain Soden (senior project manager, Northamptonshire Archaeology), Paul Thompson (museum's officer, HAGAM), Heidi Tillin, Alex Thorne (supervisor), Steve Thorpe, Tim Upton-Smith, Bryan Walker, Steve Williams and Mark Worrell.

And for their illustrations: Zenon Demidowicz, Cain Heggarty, Barry Lewis, Mark Roughley, Iain Soden and Alex Thorne.

Volunteers, too numerous to name, including members of the Coventry and District Archaeological Society supported the excavation and post-excavation teams. Both Northamptonshire Archaeology and the Phoenix Initiative team are most grateful for their invaluable assistance. Finally thanks to Derek Webb for working over the spoil heaps with his metal detector and recovering a number of small objects which would otherwise have been lost.

1 History

The history of the origins, development and destruction of the Benedictine Priory of St Mary, Coventry, can be readily found in a number of publications including; Poole (1870), Fretton (1876), Burbidge (1952), *VCH Warks.* 2 (1965), *VCH Warks.* 8 (1969), Lambert (1971) and Demidowicz (1994). Primary sources referenced in the footnotes of these works. However, a detailed examination of these histories reveals a number of inconsistencies regarding key dates and interpretation of early events. Therefore a re-assessment of the primary sources and the presentation of all the evidence in one publication would be of enormous value. Such an undertaking is sadly beyond the scope of this report. Therefore the following is a basic account of the main events in the history of the priory, which provide a framework for archaeological investigation and interpretation.

The first recorded event in Coventry's history was the dedication of the church and abbey on 4th October 1043 (Lambert 1971, 50). Early documentary sources, such as the writings of William of Malmesbury (c1125) and Roger of Hovedon (c1201), inform us that a Benedictine house for an abbot and twenty-four monks was established under the patronage of Leofric the (Saxon) Earl of Mercia and Lady Godiva his wife (*ibid*, 50). However, there is a long-standing tradition that St Osburga, a late eighth-century saint, was the abbess of a nunnery which previously stood on the site. This nunnery is said to have been destroyed by Danish raiders in 1016 (Fretton 1876, 19). Leofric died in 1057 and Godiva ten years later – both are said to have been buried in their church. Following Godiva's death their lands passed to the Crown and were subsequently granted to the Earls of Chester.

The Prior's claim to half of the town was secured by foundation charters forged during the Episcopacy of Robert de Limsey, who, in 1102, transferred his See from Chester to Coventry (Lambert 1971, 54). The late Saxon minster, now the seat of a bishop, took on cathedral status. It is from this time that the origins of the joint Bishopric of Coventry and Lichfield can be traced. The creation of one Episcopal See supporting two cathedrals was to have dire consequences for St Mary's at the Dissolution.

In the late eleventh century the first of a series of misfortunes befell the monastic house when the conventual buildings were destroyed by Peter, Bishop of Chester, or as some historians suggest, de Limsey (Clover & Gibson 1979, 110-113). The early twelfth century saw the beginning of a process of structural expansion beneath which the remains of the abbey were eventually lost. This early development was interrupted by the civil wars which broke out upon the accession to the throne of King Stephen (1135-1154). In 1143 the monks were expelled by Robert Marmion, a nobleman, who fortified the priory and laid siege to the nearby castle belonging to the Earl of Chester (*VCH Warks.*2, 52). Further disruption occurred between the years 1189-98 when Bishop Hugh de Nonant ejected the monks and demolished their lodgings (Lambert 1971, 58). These were subsequently re-built to house his newly appointed canons. The monks were eventually restored in 1198.

The history of the priory in the medieval period is marked by events such as visitations of the Black Death in 1348, 1361-2, 1368-9 and 1386. Members of the monastic community were lost to the plague, including the prior William Irreys who died in 1349 (*VCH Warks.*2, 56).

The last prior, Thomas Camswell, surrendered the monastic house on 15th January 1539. The Benedictine community at the time of the Dissolution numbered thirteen monks, including Camswell and a sub-prior. Dr London, an agent of Thomas Cromwell, wrote thus:

The prior is a sad, honest priest, as his neighbours do report him, and is a bachelor of divinity. He gave his house unto the King's grace willingly and so in like manner did all his brethren . . . (Lambert 1971, 77).

Thomas Camswell, who had only been in post for a year, was rewarded for his co-operation with a large pension.

A number of attempts were made by the mayor, aldermen and the Bishop of Coventry and Lichfield to save the cathedral – all to no avail. Accounts of these and the reasons for their failure can be found in Lambert (1971, 77-8) and Scarisbrick (1994, 164-5).

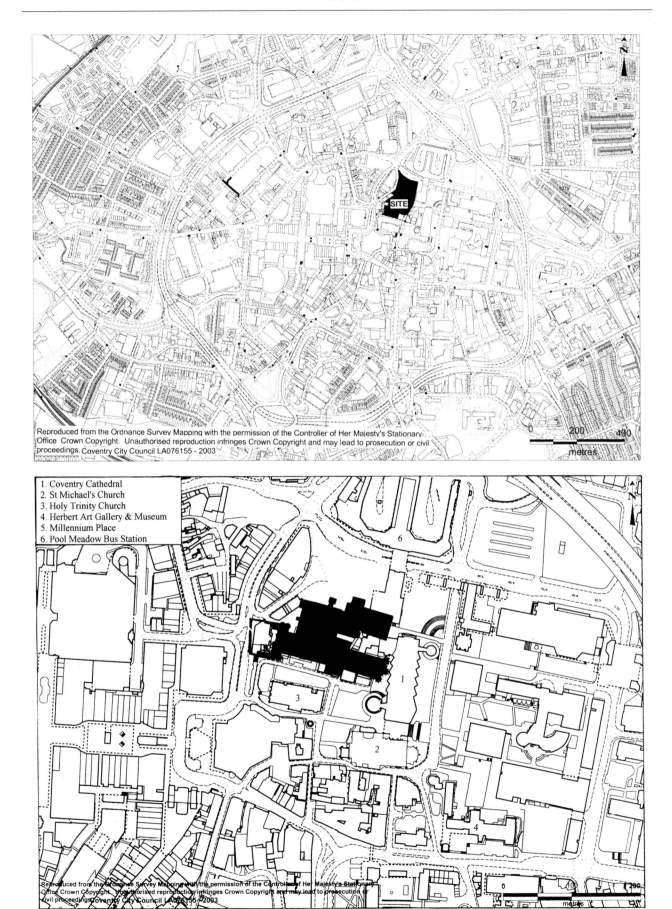

1. Coventry Cathedral
2. St Michael's Church
3. Holy Trinity Church
4. Herbert Art Gallery & Museum
5. Millennium Place
6. Pool Meadow Bus Station

Fig 2 Site Location (a) Coventry City centre (b) superimposed plan of St Mary's

2 The Site

The site occupies the northern slope of a hill which rises above the River Sherbourne to a height of 89.58m OD. The hillside is comprised of Triassic sandstone overlain by Keuper Marl. Deep alluvial deposits at the foot of the slope indicate the former flood plain of the Sherbourne, whose original course meandered around the base of the hill from west to north-east. Now culverted below ground, the river is only visible for a short distance in Palmer Lane on the west side of Trinity Street. The natural gradient of the hillside is broken by a series of artificial terraces which were created to accommodate the various buildings within the priory precinct (Fig 3).

Today, as in the medieval period, the hill forms the highest point in the centre of the city. At its summit stands the church of Holy Trinity which was built in the thirteenth/fourteenth century to replace an earlier Norman structure destroyed by fire in 1257 (*VCH Warks.* 8 1969, 326). The Cathedral of St Mary's stood less than 30m to the north, where the upstanding remains of the interior west end can be seen immediately to the east of the Lych Gate Cottages on Priory Row. The cloister and conventual buildings occupied the lower terraces to the north of the cathedral (Fig 3). The location of the cathedral church on the side of the hill, rather than at its summit is problematic. Possible explanations for this anomaly will be addressed in the discussion.

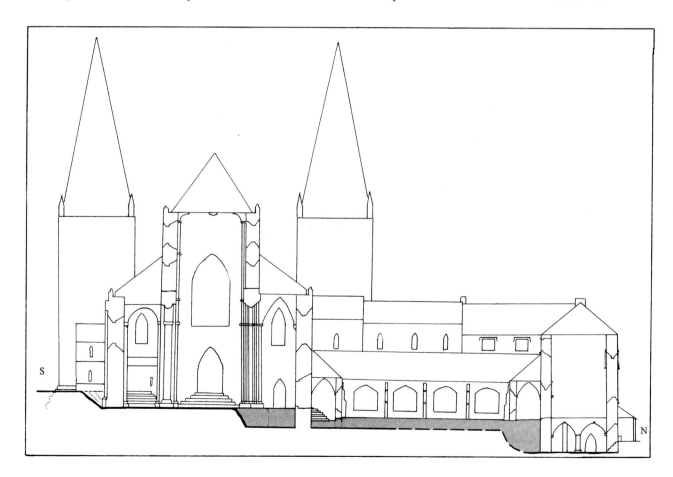

Fig 3 Site terracing (not to scale)

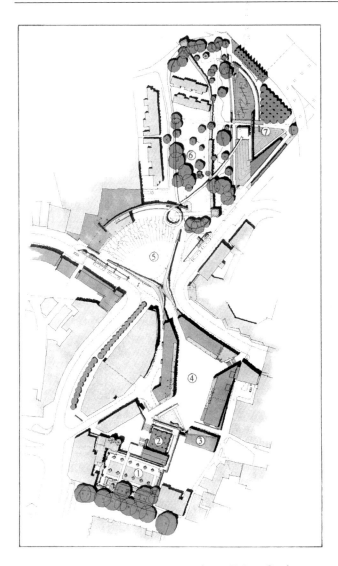

Fig 4 *Phoenix Initiative master plan: 1 Priory Gardens, 2 Visitor Centre & Priory Cloister 3 Youell House (former site of JFK House), 4 Priory Place, 5 Millennium Place, 6 Lady Herbert's Garden, 7 Garden of International Friendship (reproduced courtesy of McCormac, Jamieson & Pritchard Ltd)*

The site of the excavations of 1999-2003 lies within a parcel of land enclosed by Priory Row (south), Fairfax Street (north), Hill Top (east) and Trinity Street (west). This area covers much of the area of the Phoenix Initiative project (Fig 4), now occupied by Priory Gardens, the Visitor Centre and Cloister Garden, Priory Place and the new cathedral offices off Hill Top.

3   Previous Work

During the construction of an extension to Blue Coat School in 1856-7 the west end of the cathedral, complete with respond piers of the nave and the base of the south-west tower, was uncovered. The lower part of the north-west tower had already been incorporated into the existing building. These exposed ruins were left open to view. The remains of the east end were discovered when Coventry's new cathedral was being built in 1955. The architecture visible today enables the cathedral's total length to be calculated as c130m (425ft).

Until 1965 little was known of the extent of the monastic buildings other than those references found in documentary sources contained in the City Record Office and the Public Record Office. Poole (1870, 11) summarises these as follows:

> . . . chapter house, vaulted chamber, prior's chamber, the muniment chamber, the treasury, the herbary chamber, the synodal chamber, le seyn chamber, the princesses chamber . . . the cloisters, the refectory, the grammar school and the infirmary. Among the domestic offices and outbuildings were the larder, kitchen, porters lodge, stables and yard, outer court, malt house, kiln house, slaughter house, wood house, well yard, guests stables, guests' house, two pools within the priory wall, pool yard, St Osberg's pool, priory mill and orchards.

The first extensive excavations on the site were undertaken in 1965-7 resulting in the only published archaeological report to date (Hobley 1971). This work includes a full summary of all previous archaeological observations, including those made by Fretton (1876), Andrews (1909), Tickner (1919), Shelton (1933-54), Hemsley (1959-60) and Woodfield (1961). Most of these observations were, in the main, confined to the area of the cathedral. A comprehensive review was also made for the anniversary symposium (Morris 1994) and, therefore, it is not intended to repeat these in full in this report.

The excavations of 1965-7 were undertaken in response to plans for the re-development of the area by Coventry City Council and the Cathedral authorities. The project was designed not only to recover as much of the plan of the priory as was possible, but also to search for evidence of the late Saxon monastic house founded by the Earl Leofric and Lady Godiva. With regard to the latter the excavation was unsuccessful.

Exploratory trenches did locate sections of walls belonging to the nave, cloister and west claustral range. The entrance to the chapter house was revealed, as was a substantial section of its south wall. Stone seating was found on the inner face of the wall, as was evidence for an apsidal east end. On the east side of Hill Top stone walls were uncovered standing up to 4m high which were interpreted as being the remains of the infirmary (Hobley 1971, 98). More extensive excavation was undertaken to the north of the cloister exposing remains of the kitchen with an associated court and drains. This was the only building to be completely excavated. The kitchen appeared to be linked by a passageway to the north wall of the refectory undercroft. Parts of buildings interpreted as the reredorter (latrine block) and the dormitory undercroft were also excavated.

In his report Hobley published a useful plan of the priory complex, as he understood it, augmenting his own findings with those from the past and basing his conjectures on the plans of other Benedictine houses (especially Canterbury).

No further work on the site was undertaken until 1989-90 when Coventry Museums' Archaeology Unit located the interior floor level of the nave adjacent to the upstanding remains of the west end and the south-west tower. At this time the upstanding masonry of the west end was also recorded (Soden 1990; *West Midlands Archaeology* 33, 94-5).

4 Objectives

The symposium of 1993 stressed the importance of adopting a multi-disciplinary approach to any future work, recommending that the archaeological, architectural, documentary and topographical evidence should all be taken into consideration from the outset (Demidowicz 1994, 15). It was with this in mind that the archaeological team for the Phoenix Initiative was assembled.

Mindful of the need to preserve as many of the *in situ* remains as possible as part of the requirements of PPG 16 (planning policy guidance), the challenging role presented to the team gave the opportunity to address long standing academic issues. This duality of purpose resulted in a wide-ranging archaeological brief that sought to explore the following:

- The general plan of the priory and cathedral and extent of surviving remains, with emphasis being placed on those areas (such as the nave) selected for incorporation into the new development.
- The architectural styles used and the relationships between buildings, in order to elucidate the structural development of the priory and cathedral.
- The thinly documented early (pre-Conquest) occupation of the site hitherto unsupported by physical evidence.
- The activities taking place in separate areas of the monastic house.
- The land use in the immediate vicinity of the priory.
- The processes of destruction in the wake of the Dissolution.

From its inception, the scale of the project surpassed all expectations in terms of both its time span and in the levels of archaeological survival. Unexpected findings instigated new lines of enquiry, vastly improving our knowledge of the site. As with all such projects many questions remain unanswered as well as new ones being raised. It is hoped that this report will support and encourage new research into the history and archaeology of the Benedictine Priory of St Mary.

5   The Excavations

Mid-late Saxon/early Medieval Occupation (Fig 5)

Burials

Two earth-cut graves were discovered below the foundation level of the south cloister. The inhumations had been disturbed by the insertion of a sandstone feature, also predating the cloister. This insertion had removed the lower left side of the skeleton to its south and the upper right part of that to the north. Bone was taken from the more complete skeleton (CBP99/00 1913) (see THE HUMAN REMAINS & Fig 6) and subjected to radiocarbon dating. The same technique was applied to a sample taken from a skull fragment (SMC99 F468), found below the remains of another early structure, which in turn underlay the foundations of pier 6 of the cathedral's north aisle (Fig 7). The results of both radiocarbon determinations are as follows:

CBP99/00 1913
(Wk 11607 – Data from The University of Waikato Radiocarbon Dating Laboratory, Hamilton, New Zealand – OxCal calibration curve)

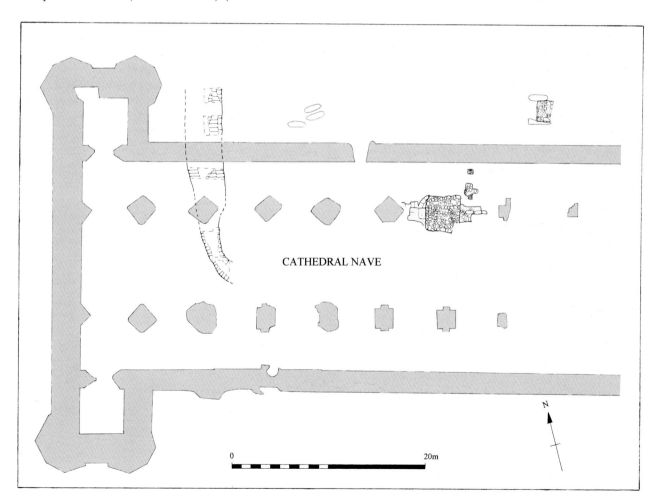

CATHEDRAL NAVE

0   20m

Fig 5   *Mid-late Saxon/early Medieval occupation*

Conventional radiocarbon age: 1104 ±51 BP
2 Sigma Calibrated result (95.4% probability): Cal **AD 780-1030**
Intercept of radiocarbon age with calibration curve: Cal **AD 900-1000**

SMC99 F468
(Beta 143957 – Data from Beta Analytic Radiocarbon Dating Laboratory, Miami, Florida – Pretoria calibration curve)
Conventional radiocarbon age: ±50 BP
2 Sigma calibrated result (95% probability): Cal **AD 700-980**
Intercept of radiocarbon age with calibration curve: Cal **AD 870**

Fig 6   Late Saxon burial

Together these results provide dating for the earliest stratified remains recovered from the site. The calibration curve relating to the skull fragment (SMC99 F468) was bold and without significant anomaly, giving a high level of confidence in the date of *c*870. The calibrated results for the skeleton (CBP99/00 1913), though less specific, strongly indicate a tenth-century date. Thus the two *in situ*

burials are the earliest evidence of occupation in Coventry. They clearly indicate that there had been Christian burial on the site since at least the tenth century. A number of disarticulated human bones recovered from the grave soil of the skeleton (CBP99/00 1913) indicate that burials were already present in the vicinity, a conclusion supported by the earlier radiocarbon date extracted from the skull fragment (SMC99 F468). Thus it would appear that Saxon inhumations were present on the site in the late ninth century and possibly earlier.

Three more potentially early graves were discovered below the southern extremity of the west range but were left unexcavated, as they were not being disturbed by the development (see **APPENDIX 3**).

Structural Remains

Beneath the north arcade of the medieval cathedral the truncated remains of an earlier stone structure were found. While its overall form is not clear, the chronological date of these remains may lie within

Fig 7   Early stonework below north aisle pier 6

the late Saxon period. These structural remains comprised a partly robbed wall foundation of well-dressed stonework on an east-west alignment set into a distinctive greenish mortar not seen anywhere else on the site. It lay to the west and east of the later north arcade pier 6 (bays 6 and 7).

Evidence of a foundation trench was discovered to the west in bay 5, on the same alignment. This had been cut into the natural sandstone forming a void which had been filled with rubble prior to the laying of the later cathedral floor. When it was built, pier 6 was set on a specially laid, two-course, unmortared rubble foundation to offset the effect of the broken ground. Protruding from the northern side of the wall, and cut by the later pier foundation, was an arc of dressed stonework comprising four closely fitting, curved blocks (Fig 7). The arc constituted about eighty degrees of what was possibly originally a semi-circle. Also on the north side an unmortared rubble foundation in a shallow trench may have supported a timber wall.

The skull fragment (SMC99 F468) was discovered below the arc of dressed stonework, thus giving us a *terminus post quem* of c870 for its construction.

Beneath the pier 6 foundation was a skeleton (SMC99 G1715), the grave of which had cut the arc of stonework. Bone from this skeleton was also sent for radiocarbon dating, producing results as follows:

SMC99 G1715 (Beta 143956 – Data from Beta Analytic Radiocarbon Dating Laboratory, Miami, Florida – Pretoria calibration curve)
Conventional radiocarbon age 900 ±100 BP
2 sigma calibrated result (95% probability): Cal **AD 970-1290**
Intercept of radiocarbon age with calibration curve: Cal **AD 1160**

The dating of the human remains, sandwiching literally (and stratigraphically) the dressed stone-work, indicate the structure was erected, put to use and demolished between c870 and c1160. The structural remains are insubstantial and therefore it is not possible to say what exactly they represent. Suffice to say that they are of high quality stonework and mortared with a distinctive greenish mortar. The arc of stonework is specific enough to relate to a particular architectural feature, such as a very small

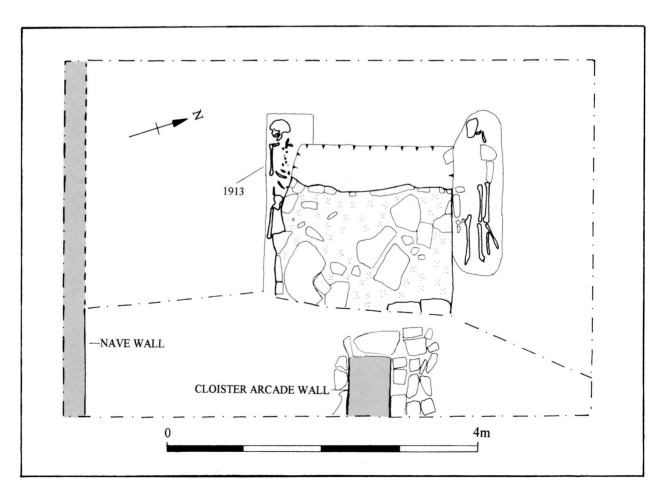

Fig 8   Raft-type foundation below south cloister alley

apse or even a turret for a spiral staircase. Unfortunately only one course survived and this was clearly at the very base of the feature. The contrasting levels of the geology to the immediate north and south of this feature indicate that it had been built on a terrace cut into the natural slope of the hillside.

A short distance to the north-west, below the cloister alley, lay the remains of the stone feature mentioned above in association with the inhumation (CBP99/00 1913). It resembled a raft-type foundation and was constructed from rough-cut blocks of sandstone set in a matrix of loose mortar and clay (Fig 8). It cut through the underlying burials and lay well below the footings of the cloister arcade. Its level was comparable to the early stonework observed in the nave, almost certainly indicating that the terrace observed there extended northwards into what became the south cloister alley. The eastern and western extent of the terrace remains unknown.

What exactly these features represent is debatable. The radiocarbon dated remains, sandwiching the stonework below the nave, provide a time-span into which fall the tradition of St Osburga's nunnery, Leofric and Godiva's monastery and the siege works of the 1140's (see THE CATHEDRAL Period 2). Likewise, the stone 'raft' could have originated from any time between the tenth century and the construction of the final cloister arcade wall.

It is possible that the remains are of the late Saxon period. The arc of stonework protruding from the wall below the nave appears to be of a quality not easily equated with a quickly erected siege-work. Furthermore the distinctive green mortar is not found in any of the features of the Romanesque church either pre- or post-dating the siege. This may indicate that the remains represent an earlier phase of construction, conceivably relating to the monastic house endowed by Leofric and Godiva.

Further Evidence

In addition to the above, two *ex situ* finds were made which have been dated to the late Saxon period. A large sandstone slab (T878) incorporating part of a semi-circular arch was found unstratified close to the priory mill (Fig 54a). Its monolithic head is typical of late Saxon work, however, this style continued to be used in the Norman period. The presence of concentric bands carved in low relief around the arch head favour the earlier date, probably eleventh century. It may have been part of a narrow arcade such as that which adorns the upper tower of All Saint's Church, Earls Barton (Audouy et al, 1995, Fig 4). Alternatively it may have been part of a small window; however, the inclusion of the carved cross above the arch head suggests that the aperture may have been internal, possibly a squint, or framing for an aumbry or holy water scoop (see THE WORKED STONES AND ARCHITECTURAL STONEWORK).

Found close by, lying on the timber base of the mill's wheel pit, was a gold coin of Alfred the Great (PP01 SF1). Issued in 886, it commemorated Alfred's capture of London from the Danes (see THE COINS).

Although both *ex situ* these finds are clearly significant. The arch fragment most probably derives from an ecclesiastical structure of the late Saxon period, possibly the religious house founded by Leofric and Godiva. The coin's significance is that it closely corresponds with the earliest radiocarbon date from the skeletal material. These two finds add to the growing body of evidence for pre-Conquest occupation of the site.

The Cathedral

Period 1

The Construction of the East End and Crossing (c1102-1140)

Investigation of the cathedral east of the nave was restricted to an area encompassing part of the northern crossing and parts of the north transept. Four piers were found *in situ* in this area; the north-west crossing pier, the north-east crossing pier, pier 8 of the north aisle and a pier standing in the north transept (Fig 9a-d). Together these enable the position of the crossing and transepts to be fixed for the first time, a significant development in the study of the cathedral. Although all of the piers, other than pier 8, were extensively robbed, enough stylistic evidence remained for dating purposes. Evidence gleaned from the base profiles suggests a construction date of c1115-40. Some of the features of the piers can be compared to those at Norwich Cathedral, Peterborough and Dunstable Priory, all of which fit into the first half of the twelfth century (see THE WORKED STONES AND ARCHITECTURAL STONEWORK).

Although the robbing of the crossing piers above base level was severe, it is apparent from what survived that their forms exhibited significant differences. Whether this was intended as part of the original build or was the result of subsequent alterations remains unclear. A number of medieval alterations to the crossing and tower are indicated by the loose architectural stones (see **Period 3** & THE WORKED STONES AND ARCHITECTURAL STONEWORK) and it is probable that the piers were altered at this time. Alternatively the differences could be the result of post-Dissolution modifications (**see Period 4**). Excavation of the area to the south and east of the piers would undoubtedly throw more light on the subject.

a

b

c

d

Fig 9 *(a) North-west crossing pier (b) north-east crossing pier (c) north aisle pier 8 (d) pier in north transept*

It is almost certain that the unexcavated eastern arm of the cathedral was constructed first and dates from this early period (the chevet chapels discovered in 1955 being late Gothic additions to the east end (Morris 1994, 32).

It would appear that the siege of 1143 interrupted the early building programme sometime after the completion of pier 8 of the north aisle. Pier 7 failed to provide dating evidence due to it being robbed out to foundation level. The radiocarbon-dated remains below pier 6 indicate that it was probably built sometime after *c*1160, therefore post-dating the siege. This westward progression of pier building in the north aisle may be of significance when considering the nature of the early stone feature found below the nave. Its location corresponds to the limit of construction at the time of the siege and thus it remains plausible that it represents some attempt to fortify the partially built cathedral.

Period 2

The Fortification of the Priory (1143)

In bays 2 and 3 of the north aisle and the nave lay a filled-in ditch which passed under the foundation of pier 2 and under the north wall of the cathedral (Fig 5). This very substantial ditch had been truncated during the terracing of the site for the cathedral and was thus much reduced at its southern end. Here it appeared to have turned eastwards. However, below the north aisle where the original ground level was less reduced by the terracing, the ditch was substantially less affected and a cut section showed it to have survived to a depth of 1.58m and being up to 7.5m wide (Fig 10). It had been cut through natural clay, deep into the sandstone bedrock and was traced a further 5m northwards outside the west cloister range where it was found to be a similar depth. Terracing for the priory buildings may have

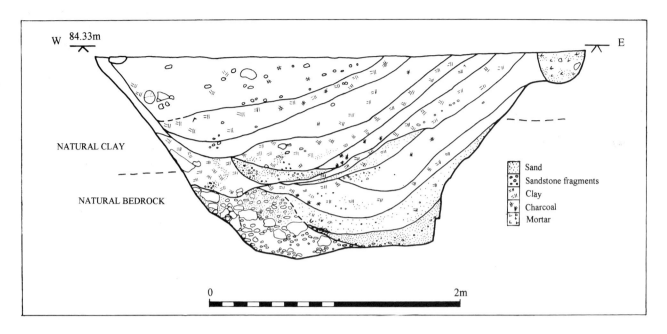

Fig 10   Section through siege (?) ditch

also reduced the ground level here so the ditch could have been substantially deeper.

Well-stratified pottery was recovered from deep within the ditch fills and comprised unglazed Coventry wares of the twelfth century. Further material was recovered from the section to the south and this included an intrusive sherd of Nuneaton A ware of 1250-1300. Material recovered further north, again from deep within the ditch, comprised glazed Coventry D wares introduced *c*1150. The ditch also contained human bone. The lack of silt in the bottom of the ditch suggests that the feature was not open for a long period of time. The pottery and the general similarity of the fills (although differentiated) indicate a rapid backfill in the twelfth century. The composition of the fills suggests that it was back-filled with re-deposited, contaminated natural material, not occupation debris. It is not inconceivable that this material represents the original up-cast thrown back in, perhaps an accompanying bank pushed over.

There was no evidence to indicate that the ditch and the early structural remains were contemporary. On the contrary, the seemingly temporary nature of the ditch indicates that it is unlikely to be an enclosure surrounding an early monastic house or church. Its short life span and spatial relationship to the partially completed Romanesque cathedral indicate that it is more likely to be part of the siege works set up by Robert Marmion II in 1143, fortifying the priory in an unsuccessful attempt to capture Coventry Castle:

In 1141 (sic) Robert Marmion possessed himself of this monastery, ejected the monks, fortified the church with its own building and cut deep entrenchments in the adjoining fields (Reader 1823, 129).

If this interpretation of the ditch is correct, then it can be seen to run southward into the area which later became the nave and then to swing eastwards to defend the partially completed Romanesque cathedral and any earlier structures still in existence.

Reader's statement in 1823 was based upon a series of contemporary or near-contemporary authors who were very much in agreement (although some shared a common source or copied each other freely) as can be seen below:

. . . two of the nobles who had converted monasteries into fortifications, expelling the monks . . . Robert Marmion was one, who had committed this iniquity in the church of Coventry (Henry of Huntingdon c1150).

. . . two persons, who had committed the offence in expelling the monks, and turning the churches of God into castles (were) punished . . . For Robert Marmion, a skilful warrior, had perversely acted thus towards the church of Coventry. Robert Marmion, while atacking the enemy, and in the very midst of a large body of his own men, was slain, singly, before that very monastery (Roger of Hoveden c1201).

The same year Robert Marmion, a warlike knight, who had expelled the monks of Coventry from their monastery and turned the church into a castle (Roger of Wendover pre-1235).

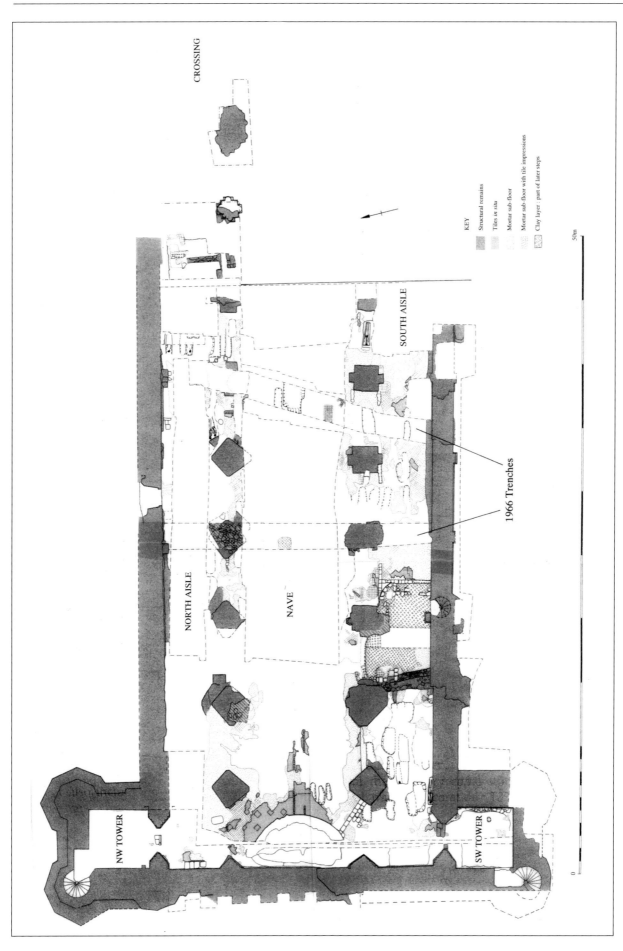

Fig 11   The excavated remains of the cathedral nave

Based upon the excavated evidence the only structure that can be confidently identified as standing at the time of the siege was the partially completed cathedral. If the ditch was cut as part of the fortification of the priory it must be viewed as an attempt to strengthen the defensive capacity of what was, in part, a grandiose building site.

If the ditch is interpreted thus, it is only the second time features relating directly to the twelfth-century siege have been identified – the first being the motte or bailey ditch under the former Baptist Chapel in Hay Lane (Rylatt & Soden 1990). The dating of the ditch fill is also crucial to the study of the later cathedral. The material in its backfill, dating to the period after 1150, indicates that the western end of the Romanesque north arcade post-dates this. As the back-filled ditch at its southern return had been truncated by the terracing to create the nave and south aisle, this indicates that the subsequently unaltered western end of the Romanesque southern arcade, the south wall and the nave must all post-date *c*1150. Furthermore, this truncation indicates that the terracing of the site was undertaken in stages dictated by the pace of construction, possibly in an attempt to delay the demolition of existing buildings until absolutely necessary.

Period 3

The Western Half of the Cathedral Church of St Mary (c1150-1539) (Fig 11)

The Cathedral Church of St Mary was *c*130m (425ft) long when complete. Evidence from the pre-cathedral features indicates that the majority of the original western half, comprising the nave (59m/193ft long) and its flanking aisles (4m/13ft wide), could not have been constructed until the second half of the twelfth century. Existing scholarship is agreed that the west front has all the architectural hallmarks of a structure dating to the second quarter of the thirteenth century. Therefore a construction programme of perhaps three to four generations is plausible, exhibiting a change in architectural style from the Romanesque to Early English Gothic. The Close Rolls (1247-51) referring to the grant of twenty oaks for the fabric of the church may relate to the completion of the west end (Lambert 1971, 63).

The central crossing supported a tower and possibly a spire, while smaller towers adorned the ends of the west front. Archaeological evidence for the form of all three is scant, but for a rather naïve drawing of 1576 (Fig 12).

The nave was much cut about by later pits and its

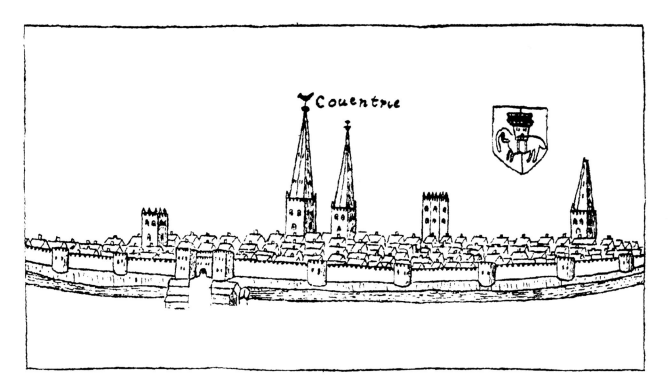

Fig 12 *Coventry in 1576 from a sketch made by William Smyth, Herald to Elizabeth I. St Mary's tower is second from right (from Burbidge 1952)*

floor smashed and dispersed during the Dissolution. Nevertheless, enough survived to indicate that the space had been used as a processional route-way unconfined by the clutter of fixtures.

Site Preparation

To build such a large structure as a great church clearly took meticulous planning. The site sloped down to the north and some account had to be taken of any buildings which already stood thereabouts. While the natural geology would prove to be suitable for founding such a structure, its varied nature meant that some improvisation was necessary.

The whole monastic complex was placed upon a series of terraces cut into the natural hillside. Terracing had evidently begun prior to the siege when the northern crossing and pier 8 of the north aisle were built. However, if interpreted as a siege work, the ditch running below pier 2 of the north aisle appears to have been truncated by post siege terracing. This indicates that the preparation of the nave site was done in at least two stages.

In addition, at least one smaller terrace already existed for the potentially earlier buildings on the site. Herein lay a problem as the old and the new did not coincide. Therefore, while the south wall, south aisle, and some of the north aisle of the Romanesque cathedral lay on natural clay or sandstone bedrock, part of the north aisle and north wall stood over earlier occupation and made ground to a depth of over 1m. The exposure of the bedrock in the south aisle meant that there was no need to build a foundation for the base of pier 6; it was simply hewn out of the natural bedrock. Thirteenth-century graves in the region of that same pier were rock-cut.

Elsewhere, pier 2 of the north arcade was dug deeply into the backfill of the wide, deep Period 2 ditch. Piers 4, 5 and 6 stood on top of made-up ground and the reduced foundations of the earlier feature (see MID-LATE SAXON/EARLY MEDIEVAL OCCUPATION). It was in this area that the cathedral builders appear to have experienced problems when setting out the foundations for the piers (see below).

Outside the south wall of the cathedral lay the edge of the first terrace dug to create the new building (Fig 3). Here the natural ground surface was reduced by 1m-1.5m just outside the wall. The terrace lay so close to the building that at the western end the south-west tower lay against the terrace side, its substantial south and east walls acting as retaining walls. The internal floors were therefore over 1m lower than the exterior ground level.

Architecture

Excavation of the north aisle was limited although the line of the north arcade itself was fully excavated.

As discussed above, pier 8 and, most probably, pier 7 were built in the Romanesque style prior to the siege of 1143. Pier 6 was built in a similar style but post-dates *c*1160. Between these piers were found ribs (T565) and wall-ribs or voussoirs (T545) from a Romanesque quadripartite vault. In bay 7 this vault had collapsed *en bloc*. Examples of a similar design span the twelfth century and can be found locally in the crypts at St Mary's, Warwick (mid-twelfth century) and Berkswell Parish Church (*c*1180-1200) (see THE WORKED STONES AND ARCHITECTURAL STONEWORK). As the construction of pier 6 post-dates *c*1160 (see above) the vault was most likely erected in the latter part of the twelfth century. It is possible that this type of rib vault had been employed in other parts of the church to the east before the siege interrupted the build. Early twelfth-century examples of this 'Lombardic' style of rib can be found at Tewkesbury Abbey (see THE WORKED STONES AND ARCHITECTURAL STONEWORK). A huge key stone relating to the vault design was found close to pier 8 (T699), its centre decorated with a *patera* of acanthus foliage carved in low relief (Fig 51a). Later medieval painted stonework was also recovered from this area, decorated with expensive pigments including vermillion and gold leaf and stencilled with finely executed *fleur-de-lys* (T877) (Plate 1a).

West of pier 6, the bases of the northern arcade exhibit a change in style from the cruciform of the Romanesque to a lozenge shape of the Early English Gothic. Excavation in the vicinity of piers 2-5 showed that their footings had been reset on two occasions. As noted above, the piers whose foundations exhibit these alterations are those which overlie the Period 2 ditch and the made-up ground over the early structural remains – ground whose broken nature was most likely to cause structural instability. It is not known to what extent the first piers were completed as the alterations are only visible at foundation level, but it is most likely that the re-jigging took place at the time of the initial build in the latter part of twelfth century. Loose architectural fragments from the nave do not indicate a substantial re-build of the arcades in any other period (Richard Morris, *pers comm*). In the case of pier 2, a robbed-out foundation trench for a cruciform pier was found underlying its base implying that all of the piers east of it were originally intended to be of the same style. Similar vestiges were not found below piers 3-5 but may have been obliterated by the subsequent lozenge-shaped footings. The foundation of pier 1 of the north arcade showed no signs of alteration and appears to have been dug, from the outset, for a lozenge-shaped pier. As a result, the pier bases located at either end of the north arcade were of different architectural styles. This is not uncommon, a number of churches incorporated different elevations, especially for their naves e.g. Romsey Abbey, Worcester Cathedral (*ibid*).

The north wall retained the vestiges of Romanesque responds opposite piers 4 and 6, both of which had been reduced and faced off at a later date, while the others had been completely removed. Other than the collapsed vault in bay 7 and the associated ribs and intersections found to the east of this, the rubble excavated from the north aisle was bereft of fragments associated with vaulting, possibly indicating that the aisle was spanned by a groin vault. A number of interesting architectural fragments not associated with vaulting were recovered and included part of a scalloped piscina (T922) (Fig 53b), the top of a lion effigy (T679) and a head stop carved in the image of a young man (T518) (Plate 2a).

In the south aisle, east of pier 2 the pier bases retained their Romanesque form, apart from some minor cosmetic additions, until the Dissolution. Each pier would have been matched with a respond on the south wall. A clear correlation was seen between the style of the base of pier 8 in the north aisle and that of the one remaining respond base opposite pier 3. In bays 3-7 of the south aisle there was not a single rib piece present in the destruction rubble, suggesting that the original Romanesque vault was, like the majority of the north aisle, a groin vault. In bays 1-2 of the rubble, clearance had been negligible and here lines of ribs could still be seen, crossing diagonally at the intersection (Fig 16a). Between them lay the upper (usually unseen) face of the vault, large portions of which were still mortared together despite having fallen up to 10m. These two bays were of Early English design of *c*1220 (Morris 1994, 51). One large amorphous mass of mortared masonry had fallen on top of the vault and may have derived from either the triforium/clerestorey or the south-west tower.

The rubble in the nave was mainly connected with the collapse or destruction of the west front and the western piers; relatively little survived to indicate the form of the triforium and clerestorey. The absence of collapsed vault material probably indicates that the nave was indeed spanned in timber, a conclusion reached by previous commentators.

Following the original Romanesque build, a number of architectural modifications took place in the crossing and north transept. Perhaps the most significant of these occurred in the fourteenth century when the south face of the transept pier was reinforced. Dating for this episode is provided by an ornate bracket for a statue (T486) coursed into the later masonry and by the chamfered mouldings of the reinforcement (T484). These alterations may be related to a tower re-build of the early fourteenth century, as indicated by architectural fragments

decorated with large ball ornaments found in the collapsed structural remains (see **THE WORKED STONES AND ARCHITECTURAL STONEWORK**). Further modifications to the architecture were undertaken in the Perpendicular style when the vault of either the transept or crossing tower was replaced. A large foliate boss (T795) dating from *c*1400 was found in the vicinity and is of a similar vault pattern to those present in the tower vault of St Michael's, Coventry (late fourteenth century).

Documentary evidence presented by Lambert (1971, 65) records building work on the cathedral taking place during the Priorate of Henry Irreys (1322-42). This may relate to the tower re-build mentioned above. Alternatively it could refer to a refenestration of the cathedral as observed in other great churches built in the Romanesque/Early English style (Richard Morris, *pers comm*). A number of fragments of window mullion and tracery characteristic of the fourteenth century (T578-86, T671-673, T682-683 and most importantly T632) were found in the demolition rubble and may attest to this activity taking place. Subsequent alterations to the

Fig 13   Evidence for semi-circular flight of steps at west end of nave

windows in the nave are suggested by the recovery of a fragment of tracery of the later fifteenth/early sixteenth century (T636).

Entrance Arrangements

The main west door to the nave was, in common with many English and French great churches, above the level of the nave floor. This accentuated the series of steps up to the east end at the pulpitum, crossing and quire, the final step being at the position of the High Altar. In pre-Reformation ecclesiology the further east within the church, the more holy the position so a progressive series of steps up towards thc High Altar was intended to produce an awareness of progress into the presence of God.

The steps from the west door had been robbed out; only part of one riser block survived *in-situ*. However the make-up behind the series of steps was undamaged and the robbing lines indicate a near semi-circular concentric flight of monumental steps stretching in an arc from one arcade to the other (Fig 13). Evidence was found to indicate the position of the lowest three steps. Amongst the rubble at the base of the steps lay a number of detached shaft fragments which probably derived from the splays of the main central door.

Alongside the main entrance stood a small doorway in the end of the north aisle which led from the suggested site of the sacristy west of the church directly into bay 1 of the north aisle. This was investigated archaeologically in 1990 (Soden 1990) where a small patch of floor tiles was found close to the threshold. This door, unlike the main entrance, was not raised up above the floor and no steps led to it. No similar flanking door was present in the end of the south aisle. A door in this position is sometimes found in other churches and most probably served as a convenient entrance for the clergy when approaching from the forecourt, rather than repeatedly opening the great west door (Morris 1994, 41-2).

A doorway, giving access to the cloister, was located in bay 5 of the north aisle (now visible in the Visitor Centre). All of the architectural detail had been robbed away on the nave-side but enough survived in the cloister to date the doorway to the period *c*1220-60 (see **THE WORKED STONES AND ARCHITECTURAL STONEWORK**). It is of the same style as the great west door of the cathedral.

In the south aisle there once existed a major (4.5m/15½ft wide) doorway out into the churchyard between the cathedral and Holy Trinity Church. It lay in the wall in bay 6 and from its remains was part of the original Romanesque build. At a late date it was blocked up and the access moved three bays westwards. The height of its blocked embrasure above the aisle floor indicates that a flight of steps

would have accompanied the original door, but no remains survived of this. The exterior ground surface hereabouts was about 1m higher than the aisle floor.

The replacement doorway lay in bay 3 of the south aisle. External foundations betray the former presence of a porch beyond, but these had been severely truncated by eighteenth/nineteenth-century graves making reconstruction of its dimensions impossible. It was probably a two-storey structure as a secondary newel stair had been cut into the aisle wall thickness hard against the respond opposite pier 3. In common with the earlier doorway the threshold level was high above the floor. Here, however, the accompanying interior flight of steps survived, extending both northwards directly into the nave between piers 2 and 3 and eastwards into the aisle. They survived as both treads and risers in places, but the majority as deep impressions left in the clay make-up when the individual blocks of the steps were robbed out after the Dissolution. Architectural fragments from within the same make-up are dated to no earlier than *c*1325 (Richard Morris, *pers comm*). This suggests that the southern entrance was moved after that date (assuming that the final steps were the only ones). The new door continued to be used for major civic and religious processions throughout the medieval period (see below for documentary references).

Floor Layout

Remnants of a sandstone-flagged floor, contemporary with the cathedral's Romanesque inception, were discovered in bay 8 of the north aisle. They survived in dispersed patches and were laid over a bed of sandstone rubble. The floor level in the vicinity of the pier had subsequently been raised, concealing the flags. This was contemporary with the construction of a stone feature, probably a monument or tomb (see below). Little remained of the later floor other than the odd broken and heavily worn tile and numerous impressions in the mortar-bedding layer. A single triangular tile survived *in situ* against pier 8 clearly indicating that the later floor would have buried the base of the pier (Fig 9c).

Of the remainder of the nave, nothing survived *in situ* of the earliest floors. That which survived (and then only in certain areas) comprised the final floor, consisting of late fourteenth-century locally made ceramic tiles (*c*84.40m above OD). There were also occasional areas of stone flags, cut from the ubiquitous local red sandstone.

The tiles that remain constitute a very worn-out floor, testament to the exceedingly widespread use of the cathedral nave and aisles by many thousands of feet over a long period of time. The laying of this floor had been carefully planned and well executed. The earlier floors had been systematically grubbed up to ensure a good base for the new one (earlier *ex-situ* floor tiles were found – see **THE FLOOR TILES**). Then the nave and aisles were subdivided into a series of panels, mainly demarcated by the piers of the arcades, but with additional subdivision into panels, outlined in very slightly raised sandstone kerbs or borders of tiles. The tiles were used to provide a guide for processions. Patterning seems to have been based largely upon the juxtaposition of these panels and its ease on the eye. At the west end concentric squares could be seen patterning the nave north of a central processional route (Fig 13). The area to the south of the processional route had been cut up by later graves and the wheels of carts used for the removal of stone at the Dissolution. The presence of lines of sandstone flags may denote an attempt at a fan effect, radiating out from the western steps.

The use of colour as an effect is assumed, on the basis of its employment on most other sites in Coventry and beyond, to provide patterns of green and yellow chequer boards with varied borders. However, the extreme wear seen on the surviving Cathedral floors makes reconstruction impossible. Colour-coded overlays were made of the site plans of the floors but these remain in archive and are not presented here as they are inconclusive. Patterned tiles were widespread but so few were *in situ* that nothing can be said about the overall desired effect. It was not possible to identify the presence of chantries from the armorial tiles found as most were *ex-situ*.

The later burial of patrons in the nave and aisles did, just as in other sites such as Charterhouse and Whitefriars (Soden 1995; Woodfield, forthcoming), wreck areas of previous pattern. Here at the cathedral the effect would have been limited by the use of the above-mentioned kerbed panels as a whole area could be effectively re-laid quite cheaply. Thus some graves were visible only because they had subsequently sunk, along with the floor, while the tiles appeared to be part of an unbroken run

The Use of Space
The nave seems to have been kept clear, at least from the date that the final floor was laid. Within the floor were tile layouts which show that no disturbance occurred within bay 1 of the nave from the day they were laid until the Dissolution. Along the central longitudinal axis of the nave lay tiles in two parallel 'tram lines', seemingly a guiding pathway for pilgrims entering by the west door or for processions entering by the same route. In much the same way 1962 pennies set into the floor mark the processional route down the central aisle of the third and present Coventry Cathedral.

South of, and possibly under this pathway, the nave appears to have received burials of those for whom the passage of feet above may have represented an act of post-mortem humility, there being arguably no greater volume of foot traffic anywhere than at the west end. The evident sinkage of graves hereabouts may have been caused not by the normal use of the floor but by cart traffic after the Dissolution.

Patrons' tombs may have been widespread but the use of the nave as burial space was probably somewhat restricted by its constant processional use although some graves were located there during the 1965-7 excavations. Such a degree of penance may not have been to many people's taste. The space beneath the arches of both arcades seems to have been a popular place for burial and a pair of building slots in bay 6 of the south aisle, directly beneath the arcade arch, seem to point to the former presence of a tomb and canopy.

A large sandstone plinth located in bay 8 of the north aisle may also indicate the site of a tomb or monument. Its presence is related to a significant re-ordering of the early Romanesque layout of the bay which involved raising the floor level in the vicinity of the feature (see above). The subsequent disparity between levels was met by the construction of a series of steps located in the centre of the bay. The stones used in their construction had been robbed away leaving impressions in the underlying mortar. At least three steps would have been required to ascend from aisle level to that of the tomb or monument.

Close by, an ashlar screen was constructed up against the west face of pier 8. This may have accompanied the laying of the stone steps. The stone fragments present in the surrounding demolition rubble represent a number of styles of architecture; however, two pieces support the assertion that a monument was indeed located in the vicinity. A single fragment of a delicately-moulded fitting (T129) and a foliate carving with bunch of grapes (T131), both hewn from grey sandstone, have been associated with monumental decoration and assigned a fourteenth/fifteenth-century date (see **THE WORKED STONES AND ARCHITECTURAL STONEWORK**).

Elsewhere, graves seem to have been largely unmarked, except by the haphazard relaying of tiles following those interments which post-date the final floor. Burials seem to have been widespread throughout the south aisle and, at least, in bays 6 and 7 of the north aisle. Bays 1 and 2 of the north aisle seem never to have been used for burials. Whether bays 3, 4 and 5 were similarly clear is unknown as the excavations did not extend far into them (certainly the space beneath the corresponding north-arcade arches was indeed clear of burials).

Patronage and Dedications

A number of chantries are known to have existed somewhere in the cathedral:

- Robert and William de Leicester's (1328; *Dugdale Warks.*, 164)
- William de Copstone's (1291; *Dugdale Warks.*, 165)
- Poley's (*Dugdale Mon.* III, 188)
- Thomas Blaby's (*Dugdale Mon.* III, 188)
- Roger Brewode's (*Dugdale Mon.* III, 188)
- Edward de Wedon's (merchant, d. after 1372 (Alcock 1990, 13)
- John Preest's (d. *c*1361) (Alcock 1990, 17)
- Wentbrige's (*Dugdale Mon.* III, 188)
- Shirland's (*Dugdale Mon.* III, 188)
- Marshall's (*Dugdale Mon.* III, 188)

Copstone's Chantry is most readily identifiable with the archaeological remains in bay 2 of the south aisle. Dugdale, quoting earlier sources, describes the chantry as *'Capella sancti Clementis iuxta porticum ecclesiae Cathedralis Coventriae'* (The chapel of St Clement next to the porch of the Cathedral at Coventry) (*Dugdale Warks.*, 165).

Fig 14   *Tomb in Copstone's Chantry, south aisle bay 2*

The remains in bay 2 of the south aisle contain all the constituent parts to qualify as an early chantry chapel, although the dedication to St Clement is otherwise unknown. The chapel contained a piscina found by Hobley (1971, Plate 9a) in his Trench 18 in 1965-7 (and by inference an altar [of St Clement]). It also lies next to the south entrance and porch, the stairwell lying hard up against the eastern wall. It contained numerous graves, including a tomb against the south wall (Fig 14) and a central cluster of graves robbed at the Dissolution. This material produced many disturbed bones, including a skull with a healed sword/axe injury (see **THE HUMAN BONE**) (Fig 73), chain mail fragments and a dagger. Hence it seems likely that amongst the burials lay an old soldier of some note.

The cathedral was, of course, the starting point or the goal of prestigious processions, both religious and civic. Because of its prominent position it was a useful place to make a point, as some disgruntled citizens decided in 1498 when they penned a petition and *'set hit up on the south durre in the Mynster'* (Harris 1907-12, 589). The same door was referred to in 1457 as the main civic entrance, *'the Mynster Durre that openeth ynto the Trynite chirchyarde'* (ibid, 299).

Most graphic of the processional descriptions also comes from June-July 1498:

> *This yere the chaptur of blak monkes was kept at Couentre about the visitation of our Lady. And many of them cam on the Seturday at nyght, and some on the Morowe and taried there unto Wensday; at which time they had a general procession. And they came forth at the south durre in the Mynstere and toke their wey thurgh the newe bildyng down the Bailly-lane. And the Maire and his brethern in their scarlet Clokes with all the Craftes in theire best araye stode under the Elme in Seynt Mighelles Chirchyard. And all the pensels of the Cite before them: which pensels there went before the Crosse, and the Maire with his Brethern and the Craftes stode styll till the presidentes cam whom the Maire toke be the handes and welcomed them to town, and so folowed the procession; which procession went down the Bailly-Lane, and so forth as is usuelly used on seynt George day; and so into the Priory; and there was a solempne sermon seyde, where the Maire there satte betwixt both presidentes, and after sermon doon they departed every man to his loggyng and som with the Maire to dyner, as dyvers of them did before. And so the departed furth of the Cite etc.* (Pantin 1937, 116-7).

As the house of God, the cathedral also provided neutral ground on which could be enacted difficult but, presumably, legitimate business as indicated by the Langley Cartulary in 1255 (Coss 1980, no 434).

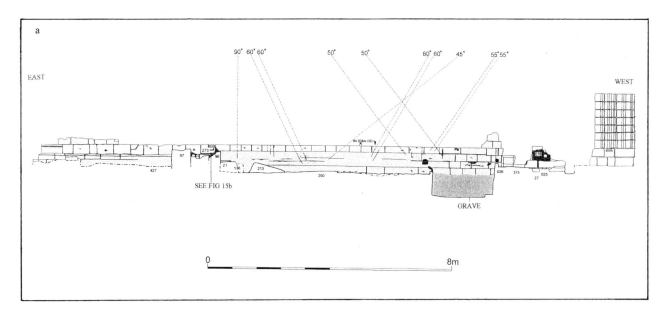

a

Fig 15   *(a) Architects tracings on south wall of nave (b) incised mason's square*

An Architect's Tracing House (Fig 15a)

Evidence suggests that bay 2 of the south aisle, before it became a chantry chapel in 1291, may have been, for some period in the thirteenth century, an architects tracing house or *chambre de traits*. Here lay the vestiges of a geometric arrangement of black lines painted into channels scored into the base-coat of thirteenth-century wall plaster. This plaster survived to a height of up to 6 courses of stonework and had been finished in lime-wash. The lines were arranged as very straight horizontals or as single or pairs of diagonals at angles of exactly 45°, 50°, 55° and 60° from the horizontal plus a single vertical. These are too regular to have been a contemporary decorative scheme and they had clearly been lime-washed over in the final wall covering. Their precision and regularity seem to indicate that they represent the vestiges of an architect's tracing, a construction aid which was usually scored into a plaster floor as at York Minster. However, they are also sometimes found on walls, examples of which can be found at Bylands Abbey (North Yorkshire) and Acton Court (Gloucester) (Richard Morris, *pers comm*). Not enough survived to suggest what items or features were being represented on the wall, but the principle was that templates could be formed from the drawings or geometric layouts from which the precision stone-work was then cut.

Here also, where much of the plaster survived, were patches of exposed stonework, their surfaces bearing a group of simple masons' or stonecutters' marks not seen anywhere else in the excavated portion of the church. They appear to have been

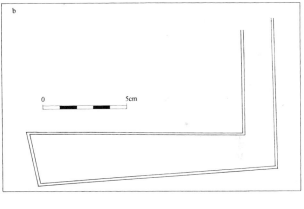

b

grouped here and are complimented by the addition of an incised mason's square on the thirteenth-century respond opposite pier 2 (Fig 15b). Such deliberate grouping can be seen locally in the tower of the gatehouse chapel adjoining Lord Leycester's Hospital in Warwick where almost every stone is marked for about three courses at just above eye-level.

Period 4

The Dissolution and After (1539-c1650)

Through documentary sources it is known that the church stood bolted and barred, but substantially undamaged until c1545, when moves to have it retained were turned down by the Crown. It was sold to agents acting for John Hales, Clerk to the

a   *b*

Fig 16   *(a) collapsed vault (b) remains of feral dogs below collapse*

Hanaper, who also bought the Coventry Whitefriars as his home; the Crown retained the rights to the materials (*L&P Henry VIII*, X, I, 1335 (51)). It is argued that the Crown would have begun dismantling soon after (Demidowicz 2000, 9). The city only finally acquired the site of the church after Hales' death in 1572, by which time it is assumed that most of the demolition had occurred and the site offered little reward for systematic, large-scale salvage by the national government. The local authorities then set about capitalising upon their investment and proceeded with the sale of remaining stone which, for them, still had a clear value in a survey of 1581 (*ibid*, 11).

During this period between the Dissolution and the wholesale demolition of the cathedral it is evident that that some slighting of the fabric took place. It is possible that acts of vandalism were, at least in part, responsible for this. The great west window was smashed upon the floor and over the robbed-out western steps before a carting ramp was laid down to remove the stone (see below). This produced a mass of high-quality painted medieval glass in very good condition (Fig 62a). Similarly the cluster of graves in the chantry chapel in the south aisle was deeply and haphazardly dug over to rob whatever might have been buried there. The resulting holes were subsequently filled with midden material and domestic rubbish, along with the disturbed human bone.

The demolition was strongly represented by a substantial layer of sandstone rubble in a sand and mortar matrix, which overlay the entire site. While there was scant evidence of squatter occupation of the ruined cathedral, in one place there was ample indication that the demolitions had left blocks of masonry, including vaulting, intact for perhaps up to fifty years until the end of the sixteenth century. This

was most obvious in bay 2 of the south aisle where the collapsed vault was recovered partly intact (Fig 16a). This sealed the crushed remains of a feral dog pack which could have used the ruined chantry as a den and may have been feeding upon the waste dumped by butchers from nearby Great Butcher Row (Fig 16b).

Elsewhere, early dismantling of the church was systematic and evidence was found at the western end of the nave for the route taken by the numerous carts necessary to take out the stone. An earthen ramp helped surmount the monumental steps leading up to the forecourt ground surface from the nave, while the heavily-laden carts left deep ruts in both the demolition trample and the exposed tile floors' mortar matrix. There was even evidence for the carts having turned and backed into the north arcade between the piers. The number of cartloads that were needed to remove the superstructure of the church probably ran into thousands. The level to which all of the structures of the nave and aisles were reduced indicates a thorough and systematic approach to making the site re-usable.

Certain parts of the cathedral are known from documents to have been left standing for some time in isolation. A sketch of 1576 by William Smythe, Herald to Queen Elizabeth, though viewed from a confused perspective, clearly shows a square tower standing close to the spires of Holy Trinity and St Michael's (Fig 12). Thereafter *c*1610, John Speed's surveyors were unimpressed and depicted merely a pile of rubble to denote the remains of the cathedral (Fig 17). In 1656 the Dutch engraver Wenceslaus Hollar, working for Sir William Dugdale, made two detailed prospects of the City. Neither showed any related towers or spires, a state of affairs which would equate to Dugdale's own lament for the result of the Dissolution:

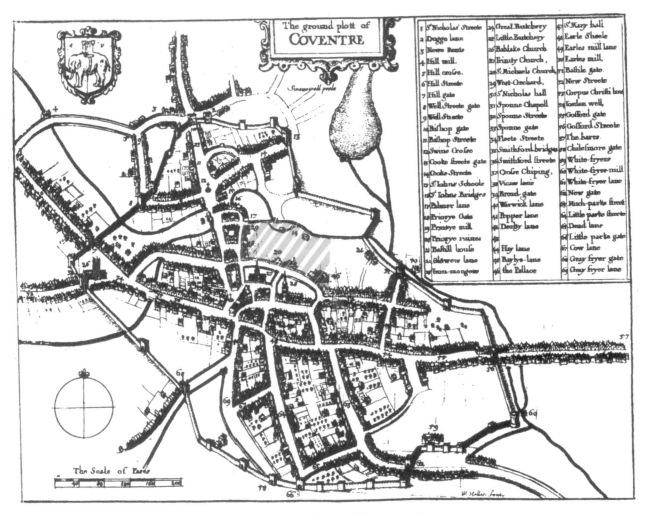

Fig 17 *John Speed's map of Coventry c1610*

At which time the very Church itself, though a most beautifull Cathedrall, and the mother-church of this City, scap't not the rude hands of the destroyers; but was pull'd in pieces and reduc't to rubbish (Dugdale Warks., 105).

However, it is clear from documentary sources that significant parts of the cathedral did survive well into the seventeenth century and beyond. Part of the south-west tower appears to have stood until at least 1654 and another 'lesser tower' stood near the crossing until c1698 (Demidowicz 2000 24-26). Surviving masonry in the vicinity of the crossing may already have been incorporated into the housing of a lead cistern by 1637 (*ibid*, 22). It is possible that the severe damage noted on the south side of the north-east crossing pier was inflicted at this time. A significant proportion of the north-west tower survived well into the nineteenth century (*ibid*, Figs 22-25) before being reduced and incorporated into the renovated Blue Coat School (1856-7).

Scrutiny of the eighteen coins or jettons recovered

from demolition contexts does little to answer questions about the exact period during which dismantling took place. Many are residual medieval coins such as two Edward III farthings of 1327-77 or French casting counters from the fourteenth century. The later jettons are generic, mainly German Nuremburg *Reichsapfel* types, the legible examples struck by the ubiquitous Hans Krauwinckel (fl 1580-1610). The only closely dateable examples comprise a Charles I Rose farthing of 1644 and a worn halfpenny of (probably) George II. It bears the partly legible date of 174 . . . The suggestion is that the nave and aisles of the cathedral were picked over for stone, certainly through the later sixteenth and seventeenth century and, in at least one place, well into the eighteenth century.

Documentary evidence suggests that the uses to which the nave was put in the 16th/17th centuries were less than fitting for a former cathedral (Poole 1870, 13). There is ample evidence for the widespread dumping of butchery waste on the west end of the nave at the end of the sixteenth-century, giving rise to the unwitting support of the above-mentioned pack of feral dogs. Dateable material from the pits hereabouts (particularly the south aisle) and the rubble deposits from where the butchery waste derives suggests this process continued for a short time at the end of the 16th to the early seventeenth century. This is in keeping with the City Annals' description of the tenancy of the site between 1611 and 1641 in which it was said:

> *Among the western ruins of this Cathedral, the butchers were accustomed to feed their animals for the supply of the public market* (Reader 1823, 140)

Rubbish pits were also dug through the middle of the nave in the late sixteenth century, the fill of the largest of them producing a jetton, probably of the Nuremburg moneyer Cornelius Lauffer, along with diagnostic sixteenth/seventeenth-century pottery. This pit was sealed by a thin topsoil trample layer which produced Manganese mottled ware of 1690-1740, suggesting that the centre of the nave was clear enough of demolition obstacles to enable pit digging perhaps by c1600, but that the entire process there was largely complete by c1700. The final layer over the nave before the introduction of a cemetery in 1776 was a poorly sorted topsoil which may be related to gardening activity. This only survived where undisturbed by later grave digging.

Period 5

Early Post-Medieval (c1650-1776)

The documented creation of a discrete garden by the Rev John Bryan outside the partly dismantled south-west tower (c1654) was probably responsible for the remarkably even final reduction of the south wall of the cathedral at its western end. This was reduced to a level of 84.9m OD, the formation level for the new garden. What lay below comprised the lowest courses of the south wall of the church on which the tracing wall lay (Fig 15a). Its vestiges were protected by the remaining build-up of rubble over the south aisle on one side and the natural ground surface on the other. Measurements appear to suggest that it formed the base for the boundary of Bryan's new garden of ten ells length (11.43m/37½ft) (Demidowicz 2000, 24 & Fig 14). The north-west tower appears to have been Bryan's dwelling by the mid-1650's and the south-west tower was intended to be turned into a gatehouse by the same lessee (*ibid, 24*). It is unclear as to whether the conversion of the latter ever took place before its eventual demolition. The presence of one of his gardens

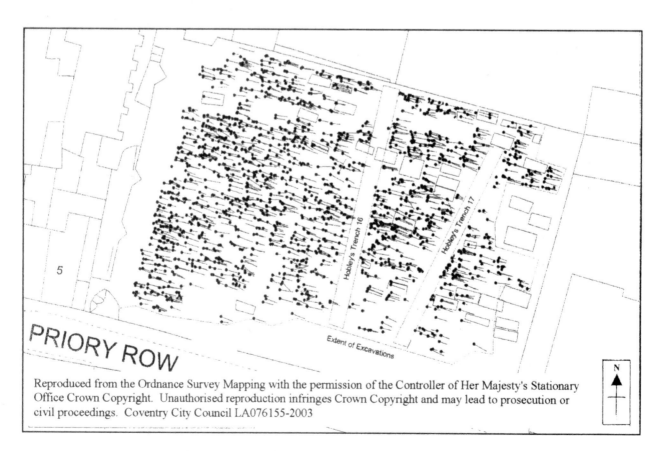

Fig 18   Position of burials excavated in Holy Trinity graveyard

running along what became Priory Row (thereby limiting profitable exploitation of a new frontage by virtue of its inherent discontinuity) would suggest that he could not at that stage align the garden north-south across the nave, perhaps because of lingering physical constraints.

Little evidence survived of the period *c*1650-*c*1776 during which cartographic and other documentary evidence indicates the presence of houses fronting Priory Row/Trinity Churchyard with gardens behind, including a possible prospect mound (*ibid*, 24-31). Physical evidence of this period comprised only the truncated bases of horticultural planting trenches noted at the base of the later burial horizon. There was residual pottery of this period in many graves, such as might have been deposited in gardens, either in pits or as horticultural crocking. The later burials had removed all but a few vestiges of such activity.

Period 6

The Graveyard (1776-1890/1975) (Fig 18)
In 1776 an extension was created to the (by then) full churchyard of Holy Trinity Church. The new extension covered the whole of the former nave and aisles of the cathedral, a plot measuring 47m (east-west) x 32m (north-south) (154 x 105ft). It was full by 1850 although family plots continued to be filled as late as 1890.

Construction in the 1850s of brick foundations for a timber bell-tower and in 1975 of the former Holy Trinity Church Centre had both caused localised damage to the cemetery as was noted during the watching brief on the latter's demolition in 1999. Drains and other service conduits had been largely left *in situ* during the demolition. Little remained of the foundations of the bell-tower. The vestiges recorded in 1965 by Hobley (1971, Fig 4) still comprise the most substantial encountered. The construction of the former church centre had removed all but an amorphous mass of brick and mortar rubble close to the surface which had once been one corner of the foundation.

The construction programme of 1975 also resulted in the truncation of a number of the extant brick burial vaults together with the removal and whole-sale *ex-situ* burial of many gravestones which were recovered and moved for safekeeping during the excavation. Parts of thirty-six further gravestones were retrieved from the back-fill of the 1965-7 trial excavation trenches and appropriately recorded. None of the gravestones could be attributed to individual skeletons excavated.

When in use the cemetery was detached from the church and flanked by buildings to the east and west. To the north was a high sandstone boundary

Fig 19   Excavation of brick-lined burial vault

wall built on top of the reduced remains of the former north aisle wall, while to the south was Priory Row, from which it was divided by a low stone wall surmounted by iron railings. The cemetery was created by the importation of thousands of tons of topsoil to augment what already overlay the cathedral ruins. By the end of its life (*c*1890) the last graves were being dug through 2.2m of topsoil.

Within the cemetery thirty-seven brick-lined burial vaults were found and eight were excavated (Fig 19) and a total of 1706 articulated inhumations were recorded. All date from the period *c*1776-*c*1890, although no new plots were allotted after *c*1850 when the cemetery was closed under ecclesiastical law. In addition the previous evaluations excavated a further forty-six articulated burials. A further *c*100 individuals were excavated during subsequent watching briefs. There was much disarticulated bone throughout the grave soils. Large blocks of cemetery deposit were left unexcavated with the potential to contain up to perhaps 200 further articulated skeletons. It is not known exactly how many burials were removed in the 1965-7 excavations which did not, apparently, record this horizon in detail.

It is likely that the graveyard contained at least 2500 inhumations of which 1855 have been excavated and recorded as above. Approximately 200 remain *in situ* with the remainder removed by unmonitored earth moving between *c*1850 and 1975.

The Monastic House

The Cloister

Original Appearance and Development

The cloister occupies the second terrace on the northern slope of the hillside. Its southern alley overlies late Saxon burials and the foundations of an earlier feature (see MID-LATE SAXON/EARLY MEDIEVAL OCCUPATION). There is no evidence for its date of construction and early appearance. As was discovered during the excavations of 1965-7, little remained of the arcade above foundation level. Of the hundreds of pieces of *ex situ* architectural stonework found in the vicinity, only two can be associated with an open Early Gothic arcade (T737 & T738). Both are double capital blocks with foliate carving and date from the late twelfth century (see THE WORKED STONES AND ARCHITECTURAL STONEWORK). Beyond these pieces the earliest remains are of the Early English style of the thirteenth century and are primarily represented by the doorway which connects the south alley to the nave of the cathedral.

The proportions of the cloister were found to differ somewhat from those presented in the 1965-7 excavation report. Here the author had conjectured a square garth with sides of 24.3m surrounded by a 3m-wide alley (Hobley 1971, 95). The revised measurements show an irregular quadrilateral cloister with alleys of varying widths (ranging between 2.40m-3.20m/8ft-10½ft).

The cloister alleys were evidently tiled during the lifetime of the priory. However, in common with the rest of the site, very few of the floor tiles survived *in situ*. A small area was found preserved in the south aisle close to the doorway to the nave. These formed a chequered pattern of alternating yellow and green (also observed in the western nave), broken by the insertion of a single tile of floral/geometric design – presumably an *ad hoc* repair. Elsewhere the presence of tiles was indicated by impressions in the surviving mortar bedding layer. The level of the tiled alley was *c*83.15m OD, roughly 1.25m lower than that of the cathedral floor. Five steps (each dropping 0.25m) within the thickness of the nave wall may have resolved the difference in levels.

Loose tiles found in the demolition rubble overlying the cloister spanned the 13th, 14th and 15th centuries, suggesting, at the very least, regular,

localised replacement (see THE FLOOR TILES). Wholesale re-flooring was indicated in the stratigraphy of the eastern alley at its north end, where two distinct mortar bedding layers were present separated by a thin layer of re-deposited natural clay. This may have become necessary due to the original floor level sinking into grave cuts located in the vicinity of the chapter house doorway (see Appendix 3).

The 1965-7 excavations also located graves in the south and west alleys. Further discoveries were made in the south aisle during the recent excavations (see THE HUMAN BONE). There was no evidence for burials in the north alley.

Excavation within the garth itself was limited and provided little evidence of its appearance in the monastic period. A possible grave cut was observed but not excavated, as was a deep rubble-filled feature towards its centre. In a similar location part of a structure comprised of large, dressed sandstone blocks was observed during development ground works. This may have been the vestige of a conduit house or cistern; close examination was impossible due to hazardous working conditions.

Access to Cloister

A number of doorways entered the cloister from the cathedral and surrounding claustral ranges. Of these, those of the chapter house and nave were well preserved and most useful in terms of elucidating phases of the cloister's development. The latter, constructed in the Early English Gothic style, provided the earliest *in situ* dating for the cloister and lay at the southern end of the west alley. The western jamb of this door (T428) (Fig 20), complete with its base block and a detached shaft, has been dated to *c*1220-50 (see THE WORKED STONES AND ARCHITECTURAL STONEWORK). The jamb is stylistically the same as both the great west door of the cathedral and another doorway discovered in the external wall of the west range. The steps which would have been required to descend from the nave into the cloister had been robbed out save for a single block preserved below the west jamb. It is possible that a corresponding doorway into the nave may have existed at the southern end of the east alley. Unfortunately the wall here had been robbed away and re-built as part of the eighteenth/nineteenth-century graveyard wall.

The doorway giving access to the chapter house was located off the eastern alley and was initially exposed during the excavations of 1965-7 when the base block of the south jamb (T228) was uncovered and removed (Hobley 1971, 95). Its architectural form was dated to the fourteenth-century Decorated period. Subsequent discoveries in the chapter house have refined this date to *c*1300-30, a time when a major re-build took place (see **The Chapter House**).

Fig 20 *Jamb of door from cloister to nave*

On the north side of the chapter house doorway, built into the wall, was a low stone bench which may have provided seating for the monks as they waited to be called before the chapter.

The space between the chapter house and the north transept is cautiously interpreted as a passageway or slype leading from the cloister to the area north of the cathedral's eastern arm. Comparison with the plans of other monastic houses show that not only passages, but libraries, vestries and sacristies are commonly found in this location. At Coventry, however, there was no evidence to suggest any function at ground floor level other than a through-passage.

Points of access were also located in the north wall of the cloister. In the north-east corner a set of steps was discovered leading down between the north and east ranges (see **Undercrofts and Courtyard**). A blocked doorway was also observed at foundation level roughly half way along the north range. This would have led to the undercroft located below the refectory. Another doorway, giving access to the refectory, may have been located in the north-west corner of the cloister (see **The Refectory**).

Only short sections of the west cloister alley were excavated and although no doorway was found, it is assumed that there would have been access from the west range into the cloister.

Refurbishment in the Perpendicular Style
A refurbishment of the cloister in the late fourteenth or fifteenth century was clearly indicated by the assemblage of architectural fragments found in the overlying demolition layer. These fragments were characterised not only by their architectural style but also by the introduction of a grey sandstone (green when first excavated) replacing the hitherto

ubiquitous red stone (Fig 49a). This soft, fine-grained stone was widely used in the fourteenth century and was well suited for carving the intricate detail exhibited by late Gothic art. Despite its softness, it survived well when not subjected to external weathering. In the cloister alley it was used to line the back wall with blind tracery. The inspiration for the new work at St Mary's may have come from Gloucester Cathedral where a similar arrangement exists (see **THE WORKED STONES AND ARCHITECTURAL STONEWORK**). The design of the arcades was also altered at this time with the introduction of glazed tracery. In one instance this was found to consist of both red and grey stone (T082 & T134) which would not have created a problem aesthetically, as all of the stonework was lime-washed.

Further elements of the cloister's Perpendicular decoration were hinted at by the discovery of fragments of a sculptured figure (T255) and an elaborate statue base (T684) (Fig 53c) found immediately inside the doorway to the nave. The latter was the lower half of a life-size figure of a soldier saint, possibly St Paul or St George. It may have originally stood in a recess in front of the east door jamb which appears to be of the same size and shape as the base of the statue. Traces of a similar recess on the other side of the doorway suggest the door was flanked by a pair of statues which had, presumably, been targeted for destruction at the Dissolution.

Evidence for a Lavatorium
Excavation revealed significant mortared footings projecting into the north alley from its north wall which may have been related to a *lavatorium*. Nothing survived above foundation level to clarify this but a drain running north from the north-east corner of the cloister could have carried water from such a feature into the main drainage system (see **Undercrofts and Courtyard**).

Use in Post-Dissolution Period
In the immediate post-Dissolution period it would appear that the demolition gangs used the open space of the cloister garth for collecting and preparing re-usable stone leaving behind patches of loose mortar, sandstone chippings and slate. Decorative pieces unsuitable for re-use, such as window tracery and mouldings, were also found in large quantities, many of which originated from the surrounding buildings rather than the cloister arcade. The dominance of decorative fragments over ashlar in the cloister assemblage was mirrored throughout the site and bears testament to the thorough, yet selective process of stone robbing.

The Chapter House

Early Form and Development

The chapter house was located on the east side of the cloister with its doorway (1.7m wide) lying slightly north of centre in relation to the alley. The internal dimensions of the building at the Dissolution measured 8m x *c*22m/26ft x *c*72ft). The eastern end of the chapter house was apsidal of part octagonal form. The majority of the excavated material from the building derives from the first half of the fourteenth century when it appears to have been entirely re-built.

The excavations revealed almost the entire length of the north wall of the chapter house. Heavily robbed in its interior, the line of its north wall survived to a great depth as it retained the third terrace of the hillside. As such, it also formed the south interior wall of a range of undercrofts which occupied the area to the north of the chapter house. Architectural features, including the responds (T487-489) built into the wall at undercroft level, have been dated to the thirteenth century. This suggests the presence of a contemporary upstanding chapter house north wall, predating the re-build by over half a century.

At ground level, nothing remained *in situ* of a Romanesque or Early English predecessor and of the mass of architectural fragments found in the vicinity only a handful predated the re-build. From this small assemblage not a single fragment can be positively assigned to the superstructure of the chapter house. However, one would expect that the fourteenth-century building reused some of the fabric from the earlier one and this would have been present in the post-Dissolution demolition rubble. Romanesque fragments with evidence of later re-use were found, including a voussoir from a small arch (T177) and two scalloped capitals (T179 & T800), one of which had been incorporated into a large fourteenth-century jamb. Early English fragments found close to the chapter house included two capitals (T747, T796) but neither of these bore evidence of re-use. Although the original provenance of these stones remains unknown, it is possible that some of them are vestiges of the original chapter house. These tenuous examples, however, do little to elucidate the appearance and size of the early building. If, as is assumed, the fourteenth-century chapter house stood on the foundations of a former structure, then it seems reasonable to postulate that they were of similar size. The scarcity of early stonework may indicate the use of timber as a building material, perhaps for the roof as observed in the nave, but it is also possible that much of the fabric of the first chapter house was completely removed from the site prior to the re-build.

The Decorated Period

Firm evidence for the physical characteristics of the chapter house dates almost entirely from the fourteenth-century re-build. As very little of the structure remained *in situ* above ground level, physical evidence is largely provided by the mass of architectural fragments found in the surrounding demolition rubble. Copious amounts of stonework carved in the Decorated style of *c*1300-30 were found in the vicinity. Many were retrieved from a *c*4m-deep deposit of rubble which filled the undercrofts to the north and buried the neighbouring yard area. The lower level of rubble appeared to represent the initial deposition of unusable architectural fragments. This was overlain by the detritus of opportunistic stone robbing and localised dumping. From this vast jumble of architectural fragments, those related to the chapter house were found to be contemporary with the significant discoveries made during the excavations of 1965-7 (Hobley 1971, 96). As well as the doorway mentioned above, a section of the south wall was also excavated at this time. Its interior face bore a low, stone bench and a single shaft – probably remnants of the seats (*sedilia*) that the brethren occupied during meetings. Perhaps the most important discovery made by Hobley was the angled return of the south wall at its eastern extremity establishing the partly polygonal plan of the east end.

Evidence from the excavations has enabled a detailed reconstruction of both the internal and external architecture. Elements of a high vault were found including springers, ribs and a boss from the apex of a window arch (T377) (Fig 49c). They indicate a vault of tierceron design similar to that of the Lady Chapel at Lichfield Cathedral which dates from 1315-30 (Gill & Morris 2001, 470). The discovery of a corner springer (T343/9) set at an angle of 135° is of vital importance as it allows, for the first time, an accurate reconstruction of the apsidal east end to be made. Based upon the vaulting pattern, the interior of the chapter house appears to have been divided into four bays – three rectangular and of equal proportion with a fourth part lying to the east (*ibid*, 471). This again parallels the design of the Lady Chapel at Lichfield.

Many of the architectural fragments relate to the window design of this period. Pre-eminent amongst the diagnostic pieces are fragments of tracery bearing ballflower decoration. In addition, pieces of window jamb (T309, T762 & T765), arch (T309/12/13) and mullion (T942, T943, T972) have all been dated to the early fourteenth century. Together they have facilitated the reconstruction of highly decorative windows with lights terminating in trefoil shapes (Plate 4b). Similar windows survive in local churches (e.g. Cubbington) and it has been suggested that these may reflect the craftsmanship of a priory workshop (see **THE WORKED STONES AND ARCHITECTURAL STONEWORK**). Another important piece, possibly associated with the chapter house window tracery, is the decapitated sculpture of an angelic figure clad in draperies (T919) (Fig 54b). It appears to have been attached to its 'block' by its upper torso leaving its feet hanging free. Carved in the 'court' style of the late thirteenth/early fourteenth century, similar figures appear in the window tracery at St Albans Abbey (Lady Chapel *c*1310-25) and Dorchester Abbey (chancel *c*1330) (Richard Morris, *pers comm*). More evidence for the splendour of the chapter house windows came from the hundreds of sherds of stained and painted glass found lying over its robbed out floor (Fig 62b).

The interior walls of the chapter house were decorated with blind arcading incorporating trefoil cusped arches topped with tall gables (Gill & Morris 2001, 470). The monk's *sedilia* were accommodated at the base of the arcade. Between the springing of each pair of gables was a niche for a statue (Fig 52 & Plate 4b). To complement the window design, ballflower carvings decorated the jambs for the arcades and canopies (T242, T346). The canopies were capped by elaborate foliate capitals (T139, T965). The blind wall panelling of the arcade appears to have been left undecorated initially, but was subsequently painted with a highly significant work of art.

Apocalypse Wall Painting (Plate 3a-d)
Many of the important architectural fragments from the chapter house were discovered at the foot of its north wall lying where they had been thrown into the undercroft. The most significant of these were two springer stones from the blind arcade, one flanked by wall plates (T698/5) and the other with only its right-hand plate surviving (T698/1). The plates were painted with finely executed polychrome designs depicting scenes of the Apocalypse from the Book of Revelations. The painting has been dated to the period *c*1360-70 (see **THE CHAPTER HOUSE APOCALYPSE PANELS**).

Floor
The floor of the chapter house had been extensively robbed leaving only dispersed patches of mortar, occasionally impressed with the outline of a group of tiles. Many fragments of broken tile were recovered from the demolition layer, some of which had identifiable decorative designs (see **THE FLOOR TILES**). Most were of the fourteenth century and decorated with heraldic, animal or floral designs – the *fleur-de-lys* being a recurrent symbol. Other tiles were identified as being part of a four- or nine-tile pattern but the total assemblage was too small to attempt a reconstruction of the overall floor design. In line with

the chapter house re-build, none of the fragments predated the fourteenth century.

Graves (Figs 21, 22 & 75)
Over half of the chapter house's internal area was excavated and two graves were discovered. The first, a stone-lined grave, was found just inside the west door (Fig 75). Its slab had evidently been broken and removed – a number of fragments were found in the upper grave fill. Interred within was a well-preserved skeleton of a *c*1.69m-tall mature adult male (Fig 21). Osteological analysis of the bones (O'Connell 1999) indicated that the individual had sustained two broken ribs during his lifetime, possibly caused by a fall or crushing injury. He also suffered from various forms of joint disease, including Diffuse Idiopathic Skeletal Hyperostosis (DISH), which is commonly found in monastic burials of mature adults.

Radiocarbon analysis dates the burial to the period 1280-1410AD (95.4% probability) (*ibid*, 6). The fill of the grave contained a floor tile of the fourteenth/fifteenth century, indicating that the inhumation probably took place took place in the second half of

Fig 21   *Stone-lined grave inside west door of chapter house*

the radiocarbon range. Further, more specific, dating evidence for this burial is provided by the style of the decoration on the fragments of grave slab. They are part of a demi-effigy of the type produced by the London brass engraving workshops *c*1350-70 (Sally Badham, *pers comm*). A similar slab can be found at Salisbury Cathedral and has been dated to *c*1360 (*ibid*).

Burial within the prestigious confines of the chapter house would have been reserved for those of the highest eminence. With this in mind it becomes difficult to ignore the possibility that the remains belong to a former Prior of St Mary's. Only two priors are known to have died within or close to the established date range; William Irreys, elected 1342, died 1349 and William de Dunstable, elected 1349, died 1361 (*VCH Warks.* 2 1965, 58). Whoever he was, after analysis, his remains were re-interred in his original grave.

The second grave was indicated by the discovery of a complete but fractured Purbeck marble grave slab measuring 1m x 2.40m (Fig 22a&b). It was located towards the east end of the building, set into the mortar floor close to the south wall (Fig 75). The slab was decorated with a central cross and had an inscription around its border. The Lomabrdic lettering was in Norman French and read as follows:

a   *b*

Fig 22   *John Aylmer's grave-slab (a) as excavated (b) reconstruction*

VOUS:KY:PASSEZ:PAR:ICY:
PRIEZ:POUR:LE:SUPPRIOR:KY:GIST:ICY:
DANS:JOHAN:AYLMER:AVOIT:NOUN:
CENT:IOURS:AVEREZ:DE:PARDOUN

This translates to:

You who pass by here
Pray for the Sub-Prior who lies here
He was named Dom John Aylmer
You shall have 100 days indulgence

Both the inscription (translated by Sally Badham) and cross were originally inlaid with brass, most of which had been robbed away leaving only a few circular 'plugs' in the colons between the words. A dark-brown clayey residue, possibly an adhesive, was found in the indent for the head of the cross.

The slab would appear to be a fairly standard product of the London marblers of the late thirteenth/early fourteenth century (Sally Badham, *pers comm*). Most have rhyming inscriptions of this sort and similarly offer indulgences for the souls of those who pray for the deceased. Although Latin inscriptions are more commonly found on the grave slabs of clerics, there are also those in Norman French. Lombardic lettering of this type was produced between *c*1270-1350 and came in three standard sizes; 36mm, 43mm and 51mm. The lettering on the slab from the chapter house used the largest of these sizes. The cross itself is unusual in that the head is not one of the two most common types of design and its mount depicts a crouched animal rather than the more widely used stepped Calvary.

No references to a sub-prior named John Aylmer have been found to date but a John Aylmer is recorded as a priest witnessing a deed in Coventry in the 1280s (Coss 1986, 199-200). The re-building of the chapter house in the early fourteenth century would, presumably have involved the replacement of the floor and the disturbance of any graves set into it. For this reason it is more likely that the slab was laid after this time, possibly in the second quarter of the century. If the priest of the 1280's was a young man it is plausible that he may have survived into old age as a sub-prior of St Mary's and died sometime after *c*1325. In 1301 it is recorded that a Brother Adam was sub-prior therefore it is likely that Aylmer became sub-prior after this date (Hughes 2001,119).

As the grave was not threatened by the development the slab was left *in situ* and its location is to be marked by a plaque.

Post-Dissolution
Following the Dissolution the chapter house appears to have been subjected to a thorough and systematic demolition. Firstly, it would appear that the floor tiles were removed. The windows were then smashed, carpeting the freshly exposed mortar-bedding layer with many hundreds of fragments of stained and painted glass (Fig 62b). As they were concentrated within the building rather than around its perimeter, it is reasonable to conclude that the windows were deliberately smashed from the outside as seen at the west end of the cathedral. Alternatively, the glass could have been deposited whilst window panels were stripped of their lead within the shell of the building. Vandalism, salvage or a combination of both (whichever process may have accounted for the destruction of the windows), the small amount of lead recovered during the excavation attests to the thoroughness of its robbing.

The remaining fabric was then dismantled and the re-usable stone taken away. Evidence for the speed and efficiency of this process was found in the lower level of rubble filling the neighbouring undercroft. It was mainly comprised of ornate pieces from the chapter house such as window tracery and sections of the upper blind arcade. In contrast, plain architectural pieces such as ashlar were all but absent. Furthermore, stonework relating to the vault of both the chapter house and the undercroft itself was scarce. The predominance of highly decorative pieces and lack of vaulting suggests that, rather than being subjected to a brutal demolition resulting in an *ad hoc* collapse, the chapter house was carefully dismantled from the roof down. Unwanted stonework was thrown into the undercroft which, having already lost its roof, now functioned as a handy repository.

Undercrofts and Courtyard (Figs 23 & 24)

The Third Terrace
Immediately to the north of the chapter house, the remains of two undercrofts were discovered, one aligned east-west (4m x *c*17.5m/13ft x *c*57½ft), the other north-south (*c*6.5m x *c*11.5m/21ft x *c*38ft). These formed an 'L' shape around a courtyard which was further enclosed by the south wall of the dormitory block on its north side. Due to the terraced nature of the hillside, the undercrofts were below ground on their southern (chapter house) side but accessible from ground level on their northern side. From these undercrofts, the cut of the third terrace continued eastward on the same line to accommodate the infirmary and westward in a dog-leg around the north-east corner of the cloister where it is retained by the south wall of the north range undercrofts below the refectory.

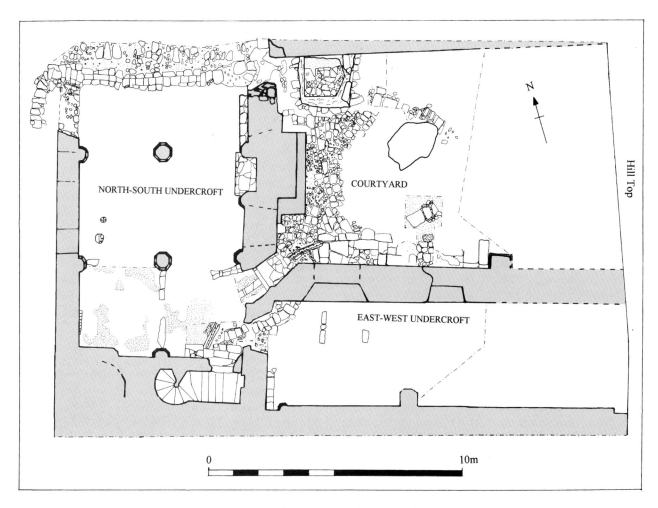

Fig 23   Excavated features in undercrofts and courtyard

Structural Evidence

The preservation of the upstanding walls in this area was exceptional and enables a relatively straight-forward reconstruction of the appearance of the undercrofts and courtyard at the time of the Dissolution. However, this final arrangement was the product of a complicated sequence of building phases and minor alterations (Fig 24a-d). There is no convincing *in situ* evidence for a Romanesque structure in this area. However, some very poorly coursed patches of stonework in the earliest walls may be remnant of such work. A handful of Romanesque architectural fragments were found in the demolition rubble (e.g. T758, T737, T738, T800) but their provenance remains unknown as the undercrofts were used for dumping in the post-Dissolution period (see below). None of the walls relating to the overlying buildings survived.

Early Thirteenth-Century Undercroft (Fig 24a)

Originally a single undercroft ran along the entire length of the north side of the chapter house terminating at the eastern cloister wall. The south

wall, despite many later alterations, has survived to within a metre of its full height (c4.70m). Its internal arrangement comprised of a row of six rectangular bays each measuring 4m x c4.35m/13ft x c14ft. The four easternmost bays together with part of the north wall survived subsequent alterations and remained intact forming a smaller undercroft. The other two bays, along with the western section of its north wall, disappeared in the wake of later alterations. The primary evidence for this early arrangement was the presence of two opposing vault springers *in situ* at the west end of the later east-west undercroft (T489 & T490). These have been dated to the first half of the thirteenth century (see **THE WORKED STONES AND ARCHITECTURAL STONEWORK**). The springers originally divided two bays but the vault was subsequently altered to span only the space to the east. Evidence for the north wall was provided by an obvious scar where it had originally met the eastern cloister wall and, in addition, robbed-out foundations were discovered on the same alignment.

It is likely that an entrance was placed somewhere in the north wall of the undercroft. The west wall

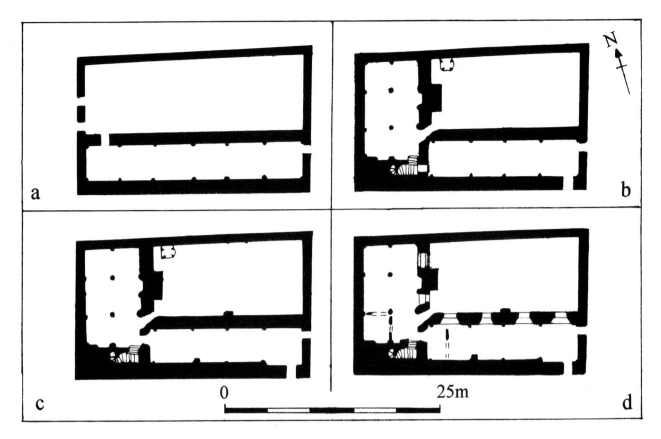

Fig 24   *Sequence of building phases in undercroft and courtyard (a) early thirteenth century (b) mid-late thirteenth century (c) early fourteenth century (d) fourteenth/fifteenth century*

continued northwards, possibly forming the original east wall of the refectory undercroft. Two doorways of thirteenth-century date were present in this wall. One may have given access to the refectory under-crofts and the other may have connected with the cloister via a flight of steps – once again lost to later alterations. At its eastern end the undercroft may have joined the infirmary, where a doorway was found during the 1960's excavations (Hobley 1971, 98). A further doorway may have led up from the south wall of the sixth bay to the area east of the chapter house (see below).

Nothing was found to suggest that this undercroft functioned as anything other than a storage area. A compacted earth floor, discovered at the lowest level of a sequence of well-stratified deposits within the later east-west undercroft, probably dates from this period. It was overlain by a deposit of organic matter interspersed with many fine lenses of sand which contained pottery dated to the period *c*1200-50 and a Long Cross Halfpenny of post-1247 (JFK00 SF15). This layer also contained a large quantity of herring bones.

To the north, running parallel with the undercroft, lies the south wall of the dormitory block, apparently already in existence by this period. Three pier bases recorded in this vicinity by J F Tickner in the

nineteenth century were interpreted by Hobley as belonging to the dormitory undercroft (Hobley 1971, 98). The multi-scallop capitals which sat over these are of a Romanesque style (Morris 1994, 50) implying that the dormitory block predated the early thirteenth-century undercroft. No evidence was recovered for a building occupying the space between the structures; however it is extremely unlikely that the western (claustral) end was left open.

Mid-late Thirteenth-Century Re-build (Fig 24b)
The latter half of the thirteenth century saw the construction of a second undercroft on a north-south alignment incorporating the western end of the earlier building. This involved the demolition of almost 9m of the earlier north wall and the construction of another wall on a north-south axis which bisected the earlier undercroft forming an 'L'-shaped structure around a courtyard.

A layer consisting of sand and fragments of building material was found overlying the robbed out remains of the north wall of the early undercroft. A single sherd of pottery, Chilvers Coton 'A' ware (1250-1300), was found in this deposit. Overlying this layer was the mortar bedding for the tiled floor of the new undercroft. The floor surface in the remaining

Fig 25   Passageway leading from undercroft to courtyard

part of the early undercroft to the east also appears to have been levelled up over the earlier occupation debris at this time.

In the newly created north-south undercroft a newel staircase was built against the south wall. Access to the cloister could now be gained by ascending this staircase and exiting through the room above. At the foot of the stairs there were doorways giving access to both undercrofts. The east-west one was accessible through a pointed archway and the north-south one could be reached by passing through a doorway and descending a few more steps. Another doorway was located in the south-east bay of the new undercroft leading into the courtyard via a short covered passageway (Fig 25).

The width of the newel staircase dictated the position of the southern end of the new vault. To support the south-west corner springer a large block of masonry was built which projected eastward as far as the apex of the vault (Fig 26). An arch spanned the gap between this and the stairwell thus creating a void below. This space probably functioned as a storage area similar to a domestic 'cupboard under the stairs'. Holes in the wall for fittings found at the entrance indicated that the space could be closed off by a gate or door.

It would appear that, before these modifications took place, the corner springer was removed from the western end of the first undercroft and re-used a

Fig 26   Elevation of south wall of north-south undercroft

80.30m
E

W

0   2m

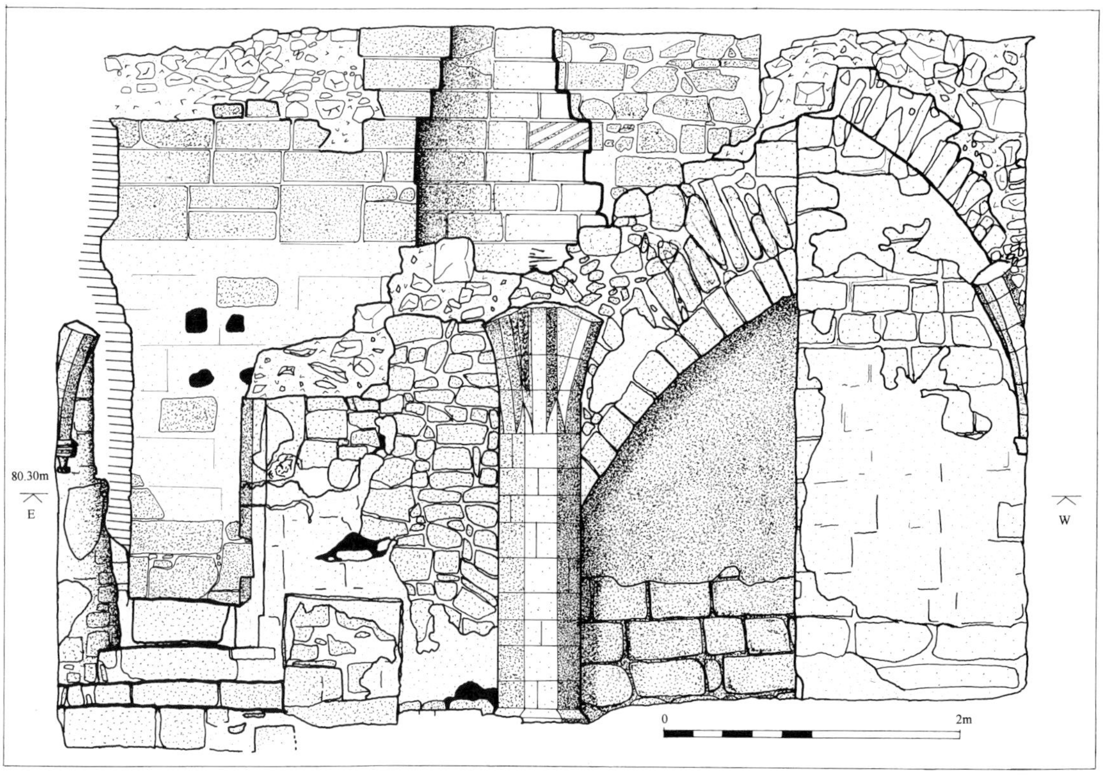

Fig 27 Fireplace in north-south undercroft

metre or so forward as part of the new vaulting arrangement. A scar can be seen on the west wall of the undercroft where the earlier corner springer was inserted. The vault of the north-south undercroft spanned three bays on its north-south axis and two on its east-west and was supported by two octagonal free-standing piers. The north and south bays measured $c3.50m^2/11\frac{1}{2}ft^2$ and flanked a slightly longer rectangular bay. To construct this vault the two doorways in the west wall had to be blocked as they corresponded with the positions of the new wall springers.

A fireplace was built into the eastern wall of the undercroft (Fig 27). Its flagged hearth projected into the room and was flanked by two polygonal jambs, one of which doubled as the respond for the northern free-standing pier. The back of the fireplace was clad with courses of bricks and roof tile. The base of the chimney breast sat upon a finely crafted masonry plinth which protruded into the courtyard.

As this was the only building discovered with a fireplace it suggests that this undercroft was a purpose-built warming room. The proximity of the infirmary would add weight to this suggestion.

Structural Instability (Fig 24c)

At some time in the early fourteenth century there would appear to have been a problem with the structural stability of the south wall. To counteract this, a number of measures were taken. In addition to a buttress being constructed around the second vaulting springer in the east-west undercroft, the whole of the south wall up to the fourth springer was thickened by $c20mm$, burying the sides of the responds (Fig 28 & 29). East of the fourth springer, corresponding with the point at which the apsidal end of the chapter house started, the wall retained its original thickness. It is also likely that both sides of the archway at the foot of the newel staircase were also blocked at this time creating, in effect, another large buttress. In doing this, the access between the undercrofts would have been cut off so a new archway was inserted to the north of the earlier one. The archway appears to have been re-used from another part of the site as the voussoirs (T460) date from the period $c1200$ thus making the 'new' arch, stylistically, over a century out of date (see THE WORKED STONES AND ARCHITECTURAL STONEWORK).

There are a number of factors which may have contributed to this instability. The wall was under considerable stress as it formed the foundation for the chapter house and also retained the deepest of the site's terraces. This created the potential for structural instability; a situation no doubt exacerbated by the major alterations made to the undercrofts throughout the thirteenth century. In many instances this involved new masonry features being chopped into the walls. The re-building of the

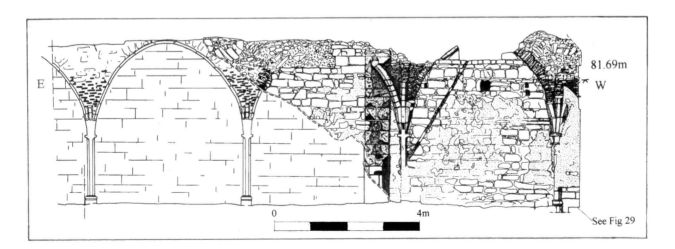

Fig 28 Elevation of south wall of east-west undercroft

Fig 29   *Wall thickening in south wall of east-west undercroft*

Fig 30   *External view of chimney breast*

chapter house during the first three decades of the fourteenth century may have brought these problems to a head. Alternatively, this extensive programme of works may have encompassed the strengthening of the wall, as its stability was vital for the longevity of the chapter house.

Later Medieval Modifications (Fig 24d)
In addition to strengthening the main walls, a series of modifications took place throughout the 14th and 15th centuries. These included the insertion of windows in both undercrofts, the construction of stone and later lead-lined drains, the raising of floor surfaces and localised partitioning of internal space.

Perhaps the most significant of these episodes was the insertion of glazed windows into those walls which faced onto the yard. This new arrangement placed a window on either side of the fireplace in the north-south undercroft and windows in the first and third bays of the east-west one. Their construction post-dates *c*1325 (see THE WORKED STONES AND ARCHITECTURAL STONEWORK). In each case the surrounding wall had been dismantled to accommodate the window, then re-built using sub-standard ashlar and core work which consisted of not only the usual stone and mortar but also soil. In the interior this poor craftsmanship was largely hidden by thick applications of mortar and lime wash. On the exterior walls, however, no attempt had been made to hide the inferior masonry work.

The insertion of the window to the south of the fireplace was complicated by the presence of the chimney breast whose southern side would have blocked part of the window (Fig 30). To avoid this, the width of the breast was reduced by half a metre. The re-build resulted in the same poor finish as that around the windows. Modifications were also made to the fireplace, probably involving the replacement of the lintel or arch over the hearth. Corbels of Perpendicular style date this work to the post-1350

period (see THE WORKED STONES AND ARCHITECTURAL STONEWORK).

The insertion of windows in the east-west undercroft may have been accompanied by the raising of the existing floor level. The new floor was comprised of a 70-80mm-thick mortar layer, over which lay an organic occupation layer containing fourteenth-century pottery.

The construction of a number of stone-lined drains also affected the undercrofts (Fig 23 & 46). The first of these ran from the north-east cloister, dropped to the third terrace and turned sharply west into the north-south undercroft (Fig 31). From here it ran parallel with the north wall before turning northwards into the dormitory block. In order to carry this drain from the cloister, a wall was built across the refectory undercroft *c*2.80m from its eastern end. The drain was supported within the resulting void by a raft of sandstone rubble. Pottery found within this deposit dates from the fourteenth century. Steps were then built in the north-east corner of the cloister over the drain and onto a flagged surface. The level of this surface did not correspond to any of the floor levels of the surrounding buildings and, furthermore, there was no evidence to suggest that related apertures had been present in any of the enclosing walls. This suggests that the surface was simply a landing and that the steps continued to descend northward. Here they could have emerged into the kitchen court or turned sharply to the right and provided access to the north-south undercroft in its north-west corner. The wall here had been robbed down to foundation level removing the evidence, if any existed, of a doorway in this location.

The remains of a door jamb, discovered on the upper west side of the steps, has been dated to the period 1320-60 (see THE WORKED STONES AND ARCHITECTURAL STONEWORK) implying that the drain was most probably inserted in the first half of the fourteenth century. A stairwell had been

Fig 31 Stone-lined drain running from cloister to undercroft

constructed to the north and east of the top steps thus permitting access from the north alley only. The north arm of the stairwell appeared to respect the position of a conjectured doorway into the room above the north-south undercroft (see below).

Another stone drain ran from a feature attached to the south wall of the north-south undercroft, through the re-used archway and out into the courtyard via the north-east corner of the east-west undercroft. The rectangular feature from which it appears to have originated was robbed down to a single course of masonry which projected *c*0.5m off the wall. The centre of this 'plinth' was hollow. A scar on the wall behind it indicated that the feature had once stood to a height of *c*0.8m. It may have supported a basin or stoup, facilitating drainage through its hollow interior. A waterspout decorated with a glaring human head (T757) was found in the rubble fill of the undercroft. It is possible that this once directed water to the feature from a lead pipe through its mouth. The wall above was very poorly constructed and has a large void in it where such a spout could have once sat.

The floor level adjacent to this feature was raised over the drain. The material deposited for this purpose contained pottery dating to the period 1400-70. Tiles remaining *in situ* against the west wall of the undercroft relate to this elevated level. Where the drain entered the east undercroft it was raised above the floor on a rubble raft before disappearing through the north wall and into the courtyard.

Towards the end of the monastic period this drain was removed in the vicinity of the wall fitting and replaced with a shallow 'u'-shaped lead drain formed around a low kerb and capped with sandstone (Fig 32a). It was inserted below the lowest step adjacent to the fitting and ran directly out into the courtyard under the threshold of the covered passage. From here it ran for a short distance uncapped before flattening out (Fig 32b). Drainage was then facilitated by the flagged surface of the courtyard which had been purposefully laid to channel water away to the east.

Other late alterations to the undercrofts included the partitioning of internal space. In both undercrofts

a　　　　　　　　　　　　　　b

Fig 32 Lead-lined drain (a) in undercroft (b) in courtyard

the remains of stone sills were found which would have carried wooden screens. In the east-west undercroft, the division lies in front of the west window bay and cuts through the final floor surface. In the other, the remnants of stone sills were found enclosing the south-west bay and slots to attach the screen are visible in the south pier and its westerly respond. The resulting enclosed area would have included the space 'under the stairs'. The partitioning appears to be contemporary with the construction of the last tiled floor in the fifteenth century.

Although the overall purpose of the alterations is unclear, their effect would have created a more pleasant environment with the introduction of light and possibly the provision of water. There was no archaeological evidence to explain the reason for the partitioning in the undercrofts.

Rooms Above
Whilst the fabric of the undercrofts was well preserved in the lee of the terrace, almost nothing remained of the buildings above. The only *in situ* evidence for an interior feature comes from a stone plinth (c83.40m OD) located at the top of the newel stair. Within the room this feature would have sat slightly to the west of the point where it emerged and may be part of a guard around the stairwell. A similar arrangement can be seen in the dormitory at Cleeve Abbey, Somerset (Dickenson 1961, Plate 19b).

A room above the east-west undercroft is indicated by a roof scar found on a window jamb from the north wall of the chapter house (T762/2). The scars of the vault indicate that the ground floor level of the room above may well have been considerably lower than that of the neighbouring room. Nothing above this level survives to elucidate the room's appearance or function. An amorphous block of masonry, observed protruding from the south wall above the fourth springer, may have been the remains of a corbel to support the floor above. A sandstone block with curved profile (T983), found in the demolition rubble, has also been interpreted as a possible corbel for a floor or roof beam (see THE WORKED STONES AND ARCHITECTURAL STONEWORK).

One or two architectural pieces discovered in the rubble provide very tentative glimpses of the rooms above. Of most significance is a corner springer (T961) for a quadripartite vault which is of a form unrelated to that of the undercrofts or chapter house. Its axial roll and fillet moulding is in keeping with the decoration of a significant room (see THE WORKED STONES AND ARCHITECTURAL STONEWORK). A springer for a double aperture (T151) bearing false ashlar painted in red may also have originated from above. It was, however, found in an area of extensive post-Dissolution disturbance and could have been

deposited here from another part of the site.

Such limited evidence does not lend itself to even the most cursory of understandings. The plans of other monastic houses often have muniment rooms, common rooms or parlours located in the corresponding position. Each of these rooms would have usually required direct access to the cloister. In this case the space available for access to the cloister is limited by the presence of the bench running along the east wall of the cloister and the stair well in its north-east corner. Between these is a gap 1m wide that could have accommodated two or three steps leading from a doorway above – a necessary measure as the cloister alley sits almost 1m below the interior floor level at this point.

The Courtyard
Enclosed by the undercrofts, dormitory block and infirmary was an open, rectangular courtyard. The fourteenth-century windows inserted into the exterior walls of the undercrofts would have looked out over this area.

Of the two yard surfaces identified, the earlier was flagged with roughly hewn sandstone slabs. Although subjected to heavy robbing, it had survived in a few areas at the same level as the bottom of the plinth course that skirted the enclosing walls (c78.30m OD). At an early date, possibly contemporary with the initial flagging of the courtyard, a stone-lined pit was cut close to its north-west corner (Fig 23 & Fig 33). The pit was surrounded on three sides by a raised sandstone 'lip' and to its north by the wall of the dormitory block. It was c1.10m deep and had two stone-lined drains built into its eastern side. The northern drain had later been purposefully sealed with a large sandstone block mortared into place. From the pit it turned sharply northward and ran into the dormitory block. The southern drain ran away to the south-east towards the infirmary.

The function of this pit remains largely obscure. Its sides were not water-tight and would therefore have required a sealant such as clay or a lead lining to effectively hold water. There was no evidence that either of these materials had been used although any lead lining would presumably have been salvaged when the feature later became redundant (see below). There was no evidence of a water supply to the pit – both the drains were designed to carry water away from it. The course of the drain to the west (see above) appears to be heading towards the feature; however, there was no evidence of an inlet in the west face and the level of the drain is such that water would have had to actually flow uphill to supply it! A tentative explanation for the function of the pit is that it was once a lead-lined tank holding rainwater running off the roofs of the surrounding

Fig 33 *Stone-lined pit in courtyard*

buildings and channelled via guttering to a down pipe and thence to the pit. It could then have functioned as a settling tank if the water was discharged at a level lower than that of the drains in its east face. This would facilitate the provision of clean(ish) water to the dormitory undercroft (before the blocking) and infirmary. A similar arrangement was found in a yard beside the warming room at Kirkstall Abbey (Bond 2002, 99).

The pit fill indicated two episodes of deliberate in-filling rather than a gradual process of silting up. The first filled the pit to the level of the bottom of the drains and pottery contained within this deposit has been dated to the fourteenth century. The large quantities of animal bone recovered from this context were the product of food waste and may indicate that the source of the material was from the kitchen or refectory.

The second period of in-filling appears to be contemporary with a universal raising of the yard level in the late fifteenth or early sixteenth century, rendering the pit useless. The final fill contained late medieval pottery, food waste and fragments of building materials.

The new yard surface was also flagged, covering over not only the pit but also the plinth courses of the surrounding walls (Fig 23 & Fig 32b). It had been laid upon a loamy layer containing occupation debris, building debris and pottery of a late medieval date. This levelling-up layer may again have been imported kitchen waste as it contained bones which had been gnawed by dogs and rats. A section of the overlying flagged surface in the south of the yard had been laid to form a channel operating as an extension to the lead drain emerging from below the threshold of the west undercroft.

Whilst the west side of the courtyard was extensively excavated, investigation of the east side was limited due to the presence of Hill Top. Post-excavation groundwork undertaken by the developer revealed what appeared to be a low wall

with an attached shaft, possibly the remains of an arcade between the infirmary undercroft and the courtyard. Close examination of this feature was, however, prevented due to hazardous working conditions.

A sketch made by Nathaniel Troughton in the nineteenth-century records a vaulted staircase found under Hill Top (Hobley 1971, Plate 26). In relating a conversation held with Troughton, Burbidge (1952, 119) locates it more specifically:

> (he) once pointed out to me a spot about half way down Hill Top . . . where during the excavations made for the sewerage the workmen came to the top of a narrow pointed doorway ten feet below the surface of the roadway at that point. On clearing away the debris it was found to lead to a stair turret, the steps descending.

Following the excavations of the 1960's, this feature was hypothetically placed at the south-west corner of the infirmary (Hobley 1971,100). In light of recent findings this staircase may have descended from ground level east of the chapter house and into the eastern bay of the east-west undercroft. Unfortunately, the extent of both the recent excavations and those of the 1960's were constrained by the presence of Hill Top, under which the solutions to many of the areas of uncertainty may lie.

Post-Dissolution
Despite being confined to a relatively small area, the undercrofts and courtyard appear to have met with differing fates in the wake of the Dissolution. As discussed in association with the chapter house, the roof of the east-west undercroft appears to have been rapidly dismantled and the resulting void used as a receptacle for unwanted stonework. The layers immediately below the rubble fill bear testament to the rapidity of this process as the pottery they contained is dated exclusively within the monastic period. The speed of the demolition did not, however, prevent the debris-strewn base of the undercroft receiving food waste including a pair of chewed eel vertebrae either spat out or deposited in faeces (see **THE ANIMAL BONE**). A fire appears to have been lit in the west window bay which was blackened by smoke. A charred deposit occupying most of the sill and spilling out into the undercroft is indicative of localised burning rather than wholesale destruction by fire, perhaps in connection with basic food preparation prior to the filling of the undercroft.

The north-south undercroft was subjected to a more intense flurry of post-Dissolution activity starting with the removal of the floor tiles. Deposits found on and around the hearth indicated at least two separate incidents of burning. The first resulted in a deposit of fine, light grey ash reminiscent of the product of paper burning. The occurrence of paper burning is supported by the discovery of a number of metal objects close to the fireplace, which may have come from the bindings of books or manuscripts. These included a trefoil headed clasp (JFK00 SF136) and a decorative stud (JFK00 SF135), possibly originating from the corner of a leather binding (Fig 70j&m). Similar objects were found during excavations at Bordesley Abbey and interpreted as attachments for manuscript bindings (Hirst *et al* 1983, 204-6). A highly decorative enamelled book mount (JFK00 SF6) (Fig 70k) was also found in the rubble fill of the undercroft. In the light of these finds it is possible that the fireplace was used by the despoilers to dispose of 'offending' or fiscally irrelevant texts.

The second episode of burning left behind a charcoal-rich deposit in the centre of the hearth which contained a large quantity of lead globules. Lead in both globular form and strips was found in abundance in the layers of debris overlying the robbed floor. It is clear the space in the undercroft was used for melting down lead. It is even possible that two shallow scoops excavated close to the fireplace were used to cast the molten lead into fothers as observed at the Dominican Friary of Beverley (Coppack 1990, 135-7). An interesting association with this activity is found in the will of a local draper named John Foxhall, dated 16th April 1539. He appeared to be operating a profitable sideline in the smelting of lead only three months after the Dissolution of St Mary's:

> *I woll that the profittes & money comyng of my office of melytng of leid shallbe delivered frome tyme to tyme to Mr Henry Over & Thomas Gregory Richard Walker & Humfre Walker and that all laboreres & others executyng the same busynes shallbe accomptable frome tyme to tyme unto the seid Henry Thomas Richard & Humfre . . . (LRO B/C/11).*

It would also appear, from the composition of the same layers in the undercroft, that birds and fish were being consumed in large quantities. The range of fish includes both freshwater and marine species (see **THE ANIMAL BONE**). The consumption of large amounts of fish is usually indicative of a monastic diet, which may suggest that the contents of the monastic fishponds were enjoyed by the men carrying out the slighting of the priory. It is likely that the fish stocks were also poached by the local populace once the monks had been expelled, perhaps indicating that the activity in the undercroft was occurring shortly after the Dissolution. This narrow time span is supported by the pottery assemblage from the area which, although containing residual sherds (presumably unearthed during the robbing of the floor), lies firmly within the

period 1470-1550. The late sherds would all appear to be associated with the consumption of drink – a trend noted throughout the courtyard and undercroft areas.

The layers of debris and burning did not extend fully into the north-south undercroft's southern bays. Their absence was particularly noticeable in the area partitioned off in the south-west corner where remains of the broken-up floor lay directly below the demolition rubble. A possible explanation for this may be that the partition was still partially *in situ* and the enclosed area used for storage of salvaged materials.

The absence of pottery post-dating the middle of the sixteenth century would suggest that the undercroft was filled with rubble shortly after the above activities took place.

In contrast to the relatively quick in-filling of these undercrofts, the courtyard appears to have remained open to the elements for a much longer period. Having said this, evidence for activity in the immediate post-Dissolution period mirrors that of the north-south undercroft. The pottery assemblage from a trample layer lying directly over the surviving flag stones dates to the period 1470-1550 and, like that of the undercroft, contains a high proportion of sherds from drink-related vessels. In addition, a significant burned deposit discovered in the southern area of the yard was noteworthy for its high lead content. These layers were not however overlain by demolition rubble, but by a thick layer of trample/soil accumulation which filled the voids created by the robbing of the yard surface. Sherds of pottery from within this deposit were of a much later date and included types running into the early eighteenth century. Other than one huge mortared mass of masonry (within which was trapped a piece of wall rib (T305/2) from the chapter house) the rubble fill lay over this post-medieval layer.

No evidence was forthcoming to account for the late filling of the courtyard; however, its very occurrence lends weight to the assertion that the surrounding buildings were systematically dismantled rather than allowed to collapse of their own accord.

The Dormitory and Reredorter

Although only a limited amount of archaeological work was possible during the latest excavations in this area, a combination of recent discoveries and re-interpretation of Hobley's findings can now be used to place the site of the dormitory to the north of the north-south undercroft and courtyard. Contrary to Hobley's belief that a huge square dormitory ran northward from the chapter house (Hobley 1971, 98), it is now clear that the dormitory corresponded with only the northern third of his projection (24.5m x 8.8m/80½ft x 30ft). The site of the reredorter has also been re-located. The evidence suggests that it was an annex adjoining the north wall of the dormitory at its western end (12.6m x 7m/41½ft x 23ft).

In the absence of evidence for buildings above the ground floor, consideration should be given as to whether the dormitory and reredorter were single-storey buildings, although such an arrangement would be most unusual. The paucity of the evidence discovered at ground level does little to clarify the situation. Three column bases recorded by J F Tickner in the nineteenth century were thought by Hobley to be the remnants of an undercroft below the dormitory (*ibid*, 98). The scalloped capitals surmounting these piers have been identified as examples of Romanesque work (Morris 1994, 50). As such, these features, if correctly located, represent the earliest recorded architecture of the conventual buildings. Hobley placed these columns within the north-west section of his undercroft. In the re-ordered plan they would, in fact, be the first, second and third central piers from the west, giving a vault with a depth of two bays on the north-south

Fig 34   Main channel of monastic sewer below reredorter

axis. Although sandstone footings were seen during development, they were too poorly preserved to assign to specific features such as pier bases. The eastern extremity of the building remains unknown, but it is possible that the structure extended as far as a robbed-out wall observed by Hobley in line with the east wall of the infirmary.

Strict observance of prayer throughout the day and night required unhindered access from the dormitory to the cloister and thence to the church. From a first-floor dormitory the cloister could be reached by entering the room above the north-south undercroft and exiting via the conjectured doorway in its western wall.

Excavations to the north of Hobley's 'dormitory undercroft' revealed the main channel of the monastic sewer (Fig 34 & Fig 46). The wall he identified as the north wall of the reredorter was in fact the south side of the sewer. Its northern (outer) side was built into a massive wall supported by a substantial buttress. The sides of the sewer were sloping inwards and appear to have been left open – in contrast to vaulted sections observed outside the reredorter (see **WATER MANAGEMENT**). This arrangement allowed the latrines to be placed directly over the sewer.

The Infirmary and Cemetery

No excavation was undertaken in this area to augment the findings of the 1960's (Hobley 1971, 98-100). However, it was noted that the configuration of springers at the junction of the main walls suggests that another room was once present to the south-east. Although the springer was indicated on his trench plan, Hobley did not attempt to explain its significance, probably because of the presence of a grave lying close by and parallel with the east-west wall. This may have led him to believe that the building was destroyed and its plot used for burial. This is unlikely to be the case as the monastic cemetery is located immediately south of the building and occupies a higher level of the terrace.

The Refectory Undercroft

Structural Evidence
Located to the north of the cloister was a large undercroft which occupied the whole of the north range (c29m x c8m/c95ft x c26ft). Its southern wall retained the third terrace which resulted in a similar level of preservation as that observed in the under-crofts north of the chapter house. The excavations of the 1960's located part of the north wall of the undercroft including a doorway flanked by windows and a small section of the south wall (Hobley 1971, 96-97). Based upon the available evidence, Hobley

mistakenly interpreted it as being the refectory. The findings of the recent excavations show that the refectory building was, in fact, located over this structure.

As noted elsewhere, clear evidence for any Romanesque build was absent. Whilst it cannot be ruled out that 'plain' elements of primary wall fabric may be remnants of this period, all of the diagnostic features found related to later architectural styles.

Features Predating Undercroft

Underlying the refectory undercroft floor were a series of linear features filled in during the thirteenth century with sandstone rubble (Fig 35). One ran east-west parallel to the main wall and the other ran north-south across the centre of the undercroft floor. The former of these features had been filled with massive stones and incorporated into the later structure as foundations as well as forming an offset shelf or seat on the interior face of the north wall (later robbed). The latter had been filled with finer rubble and levelled over. The foundation trench for the west wall of the undercroft showed close parallels with these two features. No dating evidence was recovered in the primary fills of either feature, but the pottery in the upper fill was contemporary with that found in the lower deposits of the undercroft. This would suggest that these linear features were the foundations of an earlier structure, robbed and levelled over for the construction of the later range. The upper fill was almost certainly contemporary with the earliest occupation of the undercroft floor.

Thirteenth-Century Undercroft

Whilst all of the dateable architectural evidence relates to a fourteenth-century vault (see below) it is evident that earlier undercrofts existed. The final levelling of the early features appears to have been contemporary with the deposition of later thirteenth-

Fig 35   Linear features below refectory undercroft floor

century pottery types in the base of the undercroft as a result of domestic occupation (see **THE POTTERY**).

Part of a substantial sandstone wall was found during the excavations of 1965-7 (Hobley 1971, 96) which appeared to form the western end of the structure which Hobley identified as the refectory. It ran on a north-south axis through the centre of what later became bay 3 of a re-ordered fourteenth-century undercroft. This was presumably the remnant of an earlier scheme of bay division relating to two separate undercrofts in the north range.

Re-building c1325-1360

All of the dateable architectural evidence relates to a re-ordering of the internal space in the mid-fourteenth century. This involved the demolition of the aforementioned north-south wall and the insertion of a new vaulting arrangement which created a single undercroft of six bays length and two in depth. The new central piers were of an octagonal design and supported springers (T468) for a diagonal rib of 'deep' profile indicative of a post-1325 date (Richard Morris, *pers comm*). Wall springers were also inserted at this time, which sported corbels (e.g. T469) decorated with carved human heads (Fig 36a&b). The ribs and packing stones of the vault were discovered lying undisturbed where they had collapsed in the post-Dissolution period (Fig 37).

Shortly after the re-vaulting, further modifications were made to the east end of the undercroft in order to accommodate a drain and flight of stairs leading from the north-east cloister (see **Undercrofts and Courtyard**). A large proportion of the easternmost bay was blocked off by the construction of a sand-stone wall. The eastern central respond pier was demolished, implying that the vault was removed in this newly partitioned area. A door jamb (T499) at the top of the stairs has been dated to the period c1320-60. Given that the Black Death broke out in 1348 robbing Coventry of much of its workforce, it is likely that the dating of the new refectory undercroft vault lies within the period c1325-48.

A stone wall and wooden partition later divided the internal space of the undercroft. These sub-divisions would seem to be contemporary as both were cut into the same layers. A wooden barrier was placed across the door reveal within the west wall of the undercroft. It was located too far forward to be the original door and was supported by a freestanding post. This barrier retained evidence of an iron hinge and fittings.

Access

During the excavations of 1965-7 a doorway was located in the north wall of the undercroft to the east of the kitchen (Hobley 1971, 96). An unexcavated stretch of wall located to the west of the kitchen may

| *a* | *b* |

Fig 36 *(a) & (b) Carved head corbels in refectory undercroft*

have incorporated another doorway. A single blocked aperture was observed towards the centre of the north wall of the cloister. It lay at a point where the wall was robbed below the cloister alley and would presumably have carried steps down into the undercroft. The blocking was not removed to test

Fig 37 *Collapsed refectory undercroft vault*

this theory. Internally the undercroft was connected to a neighbouring one to the west (see **The West Range**).

Monastic Occupation

The accumulation of floor layers over several centuries is evident from the base of the undercroft. These show a general homogeneity with the exception of the very last deposit, which differed significantly in having a high charcoal element and containing sixteenth-century pottery. This late deposit covered a wide area inside as well as outside the undercroft. The evidence from the underlying layers indicates that a series of rudimentary and roughly mortared floor surfaces were overlaid periodically. At least three separate surfaces were laid within the duration of the cellar's use. Either debris and dumped refuse was allowed to accumulate before being resurfaced or material was deliberately brought in to elevate the floor level. The abundant ceramic evidence suggests a widespread re-deposition of secondary ceramic refuse, possibly dumped intentionally with the soil in which they had originally been put.

The last deposit in the standing undercroft has a debatable origin. Dating from the last occupation of the undercroft, the associated assemblage of animal bones suggests a general discarding of food waste. The large amount of charcoal within this layer also points towards general dumping activity. Whilst this may have taken place in the immediate pre-Dissolution period, a more likely explanation is that it was deposited after the abandonment of the priory, maybe as a result of squatter occupation. The pottery of the period is little changed from c1525-75. Either could be argued. In any event, pottery from the vault collapse suggests that any post-Dissolution use was extremely short-lived.

Remains of a potential kitchen garden came to light in the northern area of the excavation, outside the undercroft wall. Garden soils contemporary with the monastic occupation were present within this area and they were similar to the latest monastic layers found within the interior. This area lay slightly to the west of the kitchen

Function

No clear picture has emerged concerning the function of the undercroft. The obvious use is for the storage of foodstuff due to its close proximity to the refectory and kitchen. Large quantities of jug fragments found in the floor make-up layers could be indicative of a storage facility but may have been brought in from an unknown source with the material used to raise the floors. Any storage vessels or foodstuffs present in the undercroft at the time of the Dissolution would presumably have been consumed or removed for sale. If storage was the primary function, this undercroft may have been the main storage area for the priory. Traditionally this is located in the west range, but at St Mary's this would have necessitated goods being manhandled down a steep flight of steps (see **The West Range**). The refectory undercroft, being a 'half cellar', was more readily accessible from the ground level to its north.

Post-Dissolution

The collapse of the undercroft and refectory above seems to have occurred within a short space of time

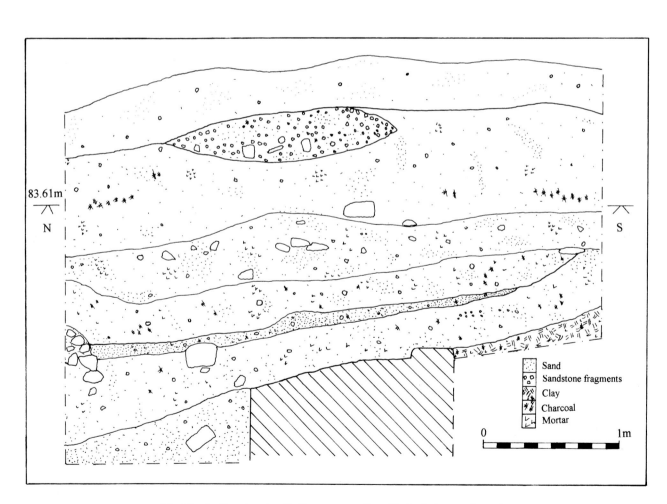

	Sand
	Sandstone fragments
	Clay
	Charcoal
	Mortar

0   1m

Fig 38   Section showing tip-lines over south wall of refectory undercroft

after the abandonment of the priory. The well-preserved condition of the internal architectural pieces contained within the rubble substantiates this. One would have expected evidence of weather damage to the sandstone if the building had stood as a shell for any significant time – unless it had retained its roof until its final demise. The undercroft vault remained *in-situ* where it had come to rest, sealing the medieval occupation layers below. Above this lay the stratified remains of the refectory super-structure (see **The Refectory**). The collapse of the building resulted in a deep deposit of unstable rubble thus making any subsequent attempt at the salvage of stonework dangerously difficult and, no doubt, quickly abandoned. Evidence that further material was then deliberately thrown over the third terrace from the cloister was indicated by substantial tip-lines seen in a section cut through the debris overlying its robbed north wall (Fig 38). Whether this took place as part of the destruction of the priory or at a later period, in an attempt to level the site, remains unclear.

The Refectory

Architectural Evidence

Glimpses of the refectory's appearance are afforded by the copious amount of diagnostic stonework recovered from the rubble layers above the undercroft collapse. They are indicative of an architecturally impressive structure with a highly decorative interior. Most of the pieces date from the fourteenth century when the building appears to have been refurbished, most probably as part of the programme of works which saw the re-vaulting of its undercroft.

Much of the stonework relates to large internal features such as doorways and windows and includes lime-washed pieces from jambs, arches and bases. Other pieces are probably associated with a large arch and include an impressive foliate finial (T331) (Fig 49f), lengths of hoodmoulding (T330, 339) and carved head-stops (T690-693). Further pieces are related to a stringcourse, maybe from a cornice surmounted by miniature crenellations (T293). Many of the fragments were painted with vivid colours, some bearing the stencilled *fleur-de-lys* design, which were also observed on pieces from the nave (T877/1) (Plate 1a).

Perhaps the most important architectural evidence was a series of large painted architectural fragments found in the rubble towards the east end of the undercroft which would appear to be the remains of the refectory pulpit (see THE WORKED STONES AND ARCHITECTURAL STONEWORK). The largest of these (T640/1) related to a fitting of polygonal plan with an elaborate miniature vault decorated with small bosses. One of these was carved with the image of a 'Green Man'. The exterior was decorated with a series of gables interspersed with side shafts and pinnacles (Plate 1b). Clear laying-out lines, inscribed by the mason, have enabled a reconstruction of the geometry of the pulpit (Fig 50a&b). It would have projected from the wall of the refectory in a manner similar to that of an oriel window with the interior space shaped like an elongated octagon. The sides would have incorporated open arches enabling the reader to address the dining monks.

A Tiled Floor (Plate 1c&d)

A little-worn floor composed of worn encaustic tiles was discovered sandwiched between the collapsed vault of the undercroft and the refectory rubble (Plate 1c). It had collapsed *en bloc* and its layout was still recognisable, as a group of over thirty tiles had come to rest on the former subdividing wall in the undercroft. The fourteenth-century tiles are of local manufacture, almost certainly Stoke, Coventry. The date is arrived at from the armorial tiles which form the centrepiece of the design, the arms of England after 1340 and the arms of Sir Thomas Beauchamp, Earl of Warwick (1360s). The tiles were laid in repeating squares offset in rows across the room, alternating in fours and nines, touching corner to corner, each separated by a border of plain green tiles (Plate 1d).

Access

Due to the total destruction of the refectory we can only theorise as to the location of its main entrance. The north-east corner can be ruled out as it was occupied by a flight of steps and a centrally placed opening would clash with the access for its undercroft. It therefore seems reasonable to propose an entrance in the north-west corner of the cloister, at the opposite end of the west alley to the doorway into the nave.

Post-Dissolution

Whereas the undercroft collapsed intact, it appears that the refectory itself had been substantially robbed prior to this event. The architectural fragments relating to the refectory were generally large, decorative pieces, mouldings and sections of tracery – all unsuitable for re-use and/or difficult to manoeuvre. There were very few ashlars and nothing relating to either a vaulted or timber roof. In light of this it is possible that the robbing left doorways, windows and arches standing in an extremely unstable condition. These could then have either collapsed or been deliberately pushed into the undercroft, breaking through its vaulted ceiling and taking with them the section of tiled floor.

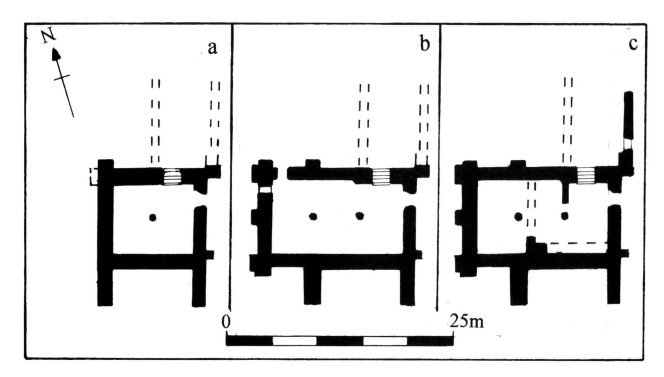

Fig 39   *Sequence of building phases in northern west range (a) early thirteenth century? (b) mid-thirteenth century (c) fourteenth century*

The Kitchen

The building (7.2m x 5m/23½ft x 16½ft) identified as the kitchen during the 1960's excavations (Hobley 1971, 97) was not re-excavated as part of the recent programme of work but nevertheless requires significant re-interpretation. As previously mentioned, the refectory was built over an undercroft and not, as Hobley thought, at ground level. He assumed that the kitchen was directly linked to the refectory by a passageway and that, in the absence of a doorway, the food was passed through a serving hatch. In the light of recent findings this would mean that the food would have been passed into an undercroft rather than directly into the refectory.

In order to facilitate the direct passage of prepared meals into the refectory, either the kitchen would have to have been at the same level or a flight of stairs connected the two buildings. A first-floor kitchen is problematic because it would require water, fuel and raw foodstuffs to be carried up from ground level. A staircase is more likely allowing prepared food to be carried to the tables direct from a ground floor kitchen. Hobley found a substantial arc of stonework bonded to the eastern side of the kitchen that, in retrospect, could be the base or foundation for an external staircase. There was no opportunity to re-excavate this feature since it was destroyed just after the 1960's excavation.

The West Range

Structural Evidence

Occupying most of the west claustral range was undercroft space measuring *c*22m/72ft on its north-south axis by *c*8.6m/28ft on its east-west. Located to the north of this was another undercroft constructed on the same building line but later extended westwards (see below). At the south end of the range, at ground level, was a small room measuring 4.2m x 8.6m/13½ft x 28ft below which lay three potentially early burials (see **MID-LATE SAXON/ EARLY MEDIEVAL OCCUPATION & APPENDIX 3**).

The make-up of the rubble fill of the undercrofts was variable throughout the west range. Large amounts of architectural fragments were recovered from the northern end whilst the southern end appears to have been subjected to much post-Dissolution stone robbing.

West Range Undercrofts (Fig 39)

The undercroft space below the west range was subject to a limited programme of excavation with only the northern and southern ends being examined in any detail. The excavation of the northern section revealed an undercroft separated from the main body of the west range by a substantial wall. In its earliest form the west wall of this undercroft was in line with the exterior wall of the west range (Fig 39a). At a later date it was extended westwards and a new vaulting arrangement inserted (Fig 39b). Whilst no evidence was found to date the original structure, the extension probably dates to the mid-thirteenth century when a tierceron vault appears to have been constructed in the room above (see below).

Plain chamfered ribs (T893 & T894) found in the demolition rubble probably belonged to the undercroft vault rather than to that of the room above. The vault was supported by two central piers, the lower courses of which were discovered *in situ*. The vault defined an area three bays long by two deep, entered from the exterior ground level by a flight of five steps which led down into the north-west bay (Fig 40). Another doorway, possibly located within a shallow external stairwell, gave access to the north-eastern bay. This, however, was significantly altered at a later date (see below). A doorway in the east wall connected the structure to the refectory undercroft. In the west wall was an aperture which resembled a window. A single rebate in this feature may have housed shutters, as there were no glazing slots.

The original floor of the undercroft was comprised of sandstone flags. These were later sealed by a number of compacted earth floor layers, probably the result of successive periods of occupation and levelling as observed in the refectory undercroft.

The appearance of the interior was altered somewhat by the insertion of partitions, shelving and the localised cladding of walls (Fig 39c). In the fourteenth century a sandstone partition wall was inserted between the eastern pier and the north wall. Another wall, constructed in the grey sandstone characteristic of the latter part of the fourteenth century, was built *c*3m to the east. This appears to have been contemporary with a cladding of the south wall of the central bay and the construction of a shelf or thrall against it – again in grey sandstone. The same material was also used to block the aperture in the exterior face of the western wall and the western doorway. A stone-lined drain was found built into the latter. It is likely that these alterations were contemporary with the partitioning of the undercroft.

The main body of the west range at undercroft level was subjected to a more limited investigation. A simple doorway was discovered at ground level towards the north of the west wall. Due to its close proximity to the northern ground floor entrance (see below) it is assumed that this gave access to the undercroft. The east wall of the range was barely touched by the excavations and no evidence of doorways to the cloister were found. The rubble fill in the south-west corner was removed, exposing the walls which had been extensively robbed of their ashlar leaving only the rubble core standing. A small

Fig 40 *Steps leading into north end of west range undercroft*

area of the floor level was uncovered but nothing remained of an actual surface. Too few architectural fragments were recovered from the demolition rubble to enable a reconstruction of the undercroft vault and fittings.

Function
As previously mentioned (see **The Refectory Undercroft**) it is unlikely that the west range undercroft functioned as the main storage area for the priory. The terraced nature of the site meant that the storage of cumbersome objects would have been more practically achieved by using the refectory undercroft, which would have been more readily accessible from ground level.

Priors Lodging and Guest Accommodation?
In Benedictine houses the first floor rooms over the west range are often used for the Prior's lodging and guest accommodation. Other rooms commonly found within the west range include lay brothers accommodation, small chapels, parlours and a guest dining hall. The accommodation was often divided

into chambers with individual names (Dickenson 1961, 40). Such an arrangement may have existed here where Poole (1870) lists various chambers (Prior's Chamber, Princess's Chamber, Le Seyn Chamber) in his summary of priory buildings. It is known that the Princess's chamber was so called following a visit from Princess Mary (later Mary 1) in 1526 (*VCH Warks*. 2 1965, 57; Burbidge 1952, 225).

Architectural evidence observed in the west range suggests the presence of high-status buildings but, in contrast to the traditional arrangement, they appear to have occupied the ground floor. Doorways giving access to the ground floor were found at each end of the west wall. Base blocks (T447, T916) for the jambs of both entrances were found *in situ* (Fig 41). They have been dated to the period *c*1220-60 (see THE WORKED STONES AND ARCHITECTURAL STONEWORK) and were of a surprisingly fine quality for this location within the conventual buildings. Door jambs of similar style and date include the main west door of the church and the doorway connecting the cloister to the nave.

Worked stone recovered from the demolition rubble that filled the north undercroft indicated the presence of an elaborate tierceron vault in the vicinity. This vault was supported by huge mono-lithic springers (T977) set upon octagonal piers (T976). The ribs which fit the springers (T315) were found in association with bosses bearing stiff-leaf foliage carving, which suggests a date of *c*1230-60 for its construction (see THE WORKED STONES AND ARCHITECTURAL STONEWORK). Other bosses bore finely carved motifs such as a cowled head (T696) and a coiled dragon (T984) and a (Fig 49e & 54d). Such work is indicative of a building of some status and would not usually be found in an undercroft. A second rib type more easily equated with an undercroft was also found in the vicinity (see above) therefore it is likely that the tierceron vault spanned the room above.

Garderobe

Further evidence indicative of the presence of high-status accommodation in the west range was found in the form of a cistern which lay just below a flagged surface immediately west of the range (Fig 42). This was probably designed to flush a garderobe projecting from the main building. It was con-structed from carefully dressed ashlar blocks and capped with large sandstone slabs. Slots for a sluice

Fig 41   Jamb of northern doorway into west range   *Fig 42   Cistern for garderobe in west range*

gate were cut into the sides of its northern end where a wooden gate would have retained a volume of water until flushing was required. A section of stone-lined drain running at ground level to the south of the cistern may have supplied it with water channelled from the roofs of the surrounding buildings. Alternatively, water could have been introduced through down pipes or by buckets, as there was no evidence for an opening in the south end or sides of the tank. Whichever medium was used, once full, a slope in the base of the cistern and a narrowing of its sides increased the water pressure behind the sluice gate. As they were lifted a torrent of water would have flushed away the waste into the main sewer (see WATER MANAGEMENT).

Parlour?

Nothing, other than the defining wall foundations, remained of the small room at the south end of the west range. Its location suggests it may have been a parlour – similar rooms are found in this position at other monastic houses e.g. Norton Priory (Coppack 1990, 67). There was no undercroft below this room.

Later Alterations to West Range

The access arrangements to both levels changed dramatically in the fourteenth century when both of the ground-floor entrances were modified. The southern one was narrowed and ten steps in grey

Fig 43   Steps leading into south end of west range undercroft

sandstone were inserted, leading down into the south-west corner of the main undercroft (Fig 43). The northern entrance was also narrowed and its jambs buried behind a secondary reveal. Although limited, the evidence indicates that steps to the undercroft were also inserted at this end. These alterations appear to have robbed the ground floor of its main entrances and must surely indicate a major re-ordering of the internal space, including perhaps the construction of an upper storey.

Post-Dissolution

In common with the refectory range, there does not appear to have been a lengthy period of occupation in the west range after the Dissolution. The architectural evidence retrieved from the rubble in the northern undercroft points towards a systematic robbing of re-usable stone. Ashlars were again conspicuous in their absence but a jumble of vaulting pieces from both ground and basement level were present in large numbers. This suggests that less useful pieces were thrown back into the robbed shell of the undercroft. However, the potential of the architectural evidence was compromised somewhat by intensive post-medieval activity in the vicinity. Much of the demolition rubble had been displaced by the foundations of later features which included an 1850 ribbon-weaving factory and a boiler room which housed the apparatus used to power the looms (field records in archive).

At the southern end of the range very few architectural fragments were found. It is clear that some time after the Dissolution the interior of the undercroft was systematically robbed of its ashlar. The evidence for the process of demolition was largely destroyed by this activity.

Shortly after the abandonment of the priory, the garderobe cistern was used as a dump for food waste and then deliberately sealed with a deep deposit of clay and roof tile. Cattle and sheep bone dominated the assemblage (see THE ANIMAL BONES). A large quantity of oyster shells and elderberry seeds was also present (see THE PLANT REMAINS). A single human vertebra, found within the material sealing the midden, may indicate that the digging for clay either disturbed a nearby grave or that disarticulated human bones were present in the ground.

The Service Buildings and Priory Property

Around the conventual buildings lay yards, gardens, pools and ancillary structures with a variety of functions. Poole (1847) summarises these as follows:

Among the domestic offices and outbuildings were the larder, kitchen, porters lodge, stables and yard, outer court, malt house, kiln house, slaughter house, wood house, well yard, guests stables, guests' house, two pools within the priory wall, pool yard, St Osberg's pool, priory mill and orchards.

These, along with a hopyard, gardens and the monastic water works were sold into private hands in 1545 whilst the fabric of the church and conventual buildings were retained by the crown (Scarisbrick 1993,161).

Archaeological evidence for service buildings north of the claustral ranges, other than the kitchen and mill, was inconclusive. A structure evidently projected from the north end of the west range where a wall with a window looking out towards the kitchen was discovered. Approximately 5m to the east of this was evidence for another heavily robbed wall built on the same alignment.

The area between the west range and the mill was watched during development. It was littered with loose sandstone rubble and isolated pockets of wall foundation. The remains were difficult to interpret but gave the general impression that buildings of some size had once stood in the vicinity. There was evidence for a latrine being present in one of the buildings (see **WATER MANAGEMENT**). Latrines often serviced buildings other than those of the claustral ranges. At Fountains Abbey, the malt house and wool house were both provided with latrines as was the guesthouse, almonry and gatehouse at Thorneholme Priory, Humberside (Coppack 1990, 99).

Fig 44   North wall of forecourt with blocked entrance

Monastic Boundaries

Cathedral Forecourt

Attached to the west face of the cathedral's north-west tower is an upstanding section of the forecourt wall (Fig 44). It stands to a height of c2.8m and runs westward for c16m. It would have originally enclosed a substantial area in front of the cathedral's west end, roughly corresponding to the parcel of land bordered by New Buildings to the north, Trinity Street to the west and Priory Row to the south. At least three entrances have been identified in the wall, one of which, albeit blocked up, still stands today (Fig 44). It was formerly an arched doorway leading into the Sacristan's room (see below). The main entrance to the forecourt lay to the west, marked on Speed's map (1610) as the Priorye Gate on Great Butcher Row (Fig 17). It appears to have survived until 1704 when it was dismantled to make way for a public house (Poole 1869, 11). Documentary sources indicate the presence of a smaller entrance to the south of this, known as the Sacristan's Gate (George Demidowicz, *pers comm*).

A number of buildings appear to have occupied the forecourt at the time of the Dissolution. One of these evidently stood in the north-east corner built into the angle created by the west side of the tower and the forecourt wall. Archaeological observations made in advance of the refurbishment of Blue Coat School (Thompson & Lewis 1999) have augmented a body of documentary and pictorial evidence suggesting the presence of a sextonry or Sacristan's store and dwelling in this location (Demidowicz 2000, 11). The blocked archway mentioned above gave access to this building from the precinct. Another range of buildings appear to have been built into a breach made in the opposite side of the forecourt wall where the Lych Gate Cottages stand at the western end of Priory Row (*ibid*, 16). Recent dendrochronological analysis of timbers from these buildings suggests that they originate from the early fifteenth century, their present form being the product of many alterations throughout the following centuries. The function of these buildings in the monastic period remains unknown.

It does, however, remain a possibility that the

fifteenth-century cottages originally stood some-where else and were re-erected on this site after 1539. It should be noted that there is no conclusive documentary reference to them prior to 1583, although a property deed of 1539 which mentions *'Woodhowses in the Sextry'* could be referring to them (*ibid*, 13).

The Precinct Wall

Five sections of a monastic wall were discovered running across the site to the north of the conventual buildings, separating them from the mill and river. Together they allowed the line of the wall to be traced for a distance of *c*38m. It appeared to have been *c*0.75m wide with an internal chamfer. A rebate for a door or gateway was found in the most westerly section. Prior to the construction of the town wall to the north, this wall may have been part of the northern precinct wall. If so, for much of the priory's existence, the precinct wall would have enclosed a rather modest area of land to the north of the conventual buildings and excluded some of the outlying buildings and monastic property.

Until the latter part of the fifteenth century, there is no archaeological evidence to suggest that the priory land to the north of the river was contained within a wall. If consistent with other priory properties in and around the city, its boundaries may have been fenced or hedged (Dormer Harris 1907-19, 444, 446). When the town wall was planned in this vicinity its original line appears to have threatened to divide the priory stews and pools from the conventual buildings to the south. In 1461 the prior appealed to the mayor requesting that it be diverted to the north to encompass them (Poole 1869, 69). His request was subsequently granted, creating, in effect, an outer precinct entered through Priory (or Swanswell) Gate.

The Priory Mill

Excavations to the north-west of the conventual buildings located the Priory Mill. The mill was not destroyed at the Dissolution but continued as a working mill under various owners until *c*1688 when it was demolished and re-built (see below). This re-building made use of some of the basic components of the monastic mill such as the wheel pit, head race and tail race, parts of which were found intact. Timbers were found *in situ* in the base of the mill features whilst their sides were pre-dominantly constructed from sandstone ashlar. The heavily robbed walls of the mill house, auxiliary buildings and a flagged yard surface were also found. They had been incorporated into later structures on the site.

The History of the Mill

It is not known when the Priory Mill was established. It was supplied by a leat leading from the River Sherbourne and the water returned via a channel to the river. The mill is first heard of in 1404 when the prior complained of the fouling of the mill's water supply by Coventrians throwing in beasts' entrails, dung and excrement (CA BA/B/1/23/1). Mills in the built-up areas of towns were always vulnerable to pollution and the constriction that the mill caused to the flow of the townsfolk's foul water eventually brought about its demise over four hundred years later.

In 1410-11 the tenant, Henry Milward, was required to grind all corn for monastic consumption without payment and paid a rent of £5 p.a., implying that he earned a living serving local people (PRO E164/21, Folio 182v). It is recorded that the mill was contained within one building – one set of stones being powered by a water wheel and another by a horse gin.

Just before the Dissolution in 1539, the prior leased *'P[ri]orie Mylne . . . being nygh unto the . . . monast[er]ie'* to Thomas Staples for forty years at £4 p.a. (PRO E303/16). The priory precinct and mill was sold by the Crown in 1545 to Richard Stansfield and John Coombes, agents acting for John Hales (*Letters and Papers Henry VIII*, vol xx, part 1, 1335(51)). The Hales family conveyed this land along with other former priory estates to Coventry Corporation in the early 1570s (CA PA96/12/1). By 1577 the leaseholder was Thomas Aston, whose name was eventually given to the mill (CA PA56/99/1). Still known as Priory Mill in 1581, the five-bay building contained two water wheels, one breast-shot, the other the more efficient overshot wheel (CA BA/A/1/2/3). In 1585 the mill was leased to Richard Aston (perhaps Thomas's son) for a term of twenty-one years and an annual rent of £8 (CA PA56/99/3). Another member of the family, John Aston, was in occupation of Aston's Mill in the mid-seventeenth century (CA BA/B/A/25/7) but it was soon to leave the family.

In 1666 the Corporation leased to Frances Perkins a *'water mill called . . . Priory Mill and since Astons Mill and a messuage . . . the . . . mill house containing in all 5 bays of building . . . all tiled'* (CA BA/B/A/28/1). There were three sets of stones: the first for grinding wheat, the second for 'maslyn' (a mixture of rye and wheat) and the third for malt. The three pairs of stones were likely powered by the two water wheels mentioned in 1581. The fact that the mill contained five bays, as in 1581, suggests that the same building was being described. It may even have been the monastic mill and the dilapidated state of the building in 1687 supports this conclusion. Richard Chaplin had been the tenant for a number of years and the Corporation were considering re-possessing the mill, pulling it down and re-building it (CA BA/H/C/17/2, 338-9). Richard Chaplin had fallen into rent arrears and his poverty had undoubtedly contributed to the mill's deterioration. In 1688 the mill was re-built and a new lease granted to Goodyer Oughton (CA BA/B/5/5/2; BA/D/A/23/9).

In 1712 the Corporation mortgaged the mill, described as '*Priory or Chaplains Mill in which are two Corne Mills . . . seven bays of building,*' (CA PA56/108/; WRO CR1709/206/1). The re-building had apparently replaced five bays with seven. In 1731 the Corporation sold '*a watermill called Priory or Chaplin's*' to John Gulson, skinner (CA PA 90/19; WRO CR1709/ 206/6-7). As the Gulsons were not millers they leased their two mills under one roof. In 1760 the tenants were William Humphreys, John Fisher, Richard Steane, John Reeves, Edward Ward and Thomas Lawson, but some of these occupied houses that had been recently built on the site (CA PA56/108/15). In this year an undivided half of the mill and premises was sold to John Fowler, who married Elizabeth Gulson, daughter of John Gulson (CA PA56/108/ 14-15). In 1796 the mill and associated premises passed to several owners, when the mill itself was tenanted by Joseph Sprigg (CA PA56/108/24-5). He was succeeded by John Clarke and by 1808 the tenants were Messrs Lant, Eagle and Bunney (CA PA56/108/32).

During the nineteenth-century ownership of the mill estate became exceedingly complex, vested in a series of benefit societies; the mill was leased in 1834 to William and Thomas Wale (of Walsgrave-on-Sowe, already in occupation), for twenty-one years at £50 p.a. (CA PA56/108/40). The lease was not to run its term as in 1845 the mill pool was sold under the Coventry Improvement Act 1844 to free the constriction of water-flow caused by the mill (CA PA56/108/70). The pool was described at this time as *a 'noisome and pestilential reservoir'* (*Coventry Herald*, 2 May 1845). The mill was retained by the trustees of the various societies hoping to use steam power, but this plan was not carried out and in 1846 William and Thomas Wale surrendered their lease and the mill was sold to the Corporation (CA PA56/108/ 71-72; CA TC/L/1/77). It appears that the buildings were demolished soon after (TC/L/1/77, deed of 1849).

The Archaeology of the Mill

Antiquarian maps (e.g. John Speed's Map of Coventry 1610) show the Priory Mill located on a mill race looping off to the south of the River Sherbourne (Fig 17). The excavations located this channel in the immediate vicinity of the mill where, to the west, it narrowed forming the head race (Fig 45a). To the east of this lay a *c*5m/16½ft-long wheel pit terminating in a tail race which widened considerably at its eastern end (Fig 45b). The bases of these features were laid with oak planks which were well preserved due to the prevailing waterlogged conditions. Their sides were constructed with ashlar, although only the lower courses appeared to be the remnants of a monastic build. Abrasions at this level were consistent with a wheel turning *in situ* and enable its diameter to be calculated as *c*4.50m/14½ft (Fig 45c). Its width, based upon the available space within the wheel pit, could have been no more than 0.8m/2½ft.

Immediately to the south of the wheel pit lay another timber-lined pit, evidently once part of the monastic mill and sharing structural elements with its neighbour (Fig 45d). The west side of the pit was overlain by an angled masonry feature which appeared to have been built to accommodate a wheel. Timbers from the pit were sampled and dated by dendrochronology. A sample taken from an integral beam provided a felling date of 1432-56 (Michael Worthington, forthcoming). Below the timbers the sides of the pit were cut through natural clay. At a lower level, cut into the clay and separate from the rest, was another substantial beam running on a north-south axis across the pit – possibly a remnant of an earlier arrangement. As only the western end of the pit was examined, its true extent remains unknown but it is conceivable that it ran the whole length of the main wheel pit. It may have originally housed a second mill wheel.

This southern wheel pit was redundant by the mid-late seventeenth century at the latest. It had been filled in with clay and flagged over. Later, a skim of mortar was applied to the flags and a brick surface laid down. A token found within the mortar (PP01 SF190) was manufactured in nearby Lutterworth during the Commonwealth period (see THE COINS). The southern wheel pit could have been sealed as part of the re-build of 1687, although the wheel may have already lain idle for some years prior to this.

The northern pit appears to have continued to function after the re-build but was substantially modified. An almost complete re-building of its sides was indicated by the presence of blocks bearing mis-aligned wheel abrasions. Bricks were used to seal apertures which had formerly connected it with the southern pit. As well as the reconstruction of its sides, the level of the base was also raised over the timber planks and re-surfaced with flagstones. An approximate *terminus post quem* for this episode is provided by a single sherd of Midland Purple Ware (fifteenth to mid-seventeenth century) recovered from a clay-bedding layer below the new surface. Thus it is probable that the alterations to the

a

b

c

d

Fig 45 *Priory Mill (a) head race (b) tail race (c) wheel abrasions (d) adjoining timber-lined pit*

northern wheel pit were contemporary with the redundancy of the southern wheel.

The Mill Buildings

To the north and south of the mill race were the remains of a number of heavily robbed sandstone walls and surfaces which may have belonged to the original Priory Mill. They had been greatly disturbed by a later period of building in brick. The walls appeared to be related to two building complexes; one centred directly over the wheel pit and the other located to the east. The former may be related to the structure housing the mill's machinery whilst the latter may be a miller's cottage or storage facility dating from the post-monastic period. They were separated by a flagged surface which sloped north-ward towards the tail race. The eastern building was constructed to respect the slope of this yard and had a doorway in its eastern wall opening onto it. In the south-west corner of the yard was a stone-lined well which appeared to be partially enclosed by a sand-stone wall – possibly the Well Yard mentioned by Poole (see THE SERVICE BUILDINGS AND PRIORY PROPERTY). Some of the sandstone walls were later incorporated into a series of brick structures as footings. Others appeared to have been subjected to localised demolition.

The Riverside Environment

A sample taken from a waterlogged deposit within the timber-lined wheel pit was found to contain large quantities of preserved plant remains and animal bone. The mineral residue of the sample was examined by Professor D Keen of Coventry University who found it to be characteristic of an alluvial deposit, therefore indicating that it had accumulated whilst the southern wheel was operating. Two sherds of pottery were recovered from the sample, one of mid-late Saxon date, the other of Chilvers Coton 'A' Ware (1250-1300). Although these were clearly residual, the absence of later sherds may place the sample within the monastic period, although it could, of course, relate to any period predating the redundancy of the over-lying mill wheel.

The plant remains support the assertion that the deposit was concordant with a working mill and provide an insight into the riverside environment in the late monastic/post-Dissolution period (see THE PLANT REMAINS). The mill stream appears to have flowed through grassland, its banks being lightly covered with hazel scrub and woods or hedgerows. The remains of a number of edible species were recovered including hazelnuts, elder, bramble, crab apple and hawthorn. Their presence might be explained by the proximity of an orchard to the west of the mill.

Flax and hemp retting for fibre extraction was evidently practised somewhere upstream, the resulting seeds being washed into the wheel pit. Very few cereals were recovered indicating that spillage of grain into the pit was avoided. The plant remains indicate that the water appears to have been relatively clean which is surprising given the predilection of the local populace to pollute the river, an act complained of by the monastic community in 1480 when it was reported in the Leet Book that:

> . . . *the seid people dayly with therr dong, fyllthe and swepyng throwen in the comien Rryver so stoppen the fflodegates and the water in the Priorye that their mille is utterly letted to go* (Harris 1913, 445).

The large quantity of animal bone recovered from the deposit may attest to the longevity of this practice and the apparent failure of the Prior's petition. Levels of pollution could have been kept in check purely by the force of the flowing water. The absence of plants favouring stagnant conditions and the presence of caddis fly larvae are both indicative of this.

Water Management

Other than that connected with the Priory Mill, only glimpses of the sophisticated system of water management employed by monastic houses were seen. These observations have been categorised using the model proposed by Bond (2001).

Supply

Undoubtedly a major influencing factor in the original siting of the house was the proximity of plentiful natural sources of water from the River Sherbourne, local springs and pools. Exactly how these resources were utilised in the early period is unknown.

The sinking of wells to supply water to the early claustral buildings cannot be ruled out. The potential for tapping groundwater was indicated by the presence of 4 wells on the site. Only one of these, stone-lined and located within the mill complex, may date to the monastic period. The others were clearly post-medieval (or at the very least re-lined in this period) but their presence alone serves to indicate the potential for supplying water to the site in this manner. Wells were not, however, favoured as the primary source of fresh water on monastic sites.

Rainwater would not have been wasted but

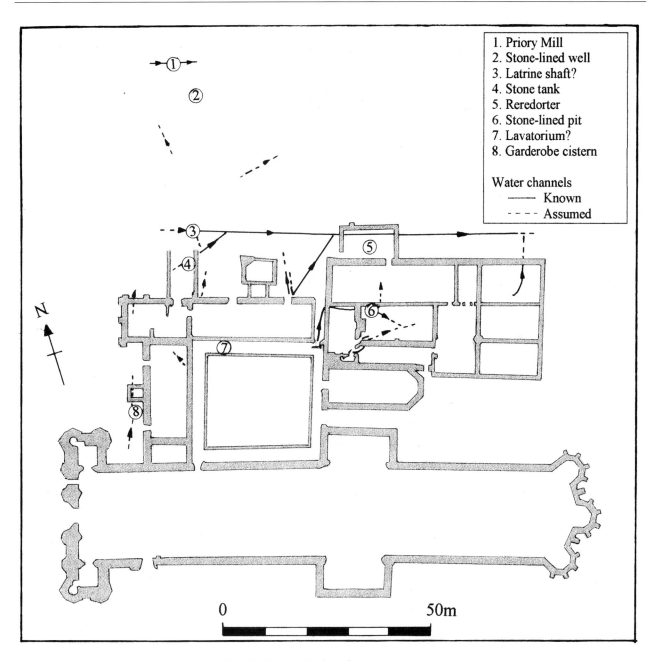

1. Priory Mill
2. Stone-lined well
3. Latrine shaft?
4. Stone tank
5. Reredorter
6. Stone-lined pit
7. Lavatorium?
8. Garderobe cistern

Water channels
——— Known
- - - - Assumed

0   50m

Fig 46   Schematic plan of water management

channelled from the roofs via guttering, a small length of which was found close to the north-west tower of the cathedral (T120). Down-pipes would then direct the water into drains and tanks. Two features, already discussed in depth (the garderobe cistern off the west range and the tank in the court-yard), may have been utilising this resource.

Throughout the country there is good evidence that there were carefully planned and engineered supplies of water to monasteries. Clean water from a spring source at a convenient level above the cloister was channelled, usually by lead pipes and using gravity flow, sometimes over considerable distances. The spring source would have its own conduit head,

and many have survived at other monastic sites with their distinctive and steeply pitched stone roofs. In Beaumont Crescent, just off Holyhead Road, about a mile from the priory, one such conduit head still stands, now known as St Catherine's Well (listed Grade II). There is no direct evidence that it supplied the priory, but it is feasible, for a course can be drawn from it to the cloister garth, gently descending contours in order to use gravity flow. It would need to cross the River Sherbourne in the area of the former Crow Lane and its course thereafter would coincide with conduit heads that are known to have been used from the sixteenth century onwards in Smithford Street and Cross Cheaping. The water would have entered the cloister garth from the west through the west range.

Distribution

In common with many monastic sites, the evidence for the storage and distribution of water within the precinct was sparse. Nothing was found to indicate the storage of water in a central cistern, although a closer examination of the massive stone feature observed below the centre of the cloister garth might have cast light on this subject (see **The Cloister**). In addition, there was no *in situ* evidence to enable the reconstruction of the mode of distribution from such a feature. Lead, the favoured material for the construction of pipes and the lining of conduits and cisterns, was systematically removed at the Dissolution. Of the hundreds of metres of lead piping that presumably once serviced the priory, only a short length was discovered lying *ex situ* in the courtyard rubble (JFK00 SF20). It was *c*700m long with an internal diameter of *c*25mm. Ceramic and wooden pipes may also have conveyed water around the site but of these no trace was found. The demand for clean water would have necessitated the inclusion of systems of filtration at certain intervals within the distribution network. As previously suggested, the stone-lined pit in the courtyard may well have served this purpose although the conclusive evidence in terms of lead lining and supply pipes is missing.

Utilisation

Other than to power the mill and flush the sewerage system (see below) the evidence for the utilisation of water within the priory was very limited. However, a few architectural fragments recovered from the cathedral were related to the ceremonial use of water. During the excavations of 1965-7 a piscina (T227) was found *in situ* on the south wall of the nave at floor level (Hobley 1971, 93). Recent discoveries indicate that it lay within a chantry chapel located to the west of the processional door-way in bay 3 of the south aisle. Another stone feature (T922), most probably a piscina, was found *ex situ* at the west end of the north aisle. Its basin was scalloped and had a central drainage hole (Fig 53b). A badly damaged convex stone object (T862), which may have been part of a basin, font or stoup, was also found. All of these features were probably supplied by a hand-held receptacle rather than direct from source.

Drinking water would have been piped to a number of locations within the priory but no evidence for its supply or storage was found. Potential evidence for washing facilities was identified in the north cloister alley where the *lavatorium* most likely stood (see **The Cloister**). In the north-south undercroft (north of the chapter house) there may have been a smaller facility for washing in the form of a basin against the south wall (Fig 23, 26 & 32a). In both instances there was little evidence of supply, although in the case of the basin it is possible that a pipe had been ripped out of the wall above. More positive evidence was found for channelling waste water away from these features in the form of drains.

Bathing and laundry facilities were considered lesser priorities in monastic houses, with the latter often being provided for outside the monastery (Bond 2001, 102). No evidence for either was found on the site. Of the known service buildings the kitchen, slaughter house, malt house and, particularly, the dye house would have all required a supply of water but as previously stated, only the kitchen was located (in 1965-7) and no evidence of water supply was found.

Poole (1870) makes reference to *'two pools within the priory wall'* which were probably artificial fishponds (stews) used for the storage and possibly breeding (Bond 2001, 73) of freshwater species bound for the monastic table. Fish bones were retrieved from the excavations in significant quantities suggesting that supplies were plentiful. Volume rather than purity would have been the primary consideration when filling and maintaining the ponds. Direct supply from the River Sherbourne is arguably the most likely source providing levels of pollution were not too excessive.

Waste Removal

Sections of the main sewer were found running across the north of the site between the claustral ranges and the inner precinct wall. To the west, close to where it would have entered the precinct, it was constructed from sandstone ashlar with a pointed vault. It was straight-sided, *c*0.7m wide and at least 1.40m tall (vaulted sections of the sewer were only observed in deep, water-filled excavations). To the north-west of the kitchen a finely constructed stone shaft was centred over the apex of the vault (Fig 47a). Its internal measurements were 0.50m x 0.62m and its 'drop' would have been at least 3.15m to the base of the sewer. It probably served a latrine located in an ancillary building. Further to the east, where the sewer ran under the reredorter, its sides rose and angled outwards to create sloping sides (Fig 34). Its northern side was built into the outer wall of the reredorter block. Its southern side also appeared to have been built into a substantial yet heavily robbed wall which probably divided the sewer from the ground floor level of the reredorter. The latrines

a   b

Fig 47   *(a) Latrine (?) shaft (b) stone chamber*

themselves were probably situated on the first floor adjoining the dormitory (see **The Dormitory and Reredorter**). Thus the waste would fall into the sewer from above and, aided by its sloping sides, be carried off by the flowing water. A similar arrangement is found in other houses, such as Canterbury, where wooden seats were placed over the drop to the sewer (Coppack 1990, 98).

The sewer in the vicinity of the reredorter was later modified in order to carry a much smaller stone-lined drain, and a circular (latrine?) pit was built into the fabric of its north wall (Fig 48). The two features appeared to be connected via a short stone channel. The new drain ran over a bed of rubble deposited in the original sewer curtailing the flow of water below. Curiously its base was not stone-lined, therefore its contents would have drained through the rubble into the original, incapacitated sewerage system. The date of these alterations is unclear, although it presumably took place in the post-Dissolution period when the walls of the reredorter had been reduced

sufficiently to allow the pit to be dug through the core of its wall.

At least two other large sewers ran into the main channel. One of these appears to have emanated from the west range garderobe and skirted the north-west wing before turning sharply to the north-east. At the point where the sewer straightened out before to joining the main culvert, a stone chamber was discovered connected to the sewer's southern side by a short vaulted channel (Fig 47b). It was evidently part of the monastic sewerage system and, judging by its size, must have been associated with a feature which utilised a substantial amount of water. The second subsidiary sewer ran below the kitchen court before joining the main channel to the west of the reredorter. Its specific origin remains unknown.

The sewerage system may have been fed from the River Sherbourne. If the known alignment of the sewer is extended in a straight line westwards, it would meet the river in the vicinity of a street called

Fig 48 *Alterations to sewer below reredorter*

Burges where the modern river culvert is bonded to the sandstone fabric of an earlier build. Perhaps coincidentally, at a corresponding point on Speed's

Map of Coventry (1610), the river disappears from view – possibly indicating that it was already culverted at this early date. Hypothetically, any localised alterations to the natural course of the river at this point may have their origins in the monastic period and represent the diversion of water into the sewerage system to flush it. Sluice gates could have been used to regulate the flow of water. Once having removed waste from the site, the sewer would have emptied into the river somewhere to the west, down-stream of the Earls Mill.

Sections of stone-lined drain were found running through the undercrofts and across the area north of the conventual buildings in the direction of the sewer. The longest traceable section of drain ran from the north-east corner of the cloister into the warming room (see **Undercrofts and Courtyard**). It is assumed that the drain served the *lavatorium* in the north cloister alley. Although it appears to be heading for the stone lined pit in the courtyard, it has been proven that this was not the case. Therefore the alternative must be that it turned northwards and cut across the dormitory undercroft *en route* to the sewer. Further sections of drain were observed to the north of the sewer where they were perhaps draining the land towards the river.

In addition to the stone-lined drains a lead-lined drain was discovered running from the fitting on the south wall of the north-south undercroft, under the threshold and out into the courtyard (Fig 32b). This was the only example of a lead-lined drain found on the site.

6   The Finds

Introduction

For the purpose of quantification and analysis, different authors have assessed the pottery assemblages from three separate parts of the site. It was felt that due to the self-contained nature of the excavations conducted by Northamptonshire Archaeology, the pottery reports from the nave and north range (which were written at an early stage of the project) would benefit from being presented separately. The data and results from these were subsequently made available to the specialist who worked upon the other assemblage.

With the exception of the nave and the north range undercrofts, only material deriving from stratified contexts sealed below the ubiquitous demolition rubble layers was selected for study (unless of extra-ordinary interest). The materials selected were those with the potential to supply corroborative dating evidence and information regarding the function of the various areas of the Priory. In addition, material from early post-Dissolution levels was included in order to shed light upon the activities of the despoilers and the initial process of demolition.

As a result of this strategy a large quantity of material recovered from the demolition rubble layers has not been studied. Although of clear interest for the study of post-medieval Coventry, it is considered that the loose stratification, lengthy period of deposition and the intrusive nature of widespread stone robbing has compromised the relevance of this material for the purpose of this report. Therefore only small amounts of closely stratified groups of demolition and post-medieval material has been considered. The remainder is present in the archive should study be considered worthwhile at a later date.

The exception to this strategy is the architectural stonework which, by its very nature, was almost entirely recovered from demolition layers.

The Worked Stones & Architectural Stonework
Dr Richard K Morris
(University of Warwick)

Preface

The cathedral priory of St. Mary's, Coventry, was the only English cathedral to be completely demolished at the Reformation.[1] The only remains of the cathedral church's architectural fabric visible today are parts of the north-west tower and west front and the foundations of one of its eastern chapels.[2] However, a multitude of worked and carved stones are available for study in one form or another, and cumulatively constitute crucial primary evidence for reconstructing the architecture of the cathedral church and monastery buildings. The potential of this evidence has never been fully realised, in contrast to the more complete application of the documentary evidence.[3] Some loose carved stones have been incorporated into buildings around the cathedral site: more stones, uncovered during building works on site, are known from visual records such as the nineteenth-century drawings of Dr Troughton and the twentieth-century photographs of Philip Chatwin; and even more stones have been found during modern excavations. In addition, various excavations have located medieval architectural features still *in situ* in the ground, which have been recorded and covered over again.

It was as a result of the quantity of stonework being discovered in the excavations that in commenced in April 1999 that the author was commissioned in May 1999 to compile a Catalogue of worked stones and architectural stonework on behalf of the City of Coventry's Phoenix Initiative. No-one could have conceived then how large was the quantity of stonework still to be discovered, and eventually the catalogue took three-and-a-half years to complete.

The recording of the worked stones has had of

necessity to be implemented as excavations proceeded over this period, so the compilation of the catalogue has been sequential. Thus the cataloguing has been undertaken in four separate 'phases', recording new finds where and when they appeared, with no predetermined area-specific or period-specific agenda to each phase. For the benefit of this report the term 'phase' has been replaced with 'stage' to avoid confusion. As far as there is coherence to each stage, the following observations may be helpful:

Stage 1　(to August 1999): mainly the 'Time Team' Trenches 1-4 in Kennedy House Garden (see APPENDIX 1); some preliminary excavations in 1998 (BCS98); and existing stones at the Blue Coat School site (mainly found in the nineteenth century). The main sites are the church north transept and the chapter house.

Stage 2　(to April 2001): mainly – firstly the cloister and some claustral buildings (including the earlier stages of Trench 10), and the refectory site (CRU00); secondly the nave site excavated by Northamptonshire Archaeology (SMC99).

Stage 3　(to October 2001): mainly the chapter house and the east range to its north (Trench 10 continuing); the church north transept re-visited; and the lower site (service buildings area). In addition, further miscellaneous finds from areas catalogued in earlier stages (e.g. the nave).

Stage 4　(to November 2002): (1) New loose stones mainly from the chapter house (later stages of Trench 10) and from the north-west monastic buildings (especially NRF01); also some miscellaneous finds, especially carved or painted fragments which had been classified as small finds, from areas catalogued previously. (2) *In situ* stonework from all stages of the 1999-2002 excavations; plus *in situ* and *ex situ* stones from previous excavations or in existence in Priory Row.

The catalogue includes entries for all extant worked stones and *in situ* stonework discovered before the present excavations, but the scope of this Report is restricted to loose worked stones and *in situ* stonework from the Phoenix Initiative excavations. This report is only an interim account, made up of the discussion sections which preface the volumes of the catalogue submitted at the end of each of the

four stages.[4] As will be evident from the Conclusion, the amount of potential information to be gained from the 1500 or so stones recorded necessitates a longer period of gestation and research than is currently available to the author to produce a final analysis worthy of the material.

The Catalogue: The catalogue consists of thirty-two volumes of ring-binders (Vol.0 + Vols 1-31). Its information is arranged as:

(1) <u>Record Forms</u>, one for each type-stone.
(2) <u>Continuation sheets</u> (optional) where more than one stone of the same type is catalogued.
(3) <u>Profile drawings</u> at full-size; optional, but drawn in most cases.
(4) <u>Photographs</u> usually one per stone; mainly monotone, but colour where appropriate.

Three copies of the catalogue have been distributed as follows:

Set 1, to the City Conservation Officer in the City Planning Directorate (intended eventually for the City Archives). Set 1 includes the photographic negatives in Volume 0.

Set 2, to the Herbert Art Gallery and Museum as part of the excavation archive.

Set 3 (including the originals of the forms and profile drawings) is retained by the author.

T-number: The Type Number (e.g. 'T164') is given to a particular stone on the basis of distinctive characteristics of its design and/or function. If there is more than one stone in a type series, then the type-stone (the model and usually the best example) is identified as T---/1, and 'continuation stones' as T---/2, etc. The catalogue entries currently run from T001 to T985.[5]

Acknowledgements

I owe special debts of gratitude to Jamie Preston, who carried out the bulk of the recording work, assisted initially by Matt Crossick, and to David Kendrick especially for the concordances, store organisation and photography. I am also grateful especially to the following – Margaret Rylatt, Chris Beck, George Demidowicz, Iain Soden, Barry Lewis, Paul Mason and Paul Thompson. In addition, there are many others who laboured in the trenches or the stores to whom my thanks are due.

Richard K Morris (June 2003)

Stage 1

The Catalogue is intended to be no more than a database, to record the worked stones to a minimum professional standard. Interpretation in the catalogue entries is generally limited to providing dating and function for each piece, as far as the formal evidence will permit, and only occasionally is further commentary provided where the comparative material was readily to hand. None the less, some preliminary observations have become apparent during the course of the work, and are presented briefly here.

The distribution of type-stones by date (see further Catalogue Stage 1, Annex 2) indicates that the majority of loose stones are later medieval (c1250-c1540) and relate particularly to the large amount of refenestration which typically was undertaken in this period to update an early medieval great church. However, the relatively smaller number of stones which can be assigned to the Romanesque and early Gothic period (twelfth and early thirteenth centuries) is the more significant find: especially in combination with the major discoveries of Romanesque fabric in the BP99 excavations in Trenches 3 (voussoir re-used in a secondary wall) and 4 (the north-west crossing pier).[6] No Romanesque fabric had come to light previously with a definite provenance from the church,[7] and very little surviving Early English stonework except for the west front of the church. Amongst the most exciting finds was the shaft-ring (annulet) with pieces of the shaft which it originally held, dating perhaps from the later twelfth century (T058, 059).

Amongst the later Gothic stones, it has been possible to identify an extensive range of window mullion types dating mainly from the fourteenth century, particularly from the later Decorated style (c1320-60). An interesting collection was recovered from the chapter house site (BP99, Trench 1), and almost certainly some of these derive from new windows inserted into the chapter house about 1330 (e.g. T040). Other important mullion and tracery stones have been identified from the Blue Coat School sites (i.e. potentially from the church). Evidence for architectural decoration from the Decorated period has been identified in ballflower ornament and in fragments of fine decorative carving (e.g. T004, 073, 087).

Amongst the window stones it has been possible to group some pieces of mullion and tracery which belong together (e.g. T040 + 081; T042 + 046 + 083 + 094), and also some stones which retain evidence for reconstructing the tracery patterns of window heads (e.g. T017, 043). A profile used for a several of the mullions is an axial roll-and-fillet with lateral hollow chamfers (e.g. T040), which is found locally on other

Decorated buildings such as the gatehouse at Stoneleigh Abbey (c1330-49). Also, pieces of large wave mouldings linked by broad fillets (T070) recovered from BP99 Trench 4 may well belong in date with examples used in the east range of the Coventry Whitefriars, in the chapter house vestibule (mid-fourteenth century). Examples like these show the potential for a more systematic comparison of all the cathedral priory stones with architecture locally and further afield. One of the most positive outcomes has been to identify enough worked stones to provide evidence for the reconstruction of much of the blind tracery decoration of the cloister east walk (T097-101, 103) (see Fig 49a for similar). Judging from the style of the stones, this was evidently a remodelling in the Perpendicular period, which involved lining the earlier back wall of the cloister walk with blind tracery probably inspired by the famous cloisters at Gloucester Cathedral. Hobley's 1965 excavations in the south cloister walk revealed further pieces there, which were not described in his published account, but which included the detail of miniature crenellations on the blind tracery. One common factor which helped in grouping together the cloister blind tracery is that all its components are cut in a soft fine-grained greyish sandstone, rather than the 'pink' sandstone predominant in earlier medieval work. It would appear that the grey stone was becoming more widely employed in Coventry during the fourteenth century, probably promoted by a greater demand for stone buildings which stretched the pre-existing local sources of pink stone. In one instance we have pieces from the same window tracery employing both kinds of stone in the fourteenth century, implying that supply was the main factor (T082 and T134). The grey stone was also very suitable for carving fine detail, which was such a characteristic of late Gothic art (e.g. T129, 131), and survived the weather perfectly well if used in interior contexts, such as the cloister walk.[8]

Stage 2

The stones recorded in Stage 2 represent such a large quantity of material, much of it as yet undigested, that no more than a few snapshots of the most obvious characteristics can be attempted here.

As the majority of the catalogue entries from T140 through the 200s are concerned with materials excavated by the Herbert Art Gallery and Museum (HAGAM) in the former Kennedy House garden area, the discussion will open with these. Thus the cloister walks and adjacent monastic buildings will be the first focus. This will lead on to discussion of stones from the refectory (frater) area (CRU00), which start to appear in the catalogue from T287 and which constitute quite a lot of the 300s and some of

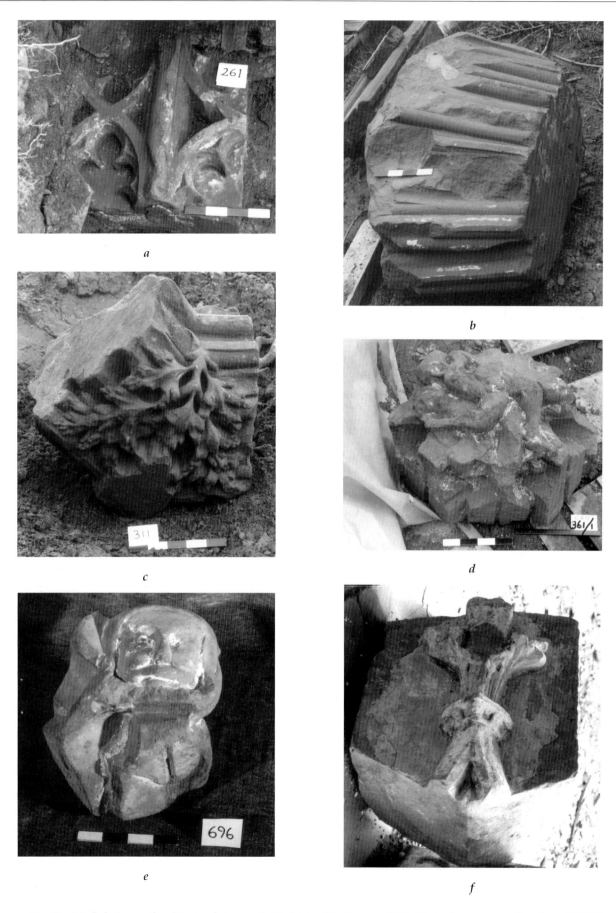

Fig 49 *Worked stone and architectural stonework (a) cloister blind tracery T261 (b) chapter house vault springer T343/1*
(c) chapter house foliage carving T377 (d) refectory undercroft vault boss T361/1 (e) refectory undercroft vault boss T696
(f) refectory? interior gable finial T331 (photos Richard K Morris)

the 600s. Finally, consideration will be given to the materials from the nave site (SMC99), which occupies all the 500s and most of the 600s.

Kennedy House Garden

The type-stones from this area include a high proportion of fragments, probably because it was early in the excavation process and we erred on the side of caution when deciding what to keep and what to reject. Also it is potentially a very mixed sample of material in terms of provenance, with trenches involving the cloister walks, the cloister garth, the immediately adjoining claustral ranges (east, south and west) and the adjacent northern parts of the church (nave north aisle and north transept). Indeed rib T140, found in Trench 6, and another example, T295 found in Trench 10, both almost certainly derive from a rib-vault in the church because more pieces have been found on the north transept site in Trench 3 (including a very large vault boss, T795 (Fig 51d)). This implies that the cloister garth had been used as a yard for displaced building materials after the Dissolution, thus adding to the potential complexity of sources for the fragments excavated there.

The two most significant assemblages of material identified so far (excluding the refectory, for which see below) are from the cloister walks and from the chapter house. From **the cloister**, more excellent examples of blind tracery were identified (e.g. T238-240, 260, 261, 262)[9] to complement the pieces catalogued in Stage 1 (T097-103), and these will be helpful in reconstructing the late Gothic panelling of the internal walls of the cloister walks (Fig 49a). There are also some substantial pieces of glazed tracery (T194, 195, 196, 197), which are related to T024 from Stage 1, which may derive from the windows between the cloister walks and the garth. All these architectural components are in a distinctive grey fine-grained sandstone (green when first excavated), and one of the post-recording assignments would be to establish whether other type-stones in this material from the Kennedy garden site also emanate from the late medieval cloister work and aid us in reconstructing other features from it. These stones include T198 (part of an arched feature), 200-204, 247, 280.

The most exciting group from this stage has been from **the chapter house**, allowing the author to be fairly confident now to propose that the whole chapter house was re-built from the foundations up in the Decorated period, *c*1300-1330; and not just updated in some features (e.g. the door) in this period, as had been assumed previously. The crucial breakthrough came in December 2000 with Margaret Rylatt's identification of the springer stone decorated with the Apocalypse painting (T698/1) as belonging

to the blind arcade running along the inside of the north wall of the chapter house (see **THE CHAPTER HOUSE APOCALYPSE PANELS** & Plate 3a&b, 4b & Fig 52). This was linked to evidence that, at demolition, the north wall of the chapter house had been pushed over on to the adjoining undercrofts to the north, the site of part of Trench 10. Thus, many of the larger and more elaborate stones being recovered from Trench 10 were likely to be from the chapter house, and some of them could be related to the 'painted stone', forming other components of the blind arcade which ran around the room and formed the sedilia for the monks. Most of these pieces will be catalogued in Stage 3, but amongst those in Stage 2 are fragments of the ballflower-studded jambs which supported the arcade arches and canopies (T242, 346).[10] One of these, T346/2, has patches of polychromy on its wall-plate which warrant further investigation by a wall-painting conservator.

Much earlier in 2000, the author had conjectured that a large vault springer (T343/1), unearthed by building contractor's machinery near the north edge of the garden, came from **the chapter house vault**, on account of its stylistic date and the fact it did not fit easily in any other obvious locations likely to be elaborately rib-vaulted (Fig 49b). This important stone can now be related to other pieces of rib and springer which have been catalogued (e.g. T305, 310, 355) and a really important stone, T377 (Fig 49c), which incorporates a vault boss and ribs meeting the apex of a window arch, thus providing us with information about the mouldings of the chapter house window jambs, which can now be identified as T309.

Also in Stage 2 are some stones of the early fourteenth century carved with plain ball ornament (e.g. T345), as well as other Decorated period stones which are from tracery decorated with ballflower (of which T168 is probably a fragment, and of which there is much more to catalogue in Stage 3 from Trench 10). It has been assumed that large stones like T345 must be from the church exterior, which is still a possibility, but a provenance from the exterior buttressing of the chapter house should also be considered. Moreover, the chapter house is the most likely provenance for the ballflower tracery.

A general perception about the Kennedy garden stones is how little Romanesque material is present, or even early Gothic, in comparison with the greater abundance of later Gothic, especially fourteenth century. The Romanesque period is represented by one worn scalloped capital (T179) and a voussoir (T177), and Early English Gothic (apart from the CRU material, see below) by a fine eaves corbel (T175), a fragment of stiff-leaf foliage carving (T314) and a triple capital (T207, from the 'Wall', and thus possibly from the church). By comparison, there are considerable quantities of later Gothic bar-tracery mullions and tracery heads, deserving of greater analysis in the post-recording assessment, e.g. T160, 165, 244, 329, 334, 338, 357, 358;[11] as well as other Decorated period components like a large ground-course moulding for a polygonal feature (T292, possibly for a lost newel stair at the north-west corner of the chapter house) and a capital block (T391).

The Refectory Site

This area proved to hold a rich deposit of architectural fragments because, like Trench 10, it sat on a lower terrace than the adjacent north cloister walk and thus retained the debris after demolition. The loose stones represent parts of an elaborate thirteenth-century rib-vault of uncertain provenance, the vaults of the refectory undercroft and a lot of material assumed to derive from a re-build of the main refectory room in the second half of the fourteenth century.[12]

The rib-vault employed rib T315, with an elegant profile of an axial chamfered mitre moulding (or 'polygonal termination')[13] flaring out of lateral hollows. This type of design was in use in the north midlands in the second half of the thirteenth century (e.g. Lichfield Cathedral nave, Hulton Abbey chapter house) and its ultimate source appears to be the works at Lincoln Cathedral in the first half of the century.[14] At Coventry there can be little doubt that the vault is thirteenth century because one of its bosses is carved with typical Early English stiff-leaf foliage (T316), fashionable before c1275 and here probably dating to c1230-60. Another of its bosses is carved with the fine 'running man' design (T361) and another with a cowled head (T696) (Figs 49d&e),[15] which indicates that this vault graced a room of reasonable status, the location of which is as yet not firmly identified.

The most tangible clue as to provenance is provided by two springer stones apparently with this rib profile *in situ* in what Hobley excavated and identified in 1965 as the western wall of the farmery (infirmary), away from the current 1999-2001 excavations, to the east of Hill Top.[16] Hobley's photo-graph shows the wall around the vault springing 'faced with secondary unmortared stonework', which is probably medieval reinforcement (of a kind found in the undercrofts in Trench 10 of the current excavations) but possibly post-Dissolution work. So one cannot be certain that the vault components of type T315 are *in situ*, rather than being re-used, but overall the evidence suggests that this vault came from an 'undercroft'; which, in the context of the terraced nature of the site at Coventry, is not as low-status a situation as the nomenclature might imply.

The survival of **the refectory undercroft** is mainly constituted by *in situ* remains, which are included in Catalogue Stage 4, but the collapsed ribs and rubble cell-stones of the vaults were retrieved during excavation.[17] Over 100 blocks of the plain chamfered rib type T320 were recorded, the majority of them incised with mason's or assembly marks, from a selection of which rubbings are included in this Stage 2 catalogue. There was also at least one undecorated keystone ('rib intersection'), though unfortunately the example retained has a damaged soffit (T288). The keystone and thirty-two of the ribs have been re-assembled as a saltire cross pattern in the garden of the Visitor Centre.

The assemblage of large stones, almost certainly from **the main room of the refectory** because of their archaeological context,[18] exhibits a variety of profiles which still need further analysis. The main group is a range of interior jamb-stones, arch-stones and bases, all lime-washed and in good condition, from a range of large apertures which might be from windows or doors or both. Generally they are characterised by profiles made up of roll mouldings and hollow mouldings separated by small fillets (e.g. T290, 291, 323, 351-353, 362, 379), and their style is reminiscent of works undertaken in the nave of St John the Baptist's church, Coventry, and for John of Gaunt at Kenilworth Castle in the last third of the fourteenth century; a lead which needs checking in more detail in due course. Certainly several of the refectory pieces derive from window jambs (T287, 351, 378) and they should provide enough information to identify pieces of the window tracery amongst the range of tracery fragments recovered from CRU00 and Kennedy garden, including Trench 10 (some of which are listed above in the previous section). One relevant tracery piece is T338.

Other significant lime-washed stones likely to be from the interior of the refectory are lengths of hood-mould (T339, 330) for a large arch finishing in an impressive foliate finial (T331 (Fig 49f), for which the outstanding series of carved heads (T690-693) are likely to have been the head-stops to the hoodmould (Plate 2b-e). Also lengths of a monumental string-course, perhaps a cornice at wall-plate level (T293), and of large miniature crenellations (T751) which would have sat on top of a stringcourse. Perhaps also from the refectory come stones from a gable with blind tracery decoration (T336-337), probably from the top of a buttress and obviously from an exterior position on account of their weathered state.

However, the outstanding stones' find from the refectory site is a large fitting of polygonal plan, which may well be **the refectory pulpit**.[19] The main piece (T640/1) (Plate 1b) indicates that internally the fitting had an elaborate miniature vault with bosses, whilst externally it had a decorative series of gables

a

b

c

Plate 1 (a) Architectural
fragment from nave [T877/1]
(b) fragment of refectory
pulpit [T640/1] (c) refectory
tiled floor as excavated (d)
refectory tiled floor

d

a

b

c

d

e

f

Plate 2 (a) Head-stop/corbel from nave [T518] (b)–(e) head-stops from refectory undercroft (f) head-stop/corbel from north-south undercroft

a

b

c

d

Plate 3 (a) & (b) Chapter house blind arcade stone [T698/1] (c) & (d) chapter house blind arcade stone [T698/5]

a

b

Plate 4 (a) Reconstruction of exterior west front of cathedral (b) reconstruction of interior east end of chapter house (will need minor revision after full architectural analysis) (*reproduced courtesy of MindWave Media*)

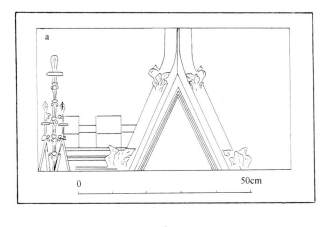
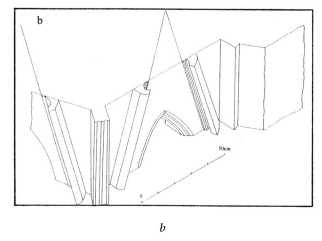

Fig 50   *Refectory pulpit canopy (a) perspective drawing of T640/1 (b) elevation of piece T641 (drawings Jamie Preston)*

interspersed with side-shafts and pinnacles (Figs 50a&b). Other pieces in the assemblage provide evidence for the tops of the gables (T641, 649), and that they were linked to the side-shafts by a miniature crenellated stringcourse; and for the existence of open-work tracery under the arches between interior and exterior (e.g. T642/1).[20] From the lower parts of the fitting survive internal vault springers (e.g. T642/1) and evidence for vault shafts with bases (e.g. T644).

In plan, T640/1 describes (part of) three sides of an octagon, the first side of which is solid and probably adjoined a wall; whereas the second and third sides contained open arches. A large piece which carried the miniature vault along the flat back wall is T344 (found earlier than and separately from the other members of this assemblage), with a vault springer in the centre for at least two miniature bays of vaulting. Altogether, these pieces suggest a space which internally was an elongated octagon, with one long side attached to a back wall, whilst 'externally' the other long side and two of the short sides at each end projected into the refectory room, probably corbelled out from the wall like an oriel window. The 'external' five sides had open arches with open-work tracery in some or all of the heads. The corbelling-out would have required some horizontal mouldings, of which T646 may be part, with a mutilated human head-stop carved at one angle.

Very substantial amounts of fourteenth-century polychromy survive on all the stones, including stencilled blue *fleur-de-lys* on the interior wall surfaces (e.g. T647), which makes this assemblage all the more remarkable. Survivals of complete refectory pulpits are rare anyway – examples are St Werburgh's Abbey, Chester (now Chester Cathedral, thirteenth century), Shrewsbury Abbey (mid-fourteenth century) and Worcester Cathedral Priory

(*c*1372) – but none retains the rich decoration of this potential example from Coventry, which must be close in date to the Worcester example.

The Nave Site
Stones from the nave site divide into two categories for cataloguing: those retained and recorded *in situ*, and loose stones of which the vast majority were removed to store. The first category will be covered in Catalogue Stage 4, and will also include *in situ* features discovered after the main contract excavation on the nave site had finished, such as north aisle pier 8 and the door to the cloister in nave north aisle bay 5.

The second category, the loose stones, is covered here. In chronological distribution, these differ from the sample from the monastic buildings in that there is a higher ratio of Romanesque and especially Early English Gothic stones to those from the later medieval periods, probably accurately reflecting how much less the main fabric of the twelfth/early thirteenth-century church had been remodelled in the later middle ages. Also, in comparison with the CRU00 and Trench 10 sites, there is a high ratio of poor stone fragments in relation to larger worked stones, presumably because the nave platform had been more thoroughly cleared after the Dissolution, as the sparse remains of most of the pier-pads testify. The exceptions were the relatively richer demolition deposits of worked stones in the areas of collapsed vaults in south aisle bay 2 and north aisle bay 7, and to a certain extent around the west door and close to the south aisle door in south aisle bays 3-4. None the less, despite the more fragmentary nature of many of the stone finds, it must be stressed that they constitute a rich vein of potentially crucial primary evidence deserving much more study than that represented by the brief account presented here.

Fig 51 *Worked stone and architectural stonework (a) church nave, vault key-stone T699 (b) church nave, tracery from large window*
T632 (c) church nave, capital and mouldings from screen or fitting T630 (d) church north transept/crossing, vault boss T795
(e) chapter house, sedilia arcade, apex of gable T722 (f) chapter house, window tracery pieces T727/15/16 (photos Richard K Morris)

The loose stones are best reviewed in chronological order, commencing with the **Romanesque materials**. The outstanding find is the massive vault key-stone ('rib intersection', T699) from north aisle bay 7, decorated in the centre with a patera of acanthus foliage carved in low relief, and which clearly indicated the existence of a quadripartite rib vault in this bay (Fig 51a). With it were found a large number of diagonal rib-stones (T565) and some related wall-ribs or voussoirs (T545), both of simple profile with plain chamfered corners. Good masons' marks were incised on them, which have been recorded (Fig 55, T565/1- /5).

This design of rib can be found throughout the twelfth century (e.g. Tewkesbury Abbey, south transept chapel, *c*1100; St Mary's, Warwick, crypt, ?mid-twelfth century; Berkswell parish church, Warks, crypt, *c*1180-1200); but here at Coventry, taken in conjunction with the style of base used on the Romanesque piers in this part of the cathedral, the date of its employment is likely to be in the first half of the twelfth century, before the fortification of the Priory in 1144 during the Anarchy. Thus this assemblage at Coventry constitutes a nationally important survival of an early rib-vault.

Other Romanesque stones include a considerable number of large attached shaft blocks from piers or responds (e.g. T508-512)[21] and at least one voussoir (T613).

The two most significant finds from **the Early English period** are the Gothic rib vault from south aisle bay 2, near the west end of the church, and a large springer and associated voussoirs almost certainly from the Early English architecture of the nave interior. The south aisle rib type (T500) is delicate in comparison with the Romanesque design (T565) and must be associated with the Gothic completion of the nave in the late twelfth and early thirteenth centuries. The stones had fallen *in situ* and enough remained to reconstruct a quadripartite rib-vault, though unfortunately the keystone has not survived.[22] The rib profile, with chamfered sides relieved by shallow hollows flanked by fillets, is hard to parallel outside Coventry and thus difficult to date with any precision. It is related to the door jamb profile of the spiral staircase in the south-west tower, and its axial termination is a less developed form of the chamfered mitre moulding introduced at Lincoln in the early thirteenth century. Overall then, T500 is likely to date to the early thirteenth century, perhaps *c*1220, and represents a possible local prototype for the chamfered mitre ribs T315 excavated in the CRU undercroft and elsewhere (see Refectory site, rib-vault).

T591 is the springer for a free-standing arcade at least about 400mm wide, perhaps from the gallery or triforium of the Gothic bays of the nave. With it belong a group of voussoirs, T638, 667. The main mouldings used in the profile are the beak, the roll-and-fillet and the beaked roll-and-fillet, a language of mouldings derived probably from the Cistercian inspired architecture of northern England of the later twelfth century, and here probably of around 1200 or slightly later.[23] Other substantial Early English architectural components, with promising mouldings for the purpose of dating and provenance, await further analysis (e.g. T524, 537). There is also an interesting stone which was originally a large Romanesque attached shaft, subsequently re-cut with Early English mouldings to be employed as a jamb of some sort (T516).

Other pieces from the interior of the early Gothic nave include a water-holding base for a triple shaft group (T573) as well as several other bases of this period, and there are sections of lime-washed triple-shaft groups as well (e.g. T523, from a nave pier or respond). Numerous pieces of moulded capital and abaci were recovered (e.g. T656-660) and fragments from a capital carved with good stiff-leaf foliage (T569). There are also several well-preserved annulets for detached shafts (e.g. T536, 662), and quite a selection of such shafts, attached and detached (e.g. T548-553), which could be either late Romanesque or early Gothic.[24]

A number of the stones are very weathered and must derive from the outside of the church, probably the west front.[25] Outstanding amongst these, despite their worn condition, are two large capital blocks (T503, 635), with the remains of sparse foliate carving and intended to sit on a triple shaft group, such as those which apparently adorned the angles of the polygonal buttresses of the west front. Sections of comparable shaft groups have also been recorded (e.g. T506, 517).

Finally amongst the outstanding stones from this period mention should be made of the almost life-size painted male head (T518) (Plate 2a) found unstratified in the south-east area of the nave site. It must originally have been a head-stop or corbel, and on stylistic grounds it is likely to date to around the mid-thirteenth century.

The main way of updating the nave in **the later Gothic period** was by refenestration, as happened in many older monastic churches. Typical assemblages of mullions and tracery pieces, to give some idea of the variety, are T578-586, 671-673, 682-683. Most of these profiles are probably fourteenth-century Decorated, which may also be the period for re-glazing the west window of the nave, judging from very preliminary investigations of the stained glass fragments excavated in the west bay of the nave.[26] The most significant piece is a long springer stone for the main mullion of a large bar tracery window (T632) (Fig 51b), incorporating a hierarchy of three mullion profiles, thus allowing it to be linked to other pieces of mullion such as T578 and 581; indicating the potential for further study of the whole tracery assemblage. The date of T632 is likely to be in the second half of the fourteenth century or early in the fifteenth century, and it might relate to new windows in the aisles or nave clerestory (assuming that the west window is earlier). A later piece of tracery is represented by T636, which has segmental pointed arches more typical of the later fifteenth century and the early Tudor period.

Apart from tracery, several other architectural components from the later Gothic period are notable, all dating to the mid-fourteenth century or later. First there is a section of splay from an aperture, carved in low relief with two trefoil-cusped blind arches, back-to-back (T530). These arches might have been returned to form bands of quatrefoils, like the ones to be found framing the choir clerestory windows of Lichfield Cathedral (work detailed by the King's Master Mason, William Ramsey, c1337-49); or they might have formed the arches of elongated cusped panels, as in the chancel clerestory of St Mary's, Warwick (c1370-1380) or in some contemporary parts of the Great Hall at Kenilworth Castle.

Second is an enormous stone, over one metre in depth, from a jamb or respond (T515).[27] Its profile is characterised by a large roll-and-fillet, rather late Gothic in the ogee treatment of the moulding, which is reminiscent in character of work in the nave of Holy Trinity church of the later fourteenth century, but is closer in specific details of style to the replacement crossing arches at Worcester Cathedral, c1354-1370s. The parallels for this stone and T530 above are clearly significant and need researching in more detail. It is possible that T515 was part of some sort of reinforcement system in the crossing or adjacent part of the nave, related to the evidence for structural strengthening in the north transept (observed in Trench 3 in the 2000 excavations, the worked stones of which will be included in the Catalogue Stage 4).

Third are four fine stones from a Perpendicular fitting (T628-631), perhaps a screen or altarpiece, which were recovered in south aisle bay 4 close to the later south door. The minuscule detail of all the pieces is delicately carved in fine-grained grey sandstone, and extensive laying-out and assembly marks are incised on some of the joint surfaces (e.g. T630) (Fig 51c). The geometry suggests projecting octagonal features linking to recessed niches, with extensive blind tracery or panelling. The delicate 'interrupted' double ogee mouldings and the soft-nosed mouldings of the capital could place the assemblage almost anywhere in the period c1360-1480; but the most likely years within this date-span would be in the first half of the fifteenth

century, when this style was popularised in the south midlands area by Master Richard Winchcombe (e.g. Oxford Divinity School, c1420-1439) and related works (e.g. the Beauchamp Chapel, St Mary's Warwick, 1444-64).

Stage 3

The Nave Site (SMC99)

The nave stones catalogued in Stage 3 tended to be odd pieces missed out in the previous stage and, like them, tended to include quite a few fragments of relatively low diagnostic potential. The most significant assemblage for further research amongst these is a series of window mullion and tracery pieces – T639, 702, 845-6, 856-7,873-5.

The most interesting type-stones all are linked to features identified in Stage 2. T826 is apparently a springer for a transverse arch for the Romanesque rib-vault in north aisle bay 7-8; and therefore related to diagonal rib T565. T704 is a vault intersection for the early Gothic rib-vault in south aisle bay 2 (rib type T500), and T824 seems to be part of a wall-rib from the same. T703 is a finely moulded Perpendicular piece in grey stone, and belongs with the important group of stones T628-631 from a screen or fitting of c1400/early fifteenth century.

Other individual stones worth comment are T823 and 847, large and small examples of Decorated period ballflower-and-tendril ornament (see also the chapter house, e.g. T346); and a large Early English triple capital block, T840, rather worn, but with good laying-out lines incised on its top surface (now in the Visitor Centre).

Church, North Transept (Trench 3)

Relatively few worked stones were recovered from this trench, but it is a significant site because it represents the only substantial excavation of a part of the church other than the nave. The trench occupied part of the north transept, in the area of the north-east crossing pier and first pier of the east arcade of the transept. An assemblage of various large-scale stones fallen from exterior features of the building provide the main theme (T781-3, 786-7, 790). Also, more stones decorated with large ball ornament were found (T784-5, 820), of which the blind tracery stone T785 is especially interesting; perhaps from a tower re-build of the early fourteenth century (see T345 from Stage 2).[28]

Two individual stones of particular significance are T772; a twelfth-century multi-scallop capital and one of only three significant Romanesque stones catalogued in Stage 3; and T795. The latter is a large foliate boss (now on display in the Visitor Centre) from a major vault inserted into the cathedral church in the Perpendicular period, probably c1400 (Fig

51d). The configuration of the four ribs meeting at the boss indicates that the vault was of tierceron or lierne type, perhaps from the north transept or from inside the crossing tower. Bosses of a generally similar type may be seen, for example, in the tower vault of St. Michael's, Coventry (later fourteenth century). Two other types of late medieval rib or mullion were also recovered from Trench 3, T778 and 779.

*Fig 52   Chapter house, sedilia arcade, reconstruction of one bay
(drawing Richard K Morris with Miriam Gill)*

Monastic Buildings (Trench 10 and its vicinity)

The material from Trench 10 constitutes the richest collection of stonework in Stage 3. This is because many more large stones had survived in the debris collapsed into the undercrofts and courtyard in this area.

A considerable quantity of these stones derives from the re-building of the chapter house in the early fourteenth century.[29] Important pieces for reconstructing the sedilia blind arcade are T720-724 (Figs 51e & 52).[30] The foliage capitals T725-726 probably also come from the chapter house (probably from the vault springing), as well as several other pieces (e.g. T736, 741, 751), of which T751 is a length of interior stringcourse with miniature battlements.

Amongst the features of the chapter house not yet reconstructed from the archaeological evidence, by far the most significant is the window tracery and window apertures. For this purpose, a wealth of potential evidence from Stage 3 awaits further assessment. A range of mullion and tracery designs survives in T727-733, initially bewildering in their variety but seemingly all (or almost all) related in their design features and therefore quite probably from one building. The seminal types are T727, of which twenty-three pieces have been recorded (Fig 51f), and T728, seventeen pieces. Linked to these by design are several other types – T753 (unglazed, relates to T811), perhaps T755 (blind exterior tracery with ballflower), 764, 792 (a mullion from blind tracery, with the same profile as T762), 804-805 (important tracery pieces), 811 (a tracery piece with an ogee foil, similar to a stone drawn by Troughton),[31] and 883. Then there are also two large window jamb stones (T762, 765) which almost certainly emanate from the chapter house window frames and should prove to be fundamental pieces in the reconstruction. Quite a few of these pieces are connected by design to other types recorded in Stages 1 and 2,[32] from earlier stages of the excavations on the Kennedy House garden site, so the total amount of tracery material for further research is now considerable.

In addition there are a number of other stones from windows, which bear no obvious resemblance to the above group and are thus likely to come from other monastic buildings. Noteworthy are several large stones, including a sill, from a fourteenth-century window employing wave mouldings in its frame (T742, 763, 788),[33] and some stones from a small aperture in a newel stair (T766-767).[34]

Very few pieces clearly identifiable as pre-fourteenth-century were found. Whereas there are at least fifteen other types (in addition to those above) which are fourteenth century or later,[35] only two types are Romanesque; three are later twelfth

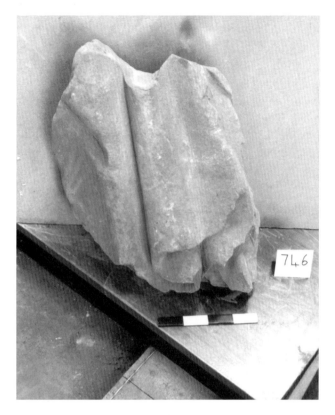

b

a

c

Fig 53 *Worked stone and architectural stonework (a) lower draperies from statue T746 (b) fragment of piscina T922 (c) statue base T684 (photos Richard K Morris)*

century; and up to eight are Early English.[36] The Romanesque examples are a fragment of voussoir carved with chevron ornament (T758), a significant stone only on account of its rarity in the monastic buildings' context; and a multi-scallop capital (T800) mainly significant because it has been re-cut as a piece of T379 and thus was probably re-used in the fourteenth century chapter house work. The most interesting later twelfth-century stones are parts of two double capital blocks (T737-738), a feature associated with Romanesque and early Gothic open arcades around cloister garths, but alternatively they could derive from any form of passage requiring an open-work arcade.[37]

Amongst the pieces of sculpture catalogued in Stage 3, pride of place must go to the almost full-size head of a tonsured monk, T678 (Plate 2f), an outstanding carving though unfortunately found unstratified in an extension to Trench 10, and of uncertain provenance and purpose. This head is now on display in the Visitor Centre, as is T746, a large fragment of the lower draperies from a near life-size later medieval statue (Fig 53a). A finely detailed hem or belt is another statuary piece (T890), and there are also two architectural stones incorporating carvings – a waterspout with a human face (T757) and a stone with traces of a clawed beast, perhaps from a gargoyle (T770); all later medieval.

Refectory Site (CRU00)
Only two stones were catalogued in Stage 3 – a damaged keystone (intersection) from the undercroft vaults (T317) and a worn face from the vault corbel on the west wall of the main undercroft (T396).

Service Buildings General Area
Of the four stones from this area, one of them (T878) must be the most significant stone catalogued in this stage – indeed in the whole cataloguing process – if its dating is confirmed (Fig 54a). This appears to be a textbook example of Anglo-Saxon work, in that it is a large slab incorporating a semi-circular arch for a small window, thus monolithic in construction; though the Normans continued to use this form for the exterior head of small windows, as still to be seen in the local churches at Wyken and Corley. However, the style of concentric bands carved in low relief around the arch head appear more typical of Anglo-Saxon work.

Parallels may be drawn, for example, with the larger arch of the west door to the famous Anglo-Saxon tower at Earls Barton, Northants, which is monolithic on its outer face and has comparable mouldings. Taylor and Taylor date the latter on stylistic grounds to late Anglo-Saxon, i.e. c950-1000,[38] though in reality the Coventry stone could predate or post-date this date-band. It is most likely to belong

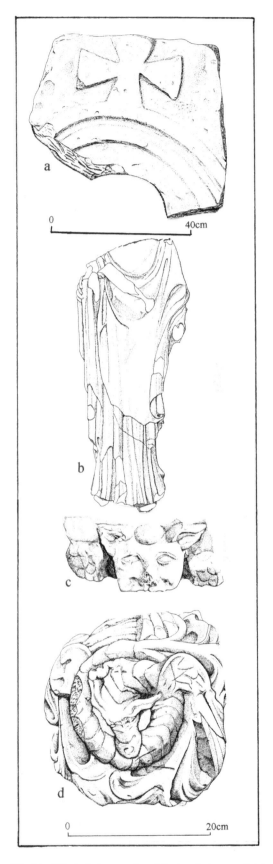

Fig 54 Worked stone and architectural stonework (a) Anglo-Saxon slab with arch T878 (b) statuette (chapter house?) T919 (c) fragment of Romanesque capital T918 (d) vault boss (prior's lodging/guest accommodation?) T984

with the monastery founded by Leofric and Godiva in the 1020s or 1030s, though it might be associated with the earlier minster church.[39] Unfortunately the stone was found unstratified amongst the remains of later medieval service buildings, so there is no clue as to its original provenance. The cross carved over the arch-head is hard to parallel amongst Anglo-Saxon window openings, and may suggest that the aperture was something internal, like a squint or framing an aumbry or holy water stoup. The stone is now on display in the Visitor Centre.

Of the other stones from this area, T881 is a capital block for a large nook shaft, carved with foliage not dissimilar to waterleaf, but different in that the leaf tips terminate in downward-facing volutes. The style suggests the later twelfth century, and has general parallels with works under way at the Cistercian abbeys of Stoneleigh and Coombe, c1160-90. T881 is the only worked stone from the whole excavation site which is definitely of pre-1350 date and which employs a grey sandstone. It is quite different, however, to the soft 'Warwick' type of grey sandstone in use in the later middle ages on the Coventry site, being an excellent fine-grained durable stone, seemingly like some of the grey stone used in the surviving twelfth-century works at Stoneleigh (e.g. parts of the processional doors in the east cloister walk). The stone is on display in the Visitor Centre.

T880 is a large springer for an undercroft vault with chamfer-moulded ribs, of a design not encountered in the other undercrofts on site. Unfortunately, neither T880 nor T881 have any provenance, having been recovered by the author unstratified.

Provenance Uncertain

The one stone worth a mention is a fragment of stringcourse decorated with ballflower and tendril carving (T289) which, on account of its style, may well belong with the chapter house pieces.

Stage 2 Stones: re-assessment and continuations

In addition to the new type-stones catalogued in Stage 3, a number of amendments have been made to those in Stage 2, by substituting new sheets in the Catalogue. The most significant of these amendments are as follows:

T140, vault rib: additional pieces were found away from the church in Trench 10, indicating that the distribution of this rib type, associated with the great church,[40] spreads across the site of the monastic buildings, perhaps as a result of collapse at demolition (if from a crossing tower) or post-demolition disturbance.

T305: now re-described as wall-rib from the chapter house; and including a new second piece,

T305/2, trapped with the chunk of fallen masonry in the courtyard of Trench 10.

T343, chapter house vault springer: more pieces have been identified.

T532, 580, 583, all nave tracery: more pieces have been identified.

Stage 4

The more interesting stones from Stage 4 will be considered in their source groups. The loose worked stones for all groups will form the first part of the discussion, and then *in situ* architectural stonework will be reviewed.

1. The Loose Stones

Church, The Nave Site (SMC99)

Several stone 'small finds', mainly sculpture are of considerable interest. T929 is apparently part of a carved lion, of the right size to belong with a later medieval tomb effigy (probably military). T932, 934 and 936 are fragments of carvings, also later medieval in date, two with good traces of polychrome decoration (932, 934). 936 is an intriguing carving of an ornamental strap or belt wrapped around a roll-type moulding, perhaps a sword-belt wrapped around a scabbard.[41]

T922 is the scalloped basin of a piscina from the west end of the north aisle, dating from the first half of the thirteenth century, with a head and foliage carving surviving on its damaged outer surfaces (Fig 53b). The quality of carving is only moderate, but it is an important piece.

T632/2-10 are nine fragments from the large tracery springer T632 (c1350-1450), noted in the Stage 2 text. Their distribution might provide more clues as to the location of this window (-type) in the nave.

The Wessex Archaeology 1997 trial excavation and a 'test pit' of 1998 produced no stones of real significance, though three small fragments with traces of painted decoration emerged from the latter (T933/1-3).

Church, North Transept

The one outstanding find for which a record was made in Stage 4 is T915, a voussoir with good mouldings of the Romanesque period, from a large arch (probably an arcade arch or crossing arch). It is very likely that it belongs with the primary assemblage of work for the Romanesque cathedral. It was deeply embedded in demolition debris in Trench 3 in 1999, and so unfortunately had to be left *in situ*.

T914 in Trench 4 was also part of this demolition debris, probably from a newel staircase which might have been in the transept or at a higher level in the superstructure – perhaps in the crossing tower. T785/3-4 are more fragments of blind tracery with ball ornament, of the Decorated period, and possibly also from the tower (as noted in Stage 3 text).

The piece of vault rib, T143/6, adds further evidence for the spread of the pieces of this vault at demolition. It is a continuation piece of wall-rib type T143, which belongs with an assemblage of ribs and vault pieces (T140-142) and a large vault boss T795, and which seems have come from a late Gothic vault in the church (Stage 3 text refers). Boss T795 was found in the north transept Trench 3, but the associated ribs have been found mainly in Trench 6, and T143/6 has added to the small number also recorded north of the chapter house in Trench 10 (see also Stage 3 text, T140).

The Chapter House and its Vicinity (Trench 10)[42]
As in Stage 3, Trench 10 provided the richest collection of stonework in Stage 4, because of the numerous large stones recovered from the debris collapsed into the undercrofts and courtyard. Most of this material can certainly or probably be associated with the re-building of the chapter house in the early fourteenth century, so these stones will be considered first.

a) The **chapter house** (see also the discussion in Stage 3)
Amongst numerous newly discovered stones from the chapter house, two stand out as of the utmost significance. The first is T698/5 (Plate 3c), another stone with well-preserved paintings from the Apocalypse cycle which came to light initially when T698/1 was found in 2000 (see **THE CHAPTER HOUSE APOCALYPSE PANELS** & Stage 2). T698/1 has since been identified and published[43] as part of the scene of Christ enthroned surrounded by the twenty-four elders of the Apocalypse (Revelation 4, 4), probably painted *c*1360-70; and T698/5 appears to depict two scenes closely following in the Book of Revelation. The stone – a springer stone from the blind arcade running around the chapter house – preserves both its panels (unlike 698/1), but their paintings are more damaged.

The second stone, T343/9, is strictly architectural. It is also a continuation stone, from the series of springers for the chapter house vault, described first in Stage 2. The significance of 343/9 is that the springer is designed for a corner situation of 135° in plan, and therefore must originally have been in one of the angles of the polygonal apsidal termination of the chapter house.[44] This termination has not been totally excavated in the current excavations, and Hobley's published and unpublished drawings from the 1960s vary in the angles they show and are thus unreliable as evidence in their own right.[45] Thus the

new stone provides the vital clue for establishing the fact that the early fourteenth-century apse was based on three sides of an octagon with angles of 135°.

Stage 4 has also recorded a valuable haul from demolition debris of additional stones of certain or likely provenance from the fourteenth-century chapter house: many of them large architectural pieces, and some others small and ornamental. In addition to the corner springer discussed above, there are several pieces of vault springer (T343/8, /10, /11). Many more pieces have been identified from the window frames and their internal rere-arches (T309/12 [an excellent piece, still with much lime-wash], T309/13, 762/7-10); and from their tracery (e.g. T719, T727/24-39, T730/3-5,), including some new variations on the mullion design (T942, 943, 972). Some of these are virtually complete pieces, and form a very significant collection.

Thus the conclusion in the Stage 3 discussion of the chapter house a year ago that 'the total amount of tracery material for further research is now considerable' is now true even more so. A very cursory survey of these pieces suggests that the Decorated tracery included ogee reticulated patterns (e.g. piece 727/3) and also lights terminating in impaled foiled shapes like trefoils (see the minor mullion profiles in e.g. 727/25, 727/26)[46] – features which can be seen in surviving early fourteenth-century fabric in local churches (e.g. Cubbington, to take a random example), almost certainly a reflection of the cathedral priory workshop. The results of such comparisons means that the tracery pattern used in the virtual-reality reconstruction of the chapter house (Plate 4b) will require revision in due course. Also, the additional evidence from the new pieces of vault springer will be of considerable assistance in fine-tuning the reconstruction of the chapter house vault, especially in the area of its apse.

Numerous new pieces have also been recorded belonging to the blind arcade (monks' sedilia) running around the chapter house walls. When the 'Apocalypse stone' (T698/5) was discovered in April 2002, other almost complete stones were found in the same area, one or two of which appear to have been the immediately adjacent pieces to it (e.g. T720/6). A few also carry important traces of the later fourteenth-century polychromy, such as the tiny painted eyes on a fragment of the spandrel of T720/5; and the bright orange paint of T720/4, on a thick layer of mortar which filled the gap between this arcade stone and the stone tympanum.

Other decorative pieces which probably relate to the blind arcade or the chapter house interior in general can only be listed briefly here. There are two foliage crockets (T038, 825) almost certainly broken off the blind arcade gables (cf. pieces T720, 722); and the charming little carved dog's head (T036) may come from a similar source, if its date is as late as the fourteenth century. T944, another fragment with carved crockets, may also belong. Three different designs of miniature gables with blind cusping (T885, 941, 985) relate in style to the arcade: T885 preserves medieval polychromy, whilst T985 might be from a statue niche. There are two foliate capitals (T139[47] and T965), both painted: the latter is relatively large and might possibly have supported a springer for the vault.

An interesting stone is a length of vault rib (T949), painted with red and white stripes running parallel with the rib's axis and with mouldings which have design similarities with the main rib profile of the chapter house vault (cf. T310, 343). The reason why it differs needs further consideration (e.g. different location, different function), but it is potentially a very useful piece in adding detail to the final reconstruction. There is also a piece of blind wall panelling (T962) with false ashlar coursing in paint, and a base (T948) which fits the mullion profile of the panelling. Stylistically both stones seem to be from the same period as the re-built chapter house (for example, compare the chapter house door bases, T228), but it is possible that they derive from another work of the fourteenth century in the east range.

b) Other **stones from other periods/features**
The distribution of stones from periods earlier than the Decorated chapter house reflects the distribution commented on previously (Stage 3).

From the late Romanesque/transitional Gothic period there is only one item, T947, a trumpet scallop capital broken in two pieces (late twelfth or early thirteenth century). Possibly the tiny carved animal head (fragment T037) is also Romanesque, but it could as well be later.

The Early English period/thirteenth century is represented by six type-stones. T939 is an annulet for a shaft. T961 is a corner springer for a quadripartite vault, and the profile of its wall-ribs should place it in the thirteenth century. However, unlike other vaults of this design and date in Trench 10 (i.e. the under-croft vaults), its diagonal rib is distinguished by an axial roll-and-fillet moulding, suggesting that it derives from a more significant type of room. The corner block with moulded corbel (T978) may also belong with this springer. Finally, there is a springer for some sort of double aperture (T151) which has excellent painted false ashlar with alternating blocks of red and white. The simple chamfer moulding of this piece suggests it could be thirteenth century. The less interesting stones T979 and 982 are probably also from the same century.

The few stones assigned to the late Gothic period, *c*1350-*c*1500 include several ornamental fragments, all with polychromy, from fittings or sculptures. T245

is the centre of a miniature vault from a niche canopy, with bright scarlet background in the vault cells. T246 may also be from a canopy, and its goldish paint and moulding profiles strongly suggest that it relates to the refectory pulpit canopy (T640 etc). If so, this is the furthest away from the refectory site that a piece has been found, though the large springer T344 was discovered in the vicinity of Trench 5. T890/2 is piece of carved belt or hem, perhaps from a statue, and is differentiated from the piece (T890/1) found in Stage 3 by including a band of vivid orange paint. Both T245 and T890/1-2 are carved from the soft fine-grained grey sandstone which is characteristic of much of the late Gothic work in the cathedral priory. The only larger architectural piece from this period (T969) appears to a vault springer, with a simple rib profile perhaps from the mid-fourteenth century, but badly damaged.

A stone which is not easy to date is T983, which seems to be a large plain corbel for a floor- or roof-beam: a functional design popular through much of the middle ages. Equally a very damaged vault springer (T973) is difficult to date closely, though likely to be thirteenth century or later.

The Cloister Area
The most significant piece from the very few stones found in the cloister area is T974, an early thirteenth-century voussoir. This was re-used in the foundations of the cloister garth wall at its north-east corner, and thus provides a useful *terminus post quem* for building activity in this area of the cloister – which might be local work occasioned by structural problems, or a more general remodelling. If the latter, it might actually be the late Gothic re-casing attested by numerous surviving pieces of Perpendicular panelling in grey stone (see Stage 2 text). A new stone which deserves consideration as part of this Perpendicular remodelling is T975, which is part of the springing for a tracery light, carved from the same grey sandstone as the cloister panels.

Three fragments of carvings have also been catalogued in the assemblage from trenches in the cloister. T255/1-2 may be pieces of carved drapery from a figure sculpture, and are also in the grey stone. T259 incorporates foliage carving in a style which suggests the Decorated period, in the fourteenth century, and has the additional interest that it appears to be carved from grey lias; the only recorded occurrence of this stone in the Catalogue. All three pieces preserve significant traces of polychromy.

The West Range and North-west Area of the Conventual Buildings
One interesting piece excavated two years ago in this area has been catalogued in Stage 4. This is T241,

from Trench 16 in the west range ('cellarium'), a short length of mullion with stiff-leaf carving on its surfaces. It is designed for a pair of unglazed apertures, not of monumental scale and so probably derives from some sort of fitting.

Otherwise the finds from this area result from more recent watching briefs and minor excavations in and around the North Ribbon Factory (NRF01), i.e. the northern end of the western conventual buildings. These investigations have produced some important architectural materials, indicative of high status building in this area, provided that these stones belong where they were found (which seems very likely with large stones like T979, 977). Most of the significant stones are mid-thirteenth century or later. A strong possibility is that they indicate the presence in this area of the prior's lodging or/and well-built guest accommodation of a quality which Stoneleigh Abbey added in its entrance courtyard around 1300.[48]

The main architectural finds are two stones from a large octagonal pier (T976/1-2), 0.535m wide, and a massive monolithic vault springer (T977) which sat on top of it.[49] The springer provides the dating evidence, because it employs the same rib profile as T315, which has been found in conjunction with a vault boss with stiff-leaf foliage (T316), hence a date of c1230-60 has been proposed (see Stage 2 text). The sixteen ribs on the springer are grouped singly and in threes, leaving little doubt that the vault design included tierceron ribs (i.e. additional diagonal ribs) as well as main diagonal ribs to produce a star-patterned vault. Decorative tierceron vaults had been developed in England at Lincoln Minster at the beginning of the thirteenth century, and the idea had begun to spread from there to other centres only in the second quarter of the century (the eastern arm of Ely Cathedral, 1234-52, is the first significant example amongst great churches).[50] So the Coventry vault is a remarkable discovery, not only for its relatively early date but also because it must belong in the undercroft or ground floor of its building; the size of the pier argues for this. In this respect the most comparable example in this time frame is the inner crypt of Glasgow Cathedral (1240s-50s),[51] but there is no indication that the Coventry context was ecclesiastical: though it might possibly be the lower storey of a chapel (in the prior's lodging?).

Corroboration that early stellar vaults were in existence at the cathedral priory comes from the vault boss T984. This exciting find was made in an unstratified context close to the Ribbon Factory, and it almost certainly belongs with the vaults of springer T977 discussed above. Its carving depicts a coiling dragon, biting its tail (Fig 54b), a subject not dissimilar in composition and style to a boss re-used

in the cellar of No.9 Priory Row (T905). Behind the sculpture, the stubs for two diagonal ribs of T315-type converge on a length of horizontal ridge-rib with a variant profile. In this instance the diagonals can only be interpreted as tierceron ribs.

The other architectural assemblage worth comment is of three type-stones (T895, 896, 899), from a feature with glazed and open cusped tracery, probably a two-light window. A date of c1250-1350 seems reasonable, but the assemblage needs more research.

T898 is a fragment of carved drapery, hollowed at the back and therefore likely to be from a sizeable external statue. From what little one can judge from the style of drapery, a date in the mid- to late thirteenth century is possible. The figure might have graced a major facade in the outer court (such as a gatehouse or porch), but it could also be a displaced statue from the neighbouring north-west tower of the cathedral church facade. It would be very surprising if the facade was not decorated with at least some statues, as at Lichfield Cathedral.

The Lower Site (service buildings etc)

In this group, the two worthwhile stones from the lower site were found unstratified by building contractors during construction, apparently on the western part of the site in the vicinity of the Ribbon Factory. This is significant, because the stones are very likely to be part of the stellar vaults described in the previous section, both having the distinctive T315-type rib profile. T957 is a large piece of mutilated vault springer, similar but not identical to T977. Seven rib-stubs are discernible in a stone which describes almost a semi-circle, which suggests the presence of tierceron ribs. T958 is a badly damaged boss carved with coarse stiff-leaf foliage, but enough survives to show that it was placed at the apex of a vault, where four diagonal ribs and four ridge-ribs converged.

Stones with Polychromy

In the Stage 3 discussion, it was thought worthwhile to list stones with traces of medieval polychromy catalogued in that stage. It is now evident that the excavations have produced a substantial collection of painted stones, with many important traces of medieval polychromy in addition to the best-known of examples of the two Apocalypse stones (T698/1, 698/5) and the refectory pulpit canopy (T640 etc) (Plate 3a-d & 1b).

A total of seventy-nine stones bore remains of medieval paint when catalogued, which is almost 10% of the total number of type-stones;[52] or an estimated 5% of the total if one includes continuation stones in it.[53] A full list of all the painted stones is given in Annex 4 of the Stage 4 Catalogue, together with an additional thirty-four stones which preserved substantial areas of lime-wash.

The painted stones are potentially significant to art historians and conservators not least because they are in their medieval un-restored state, in contrast to wall paintings surviving in extant buildings, such as the Doom painting in neighbouring Holy Trinity church.

2 In Situ *Architectural Stonework*

The features of the highest significance from a national and international perspective are the Romanesque piers where worked masonry has survived above foundation level. The best of these are the north aisle pier 8 (T470), together with its bases (T471, 472); and the north-west crossing pier (T474), also with its bases (T475, 476) (Figs 9a&c). There were also significant survivals of fabric from the north-east crossing pier (the base T478) and from a pier in the north transept (T482) (Figs 9b&9d). The base profiles supply the most helpful evidence for dating, providing comparisons in the date-span *c*1115-1140,[54] which is what one would expect for the new church was commissioned in the early twelfth century and work commenced with the building of the eastern arm first.

Features of the nave and north-west crossing piers (T470, 474) may be compared with piers at a number of important churches in the east and south-east of England in the first half of the twelfth century, such as Norwich Cathedral (begun 1096), Peterborough (begun *c*1110) and Dunstable Priory nave (f.1131).[55] The use of a large quadrant section in these piers suggests that at one stage the designs for Coventry's cathedral might have included a giant order in the elevation, as in the surviving nave at Dunstable.

Also of outstanding interest in the nave is the wall-respond base (T433) in the south aisle opposite pier 3, and which is still visible in the landscaped nave site. Its pronounced attic ('water-holding') profile would fit well with a resumption of work on the western parts of nave in the 1160s or later in the century. Also outstanding is the jamb (T428) of the processional door from the nave to the cloister west walk, now protected within the Visitor Centre together with its base block and part of a detached shaft (T429, 430). This is the best preserved of the lower parts of several impressive doors in the same Early English Gothic style of *c*1220-60, others being in the west range ('cellarium', T447) and for the main west door of the church (T411, 412). Moreover, T430 is the only survival of part of a detached (sandstone) shaft still *in situ*, of which there must have been many other examples originally, as numerous bases and annulets with empty socles testify.[56]

The one other feature of outstanding interest is a vault corbel carved with a human head (T469), in the undercrofts of the north range. The dating of the refectory undercroft vaults is ambivalent between the thirteenth or fourteenth centuries, but on the basis of the rib profile I have provisionally suggested the latter, and therefore probably part of the later fourteenth century campaign which saw the refectory above remodelled as well.

Otherwise there are numerous good features amongst the *in situ* masonry, almost entirely in the area of the conventual buildings, and these stones are listed in Annex 3 of the Stage 4 Catalogue, under B Grade, section 2.

Addendum (January 2003)

Since completion of what was felt to be the last phase of cataloguing, thirteen more stones have been located in the stores and their records added in the appropriate volumes of the Catalogue. The sources of these stones are mainly – the church nave, the chapter house and buildings at the north end of the east range, and the west range.

Most of these stones are significant. This is largely explained by the fact that they are sculptures or decorative carvings which were removed from the excavations with the small finds, and thus were not entered in the Catalogue in an earlier stage.

The outstanding piece is T919, an early fourteenth-century headless statuette probably depicting an Old Testament prophet, and probably from the chapter house (Fig 54c). Also outstanding is T918, a Romanesque capital carved with a devil's head, from Trench 10 (Fig 54d); and T679, a second part of the lion carving found in the church nave, from a fourteenth- or fifteenth-century tomb effigy. Other pieces with decorative carving are T890/3, 920 and 921: the last a rare example from these excavations of a carving in lias stone (see also T259 from Stage 4).

T343/12 is another good piece of vault springer from the fourteenth-century chapter house vault, which will be helpful in the final reconstruction of this feature. T219 is a block with quite good traces of painted false ashlar.

Conclusions

The Future of the Stones and their Study

The Catalogue is completed, as far as it was intended to go in the lifetime of the Phoenix Initiative. However, numerous essential things remain to be done, if we are do justice to this very significant collection of primary evidence from what has been one of the most extensive monastic excavations in this country for almost one hundred years.

Further Recording
Some assemblages of stone need to studied further for interpretation purposes, e.g. the tracery assemblages (especially chapter house), the stones provisionally assigned to the architecture of the refectory, and the grey stonework from the re-modelling of the cloister walks.

Academic Study and Publication
a) All the data in the Catalogue needs to be digested and refined into a full account of the architectural evidence, arranged by period and by location.
b) This needs to be integrated into a survey of the wider architectural context – locally, regionally and nationally – based on church and monastic buildings at all these levels and leading particularly with moulding profile comparisons from the Warwick Mouldings Archive.
c) These programmes of research should lead to the publication of a monograph on the architectural history of the cathedral priory, as well as articles in major periodicals.

The Archive
The stones not on display at the Priory Visitor Centre, or in the glass boxes in Priory Gardens (T239/3, 512/3, 727/26, 274), are in three storage areas in the care of Coventry City Council. The best stones (Grade A), including those with polychromy, are kept in the Herbert Art Gallery and Museum's store at the Whitefriars. Important stones with research and/or possible display potential (mainly Grade B) will eventually be stored in a space below the path-way between Hill Top and Priory Place which is accessible via the undercroft. The other stones (most Grade C and all Grade D) will be stacked in a storage 'void' off the car-park in Priory Place.

Display
The collection has great potential for further display, and much more of the collection than is currently on view is worthy of permanent exhibition. Display can take a variety of forms, such as rotating the selection of loose stones on exhibition at regular intervals; setting some of the repetitive pieces in a lapidarium wall; and physical reconstructions of parts of the medieval buildings, using surviving stones and replicas.

Notes

1 See further G. Demidowicz, ed., *Coventry's First Cathedral: the Cathedral and Priory of St. Mary* (Stamford, 1994).
2 See further R.K. Morris, 'The Lost Cathedral Priory Church of St. Mary, Coventry', in Demidowicz (1994).
3 See, for example, M.W. Lambert in B. Hobley, 'The Cathedral and Priory Church of St. Mary, Coventry', *Birm. & Warks Archaeol. Soc Trans*. 84 (1967-70, publ. 1971), 50-78.
4 The texts here have been slightly edited and updated; the reader should bear in mind that originally the text for Stage 1 was written without knowledge of Stage 2, that for Stage 2 without Stage 3, and so on.
5 With a few minor gaps in this number series.
6 See further Stage 4 text below.
7 Morris in Demidowicz (1994), 42, 46-48.
8 As noted in Hobley (1971), 100-101.
9 T239/3 is on display in one of the glass boxes over the pier positions in the garden on the site of the nave.
10 These can be linked to the ballflower fragment found by Brian Hobley on the chapter house site in 1965; Hobley (1971), fig.19.15. Also, a fragment of a small statue illustrated in ibid., fig.18.7, may be from one of the carved figures in the niches between the sedilia gables.
11 A lot more pieces, better preserved, of tracery in the style of T357-358, have recently appeared in Tr.10 and will be catalogued in Stage 3.
12 Of which the fine tile pavement collapsed into the undercroft was also part, preliminarily dated by Iain Soden to *c*1360-1400 (pers.comm.).
13 For mouldings terminology, see R.K. Morris, 'An English glossary of medieval mouldings', *Architectural History*, 35 (1992), 11-15.
14 See further R.K. Morris, *Hulton Abbey, Staffordshire: the architecture and the worked stones* (specialist report for The Potteries Art Gallery and Museum, Stoke-on-Trent, 31.12.99), 18; for publication in W.D. Klemperer & N. Boothroyd (eds), *Hulton Abbey, Staffordshire: excavations 1987-1994*, Medieval Archaeology monograph (in preparation).
15 Other fine carved bosses from a vault with rib type T315 were drawn by Nathaniel Troughton, Volume IX, reproduced in Hobley (1971), plate 29.
16 See Hobley (1971), plate 20 and fig.5 (right). There are also four photographs of loose ribs of this type, apparently in the same farmery area, in the 'CBP Archive' of Hobley's 1965-67 excavations, labelled 'CBP. 1965 R.E. T.I 539Q 48 817' and three other '81-' numbers not legible.
17 See T. Hallam and I. Soden, *Excavations in the Frater Undercroft, St Mary's Benedictine Priory, Coventry: March-April 2000* (Northamptonshire Archaeology, unpublished summary report, n.d.), figs 3, 4.
18 Ibid., 5-6.
19 To my knowledge, this identification was first suggested by David Kendrick.
20 If the fitting was indeed a pulpit and therefore would need to keep the main area of the openings uncluttered for communication, then perhaps the tracery was retained by a lower segmental arch at the springing of the head, as in the 14th-century chapter house vestibule of the Coventry Whitefriars.
21 T512 is exhibited in one of the glass boxes over the pier positions in the garden on the nave site.
22 See further I. Soden, *Excavations at the Cathedral Church of St Mary, Coventry, 1999-2000: Summary Report*

(Northamptonshire Archaeology, unpublished report, n.d.), 9, 16 (passim), plate 6.

23 For a summary of the context of these moulding types, see Morris, 'Glossary', 5, 8.

24 Some more shafts from the nave will be catalogued in Stage 3.

25 See various 19th-century views of the NW tower, illustrated in G. Demidowicz, *A History of the Blue Coat School and the Lych Gate Cottages, Coventry* (Coventry City Council, 2000), e.g. figs 20-25.

26 See Soden, *Cathedral Church 1999-2000*, 16 (passim), 23; and a recent reconstruction of a female head from these fragments (drawing, Barry Lewis, HAGAM), suggesting a stylistic date of *c*1320-50.

27 A similar piece, saved by the Victorians, was recorded in Stage 1 (T007).

28 The matter of whether these stones are from the exterior of the church or from a monastic building remains unresolved without further research; cf. Stage 2 text.

29 For the chapter house, see also Stage 2.

30 T724 is in the Visitor Centre; the important stone T722 is the only piece of this kind.

31 Troughton Collection, IX, No.19; the stone survives as T017 in the Stage 1 Catalogue.

32 For example, T727 is the same as T357; T730 is the same as T040; T762 is the same as T378-379; T765 relates to T352-353, which in turn link to T291.

33 Some similar stones were catalogued in Stage 2, see T347-348.

34 Other tracery pieces from Trench 10 include: T734, 735, 754, 789, 791, 803, 806 (relates to 803), 807, 808, 821, 882, 884.

35 e.g. T742, 745, 746, ?752, 757, 760, ?761, ?768, 770, 771, 789, 794, 813, 886, 890.

36 e.g. T740, 743, 747-750, 796, 797.

37 The other later(?) 12th-century type is T739.

38 H. M. and J. Taylor, *Anglo-Saxon Architecture* (1965), Vol.1, 222-3.

39 For example, the burial dated to *c*870.

40 It is the type found on boss T795; see above, the Church North Transept (Trench 3).

41 I owe this suggestion to Paul Thompson.

42 The only two pieces from Trench 1, T256, 257, are insignificant fragments of mouldings, except that 257 has traces of polychromy.

43 M Gill and R K Morris, 'A wall painting of the Apocalypse in Coventry rediscovered', *The Burlington Magazine* (August 2001), 467-73.

44 It lies mainly under Hill Top. Foundations at the east end of the north wall, where it starts to return into the apse, have been uncovered, but they are too roughly laid to calculate the angle of the return to any degree of accuracy.

45 For example, the angle in Hobley (1971), Fig.6 (plan) is approximately 140°.

46 T727/26 is on display in a glass box on one of the pier positions in the garden on the nave site.

47 T139 bears a HAGAM label 'CBP 99 unstrat.'; it is assumed here to have been excavated in the vicinity of the chapter house.

48 See further R. Rowell, 'An archaeology of hospitality: the Stoneleigh Abbey gatehouse', in R Bearman (ed) *Stoneleigh Abbey* (Shakespeare Birthplace Trust & Stoneleigh Abbey Ltd, forthcoming 2003).

49 These stones are currently on display in the small modern cloister in front of the Visitor Centre.

50 For a recent account of the development of early decorative vaults, see C Wilson, 'The stellar vaults of Glasgow Cathedral's inner crypt and Villard de Honnecourt's chapter-house plan: a conundrum revisited', in R Fawcett (ed), *Medieval Art and Architecture in the Diocese of Glasgow* (British Archaeol. Assoc Conference Transactions XXIII, Leeds 1998), 55-76.

51 See further ibid.

52 The total of relevant type-stones (i.e. loose worked stones) from the recent excavations is estimated at 812.

53 The figure of 79 painted stones includes 28 continuation stones, so a percentage calculated in proportion to a total made up of all relevant type-stones + continuation stones (assumed here to be almost as many as the type-stones) is probably more representative.

54 See S. Rigold, 'Romanesque bases in and south-east of the limestone belt', in M Apted *et al* (eds), *Ancient Monuments and their interpretation* (London and Chichester 1977), 99-138 (e.g. p.123, top).

55 For Norwich and Peterborough, see E. Fernie, *An Architectural History of Norwich Cathedral* (Oxford 1993), and L. Reilly, *An Architectural History of Peterborough Cathedral* (1997). For a discussion of Romanesque pier forms in the east of England, see B. Cherry, 'Romanesque Architecture in Eastern England', *British Archaeol. Assoc Journal*, CXXXI (1978), 1-29.

56 A stub of a sandstone shaft was exposed by Iain Soden in 1989 in the north door jamb of the cathedral's west front, but it has since been reburied and may not have survived intact. See T409; and R K Morris, 'The lost Cathedral Priory church of St Mary, Coventry', in G. Demidowicz (1994), 41.

The Masons' Marks
Margaret Rylatt & Paul Mason

A variety of masons' marks were found on *ex situ* worked stones, recovered from across the site. Others were discovered adorning *in situ* architecture. Many of the marks were found repeated in numerous contexts. In addition to the selection illustrated below a number of examples can be found on the elevation of the architects' tracing house (Fig 15a).

a   vault rib (T320/19), collapsed vault, refectory undercroft (CRU00 013)

b   window jamb (T762/9), rubble in undercrofts/ courtyard (JFK00)

c   vault rib (T320/44), collapsed vault, refectory undercroft (CRU00 013) d   grey sandstone (T937), rubble, south cloister alley (CBP99/00 808)

e   door(?) jamb (T966), rubble, east-west undercroft (JFK00 1061)

f   block (T079), rubble, vicinity of north transept (BP99 201)

g   vault rib (T565/1), rubble, north aisle bay 7 (SMC99 1708)

h   vault rib (T320/99), collapsed vault, refectory undercroft (CRU00 013)

i   vault rib (T500), rubble, south aisle bay 2 (SMC99 1169)

j   vault rib (T320/71), collapsed vault, refectory undercroft (CRU00 013)

k   vault rib (T500), rubble, south aisle bay 2 (SMC99 1169)

l   vault rib (T320/68), collapsed vault, refectory undercroft (CRU00 013)

m   vault rib (T320/1), collapsed vault, refectory undercroft (CRU00 013)

n   voussoir/wall rib (T545/1), rubble in nave (SMC99 1708)

o   respond (T488), south wall of east-west undercroft (JFK00 1117)

p   vault rib (T565/2), rubble, north aisle bay 7 (SMC99 1708)

q   vault rib (T320/88), collapsed vault, refectory undercroft (CRU00 013)

r   vault springer (T961), rubble, east-west undercroft (JFK00 1061)

s   vault rib (T320/88), collapsed vault, refectory undercroft (CRU00 013)

t   vault rib (T565/3), rubble, north aisle bay 7 (SMC99 1708)

u   base block (T477), north-east crossing pier (JFK00 307a)

v   newel block (T454/1), north-south undercroft (CBP99/00 1012)

w   vault rib (T500), rubble, south aisle bay 2 (SMC99 1169)

x   vault rib (T320/68), collapsed vault, refectory undercroft (CRU00 013)

The Chapter House Apocalypse Panels
(Plate 3a-d)
Dr Miriam Gill

Three masonry fragments found during the Phoenix Initiative excavation of the site of Coventry's medieval cathedral priory retain significant figurative painting. They seem to have been part of an elaborate cycle executed on the lower walls of the Chapter House (Fig 52 & Plate 4b). The high artistic quality and sophisticated iconography of these unexpected discoveries gives them an art historical significance which extends far beyond their obvious

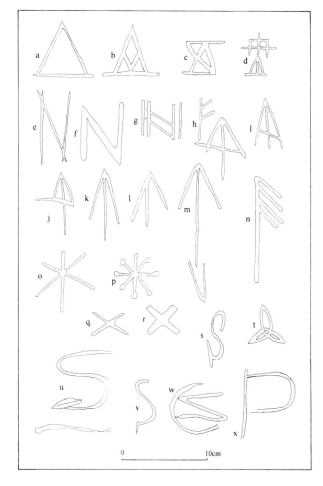

Fig 55 *Masons' marks*

importance in the cultural history of Coventry's medieval cathedral.

The second of the three panels is now a focal exhibit in the Priory Visitor Centre, Coventry and together with the first fragment discovered formed the focus of a previous publication (co-authored by Dr R K Morris) in which much of the general analysis offered here was first presented (Gill & Morris 2001, 467-473). However, this is the first art historical and iconographic analysis of the third fragment. The examination of this panel makes a significant contribution to our understanding of what appears to have been a major Apocalypse cycle.

This report analyses the fragments in the order in which they were excavated, describing each in turn and outlining how each discovery contributed to an understanding of the painted scheme. It will then offer a brief evaluation of the artistic style and quality of the painting, its date and possible patrons. The cycle will then be considered in the context of other known Apocalypse cycles, particularly later fourteenth-century examples, so that its significance and iconographic distinctiveness can be established.

Description and Identification

The first masonry fragment was found early in December 2000 by a team working for the City Archaeologist, Mrs Margaret Rylatt. It came to light during the mechanical removal of post-Reformation debris from the undercroft adjacent to the chapter house site. A small piece of masonry, preserving traces of an exquisitely painted crowned head (Fragment 1) served to alert those supervising the clearance operation to the possibility of surviving polychromy. Subsequently, on December 7th, Mr Barry Lewis spotted a stone with a patch of gilding in an area being cleared by a mechanical digger. Work stopped immediately as he found himself examining what he described as the most exciting find he had ever made; a large masonry fragment with a significant area of figurative painting (Fragment 2) (Gill & Morris 2001, 467). The stone was removed to Coventry's Herbert Art Gallery and Dr Richard K Morris and the author were contacted by Mrs Rylatt to advise on its identity and conservation. The third and most substantial fragment was not unearthed till over a year later in April 2002. It was discovered during the excavation of pile holes in the same location as the first two pieces. This third fragment preserved two significant areas of painting. Although for reasons of convenience this paper makes reference to an 'artist' of the cycle, such large schemes were almost always executed by a workshop and it is possible that the third fragment includes the work of a different hand.

Fragment 1 (T698/2) (not illustrated)
This is a relatively small piece of masonry, retaining no significant architectural elements. It preserved a fragment of painting showing the head of a venerable bearded figure with a golden crown. The man was presented in three-quarter profile and looking to the left. Comparison with subsequent discoveries suggests that this painted fragment comes from the wall plate which formed part of the blind arcade in the chapter house. The figure looking to the left corresponds in scale and appearance to the group of figures looking to the right preserved on the second fragment. It is quite probable that it originally formed part of the right hand side of the subject partially preserved on Fragment 2. This fragment also included a small pinkish area which may have been part of a tower resembling that found and described in Fragment 2.

Fragment 2 (T698/1) (Plate 3a&b)
This comprises of the central springer from a Gothic blind arcade and a portion of a wall plate to the right on which an area of painting measuring approximately 30cm by 20cm survives. This painting is characterised by a high level of detail and wide range of colour, including the dramatic use of gold. In the bottom left hand corner it depicts a bearded figure with a large gold halo accompanied by a scroll. This is as yet undeciphered but it clearly contained a lubricated first word, followed by an inscription in black letter. This face is divided from the other figures by an illusionistically rendered tower of a startling pink colour the door of which stands open. To the right of this tower are the remains of three tiers of male figures in a smaller scale. In addition to three well-preserved faces, two in the uppermost tier, and one in the middle, a further four figures are partially preserved, one at the right end of the upper tier, two at the right end of the damaged middle tier and the crown of a fourth in the lower tier. From the surviving painting, they appear to be a homogeneous group with golden crowns, long wavy grey hair and beards. They all look to the right. Above them in the top right hand corner of the fragment is a whitish wing covered with eyes. On the far-right edge of the panel is the left side of a gilded halo containing a fragment of golden-brown pigment, reminiscent of fur. The tower, the grey-haired figures and the wing are all set against a striking orange/red background diapered with freehand six-pointed stars.

Sufficient iconographic detail remains for this subject to be identified as a scene from the *Apocalypse* or *Book of Revelation* and more particularly a representation of Chapter 4 which recounts a vision of Heavenly worship. The larger-scale bearded figure can be identified as St John the Divine, whose vision is recorded in the *Apocalypse*. The door with its iron-work and the pink turret is thus a rather literal image of the 'door opened in Heaven' described in verse 1. The golden crowns and venerable features of the group of figures identify them as some of the twenty-four elders described as seated on thrones surrounding the throne of God in verse 4. The wing with its eyes is thus part of one of the four winged creatures which surround the throne of God: the man, the lion, the ox and the eagle. These apocalyptic beasts are described in the Old Testament (*Ezekiel*, Chapter 1, verses 5-10) and they were associated with the four Gospel writers from the fourth century onwards. The position of the wing (at the left foot of the lost figure of Christ) and the appearance of fur on the edge of the halo suggest that it may have shown the lion of St Mark.

Fragment 3 (T689/5) (Plate 3c&d)
The third piece of painted masonry is the most substantial. It comprises of a central springer and with adjoining portions of painted wall plate on both sides. Both wall plates preserve significant areas of painting. There are also traces of polychromy,

including what appears to be very intricate decorative work executed at a small scale in the interstices of the cusping. The discovery of this stone significantly enhances our knowledge of the painted scheme. Most importantly, this piece confirmed the hypothesis that the two earlier fragments had been part of a detailed and extensive Apocalypse cycle. This stone also displays more clearly the relationship between the architecture and the painted scheme.

The area of painting to the left contains a wing with eyes at the top of the surviving area of painting. The tips of the wing face downward and from its appearance and position it seems reasonable to infer the presence of a winged creature to the left and possibly slightly above the surviving portion of the image. This wing is separated from the remaining portion of the surviving image by a band of stylised cloud. This appears to form a gentle curve below the winged figure and may originally have been shown surrounding and containing it. Below this 'hover' slightly mysterious whitish 'blobs' more reminiscent of naturalistic depictions of cloud. The exact meaning of these elements is uncertain: they could be attempts to show meteorological phenomena or the remains of upturned faces associated with the group of figures below. Three identifiable figures remain. The first from the left has grey hair flowing down from a central parting and a grey beard. The second with the same long grey hair, beard and moustache is uniquely shown facing the viewer, his head a little to one side. He is wearing a garment which appears grey but with a distinct band of gold at the neck. The third is a white-haired figure with a long beard. He is shown with his face dramatically tilted upwards and apparently slightly foreshortened.

The area of painting to the right contains the damaged head of a venerable grey-haired bearded man with a gilded halo. Comparison with the second fragment identifies this as the visionary St John. The face has a slightly 'squashed' appearance, as if it was difficult to fit it into this far-left corner of the composition. It is divided from the rest of the scene by a further band of stylised cloud, this time vertical. To the right of this the remains of four faces are visible in the lower part of the painting. Reading from the top left, the first is shown directly to the right of the band of cloud, his lips and beard and his right eye survive and he looks to the right. The second and most extensively preserved is shown with a slightly lower eye line; the left side of his face is well preserved and he has waves of long grey hair coming down from a central parting. Similar hair is shown on the final figure on this row, although only the left edge of his head is visible. Significantly, what appears to be the top of a fourth grey head is visible at the bottom edge of the fragment between the first and second figures, suggesting a further tier of figures. Above these figures in the top right hand corner of the stone is a wing full of eyes, shown with its tips pointing down. On the right edge of the stone there are two small fragments of colour which may have belonged to the winged creature which was presumably depicted to the right of the surviving wing. These are too slight to be definitively identified, but are reminiscent of fur or feathers. The area between the group of figures and the remains of the winged creature is an orange/red colour a diaper of stars – it closely resembles the background of the second fragment (*Revelation* 4).

Although the third fragment preserves portions of two scenes similar in size to the second fragment, their precise subject matter is less easily identified from the surviving content. Several aspects of the imagery, most significantly the venerable face of St John the Divine and the apparent presence of the apocalyptic creatures with their wings full of eyes, make it clear that these were further scenes from the *Book of Revelation*. This represents a vital confirmation of the existence of an elaborate Apocalypse cycle proposed after the initial discovery of the first two fragments. As to the exact content of the two lost scenes, careful study of the remaining details does allow for a tentative identification.

The figure groups on the third fragment contrast with the massed and homogenous presentation of the elders found on the two earlier fragments. Although they too are shown looking upward it is with more differentiated poses, particularly on the left-hand fragment where the most ambitious portrayal of foreshortening is found. The three remaining figures on this left-hand portion suggest perhaps a group of witnesses to, or victims of, an apocalyptic event rather than a serried rank of worshippers. While several of the figures on the right-hand panel appear to have long grey hair like the elders, no trace of their garments is preserved. They appear to be in a larger scale and less closely packed than the adoring elders of Fragment 2. The evidently bare head of the second figure suggests that if they are meant to be elders, they have removed their crowns.

A wing decorated with multiple eyes is found in both scenes. If we attribute to the artist a degree of iconographic precision (an assumption which seems compatible with the artistic sophistication of the cycle) then both of these wings must indicate the presence not simply of an intervening angel (a frequent visual motif in the Apocalypse), but one of the four winged creatures first described in *Revelation* 4. Given the relatively small number of incidents in which these creatures are mentioned, their presence in both scenes is diagnostically important.

Both scenes include a stylised depiction of a band of cloud. The position of this cloud is a significant element for the possible identification of the individual scenes. In the left-hand scene the cloud surrounds the wing of the apocalyptic beast, implying that this image showed the 'heavenly' creature manifesting itself above the earth. The text of *Revelation* situates the apocalyptic creatures exclusively in Heaven and does not identify their presence specifically in any of the earthbound sections of the vision. However, the visual tradition found in thirteenth-century French and English Apocalypse Books includes one of the creatures in each of the scenes of the Four Horsemen of the Apocalypse (*Revelation* Chapter 6, verses 1-7) (Lewis 1995, 78-85). This motif gave visual expression to the Biblical description *'one of the four living creatures'* ordering each of the horsemen to ride forth (see *Revelation* Chapter 6, verses 1, 3, 5, 7).

By contrast in the scene to the right the band of cloud is not exclusively associated with the wing of the apocalyptic creature but rather forms a division between the head of the visionary St John the Divine (on the far left) and the rest of the surviving scene. Just as the fragmentary scene of *Revelation* 4 shows St John on the edge of the image looking through the door opened in Heaven, the position of the cloud in this fragment implies that the saint is shown witnessing a scene occurring in Heaven. This supposition is confirmed by the use of the same orange/red background colour and diaper of stars (perhaps originally attached silver leaf) found in the depiction of Heaven in the scene of *Revelation* Chapter 4. Such a diaper of stars is a prominent element in the depiction of Heaven in the Hamburg altarpiece of *c*1400 attributed to Master Bertram and now in the Victoria and Albert Museum (Kauffmann 1968, Plate 4).

From this analysis it is possible to move to some tentative identifications. To consider the left-hand scene first; this appears to show an event on the earth including what appears to be a group of lay people possibly in contemporary costume. The presence of an apocalyptic creature emerging from Heaven implies that this scene must have shown the events which follow the opening of one of the first four scrolls, namely the unleashing of the Four Horsemen of the Apocalypse. These four horsemen were respectively associated with conquest, war, famine and death. In the commentary of Berengaudus the four beasts which 'introduce' them were identified in the order derived from their association with the four Gospels (i.e. the man for Matthew, the lion for Mark, the ox for Luke and the eagle for John) (Lewis 1995, 78). Unfortunately the details preserved in the scene do not help a great deal. The fragment of the body of the living creature is too slight to definitively identify it and the human figures, while not exactly jubilant, give no direct

indication of the catastrophe which they are witnessing or succumbing to. Given the drama of this subject, surprisingly few Apocalypse Book images of the Four Horsemen include human figures, although figures standing near or swallowed by the Mouth of Hell are relatively common in the image of the final rider, Death. This is one of the circumstantial factors which tends to favour the identification of this scene as the Fourth Horseman.

The other such factor, the relationship between the two scenes, is more problematic. Our present ignorance of the original extent of the scenes and, most significantly, the number of scenes in each bay (we do not know if there were there two tiers or whether there were two scenes across the width of the bay) limits our interpretation of the composition here. The fact that St John is twice depicted on the far left of a scene may imply that the images and the cycle read from left to right (like a book). This pattern of reading is confirmed by the likelihood that the image of Chapter 4 appears to have come from the north wall of the chapter house (Margaret Rylatt, *pers comm*; Gill & Morris, 2001, 470), suggesting that the narrative began on that wall, and was presented clockwise. This suggests that the scene to the right of the niche should come after (but not necessarily directly after) the scene tentatively identified above. The iconographic relationship between Fragment 1 and Fragment 2 was previously regarded by the author as probable evidence that each scene was the width of the bay, although Fragment 1 was devoid of any diagnostic architectural detail (Gill & Morris 2001, Fig 6). However, there are some instances, such as the Hamburg altarpiece, where the scene of the twenty-four elders is singled out for presentation on a larger panel (Kauffmann 1968, Plate 4).

This question of the number of tiers and scenes in each bay clearly impacts on the identification of the second subject portrayed on the third fragment. If the position of the cloud band does imply that this scene is set in Heaven, then the next such incident in the narrative sequence is the Adoration of the Lamb by those sealed by the angels of God, an event which separates the opening of the sixth and the seventh seals (*Revelation* Chapter 7 verses 9-17). The un-crowned venerable worshippers resemble the saints depicted in conventional Apocalypse book representations of this scene (Lewis 1995, 90-5). There are no signs of their attribute of palm branches (*Revelation*, Chapter 7 verse 9), but their upturned faces (reminiscent of the elders of Fragment 2) and the presence of one of the four winged creatures who surround the throne of God are both compatible with this identification. This fragment contains no trace of the figure of the elder who accompanies St John in this vision. However, the elder may have been positioned below John's head, as in some thirteenth-century representations of the scene (Lewis 1995, Fig 54).

The only possible problem is the number of important scenes which would divide the two identified subjects: the opening of the fifth seal (saints below the altar), the sixth seal (earthquake) and the four winds. The identification proposed above suggests a more crowded programme than either two tiers of double scenes or three tiers of single scenes, although it is possible that the fifth and sixth seals were combined into a single scene or the image of the four winds omitted.

Style, Quality, Date and Patronage

All the surviving fragments indicate a mural cycle of the highest artistic quality. The delicacy of the paintwork and the range of colours deployed are immediately impressive, as is the extensive use of gold. The pigments and techniques of the second fragment have been the subject of a detailed scientific study by Dr Helen Howard who sets them in the context of the techniques found in the Westminster Chapter House cycle. No documentary evidence for the execution and patronage of this important cycle has yet been identified. However, a contextual and comparative study of the paintings suggests their probable date and may even indicate the identity of possible patrons.

The architectural detail preserved in Fragments 2 and 3 and the location of their discovery suggest that they probably formed part of the blind arcade of the north wall of the Chapter House (Margaret Rylatt, *pers comm*; Gill & Morris, 2001, 470). This building has been dated to the period *c*1300 to 1330 on the basis of stylistic analysis and the Apocalypse painting appears to be the first layer of polychromy applied to the stone work (Mark Perry, conservation report in archive; Gill & Morris 2001, 470). However, the style of the painting, in particular the naturalistic rendering of faces (including foreshortening) and the perspectival presentation of architecture, suggests a date after 1350. English painting in the decades after the Black Death was stylistically diverse and subject to a range of continental influences. Although considerable schemes of mural painting survive from this period, very little of it reaches the artistic sophistication found at Coventry. Moreover, the limited content of the painted fragments prevents any examination of common diagnostic features such as the treatment of drapery.

The scheme of painting with which comparison can most reasonably be drawn is that of the lives of Job and Tobit from St Stephen's Chapel, Westminster Palace (*c*1350-63) (fragments of which are preserved in the British Museum) (Howe 2001, 259-303). Although apparently the work of English artists, the style of these paintings was clearly derived from Italian, particularly Sienese, painting from the first half of the fourteenth century (Howe 2001, 286). This influence shows itself in general characteristics, such as a preference for warm orange and pink tones, architectural settings which are complex and perspectival, but presented in a slightly smaller scale than the figures which inhabit them, and faces which are naturalistic and subtly modelled, but lacking the soft and bulbous quality of the late fourteenth-century International Style. More specific similarities are evident in the comparison of the scene of Job rebuking his comforters with Fragment 2 (Gill & Morris 2001, 472-3). The profile and form of the turrets in Westminster scene closely resemble the tower which frames the doorway into Heaven in the Coventry fragment. The pink colour of the Coventry tower recalls elements of the architecture in the Westminster scene. While most of the faces in the Westminster paintings do not resemble those at Coventry (the concave nose and swept back hair of the young boy in the scene of Job addressing his sons are a notable exception), the foreshortened faces on the third fragment do recall the dramatic, Italian-inspired style found in some English manuscripts dated to the 1360s, most particularly the Egerton Genesis (Sandler 1986: I, 22-3). More generally, the ovoid heads and striking pink and orange palette of the Coventry scenes recalls the predominant styles of the group of manuscripts executed for the Bohun family between 1361 and 1399 (Sandler 1986, I, 34-6).

The Coventry paintings naturally invite comparison with the extensive and ambitious scheme of painting in the chapter house of Westminster Abbey. This cycle of ninety-six scenes was financed (in part at least) by the monk John of Northampton (Turner 1985, 89-92) and appears to date from the 1380s (Babington *et al* 1999, 10-11, 30-32). Interestingly, despite their prestigious location and complex technique, the Westminster paintings are artistically inferior to the Coventry cycle. The treatment of detail, evident in the figures of the elders (Babington *et al* 1999, 31), is much coarser, with a rather heavy-handed use of black outline and white highlights which contrasts with the delicate precision and subtle modulation of the Coventry murals.

In terms of both quality and date, the Coventry paintings lie between the scheme at St Stephen's Chapel and the Apocalypse cycle at Westminster. Stylistic comparison with manuscripts suggests that the paintings were probably executed in the period *c*1360-70. This date does in turn help to suggest some possible elite patrons: dowager Queen Isabella (d. 1358), the Black Prince (d. 1376), Henry Duke of Lancaster (d. 1361), John of Gaunt (d. 1399), and the earls of Warwick (Thomas Beauchamp the elder (d. 1369) and his son, Thomas (d. 1401) (Morris: Gill and

Morris 2001, 472). No documentary evidence survives of any donations to the Priory from these illustrious individuals, although the arms of the Beauchamp earls of Warwick appear in a pavement of *c*1360-1400 in the recently excavated monastic refectory undercroft (Morris: Gill & Morris 2001, 473), possibly suggesting a contemporary benefaction to the Abbey. The scheme was almost certainly painted in the time of Prior William de Greneburgh who was elected in 1361 and held the office till his death in 1390 (Morris: Gill & Morris 2001, 473). Given the evidence for monastic patronage at Westminster the patronal involvement of the monastic community cannot be ruled out.

The discovery of an extensive Apocalypse cycle at Coventry may also throw light on the significance of this subject in a monastic context. Although the Apocalypse was depicted in several significant monumental schemes in the late fourteenth-century, most strikingly the Angers Tapestries created for Louis, Duke of Anjou in 1377, the choice of this complex subject for the chapter house at Westminster had been considered a little idiosyncratic (Binski 1995, 192). The identification of an apparently earlier and more accomplished cycle suggests that the Westminster scheme may be an act of emulation. In general terms, the theme of judgement can be related to the function of a chapter house; at Westminster the Abbot sat in a seat directly beneath the image of Christ the Judge (Binski 1995, 188). The Twelfth Chapter of the *Rule of St Benedict* states that the Sunday celebration of the Office of Lauds should include the recitation by heart of one chapter of the *Apocalypse*. This would require an intimate knowledge of the book, one which would enhance and be refreshed by the presence of such a detailed monumental cycle.

Given the complexity of their subject matter, most monumental Apocalypse schemes were based on cycles developed in book illumination, particularly the lavishly illustrated Apocalypse books produced in England from the mid-thirteenth century. For example, the cycle at Westminster is derived from a later fourteenth-century version of the 'expanded Metz' cycle (Cambridge Trinity College MS B. 10. 2) (Noppen 1932, 154). However, the visual source for the Coventry scheme remains elusive. A comparison between the images of the adoring elders at Westminster and Coventry highlights the former's dependence on the compartmentalised framework of its thirteenth-century exemplar, in contrast to the more naturalistic and complex rendition of space in the later. Moreover, the precise scene shown on Fragment 2 is omitted from the Westminster scheme, possibly suggesting that the Coventry cycle was originally more extensive than Westminster's ninety-six scenes. While it is possible that the Coventry cycle

represents a visual recasting of a conventional Apocalypse cycle in a more contemporary artistic idiom – an approach suggested in the case of the cycle of eighty early fifteenth-century panels in the great east window at York (French 1995, 10), it may be more directly derived from a source as yet unidentified.

The refectory painting from the Coventry Charter-house (*c*1411-17) with its refined use of the International Style (Gill 1999, 127-9) and the more forceful and intense Doom painting (*c*1435) now emerging from over a century of obscurity in Holy Trinity, Coventry indicate a high level of artistic production in the city in the first half of the fifteenth century. A similar richness is found in the surviving corpus of sculpture and stained glass (Davidson & Alexander 1985), a corpus which archaeological work on the sites of the Whitefriars and the Priory has significantly augmented. The prominence of local painters may be indicated by the 1435 requirement that they and the saddlers should contribute to the card-makers' pageant (Ingram 1981, 11). Moreover, Coventry was the home town of the famous glass painter John Thornton who executed the great east window at York Minster (*c*1405-8) (French 1995) and is credited with the promotion of the International Style in that city. The Apocalypse panels indicate that a similar level of innovation and sophistication was present in Coventry in the later fourteenth century. Although there is little evidence of a direct iconographic relationship between the Coventry panels and the York east window Apocalypse cycle, some early fifteenth-century Coventry glass (formerly in St Michael's Church – the Old Cathedral) does seem to preserve stylistic elements, such as concave noses, evident in the Coventry panels perhaps indicating their sustained influence on local style (Marks 1993, Fig 147).

To conclude: the three panels from the Priory excavation appear to have formed part of a very extensive and detailed Apocalypse cycle, the exact visual source of which remains to be identified. The surviving scenes show the Adoration of the Elders (*Revelation,* Chapter 4, vv. 1-9) and possibly Death, the last of the four horsemen of the Apocalypse (*Revelation* Chapter 6 vv. 7-8) and the Adoration of God by the redeemed (*Revelation* Chapter 7 vv. 9-17). The cycle is executed in a sophisticated style, derived from early fourteenth-century Italian art, and characterised by illusionistic space, perspectival architecture and naturalistic modelling of figures. Probably dating from *c*1360-70 it predates the famous but less artistically accomplished Apocalypse cycle in the chapter house at Westminster, and may even have been the inspiration for it. Its identification suggests a monastic interest in the Apocalypse as a monumental subject; one related to the importance of this book in monastic offices, and possibly to the specific role of the chapter house. The discovery of such an important and sophisticated painted cycle in later fourteenth-century Coventry indicates not only the artistic importance of the city at that time, but provides a context for the city's status as an artistic centre in the fifteenth century.

The Floor Tiles
Zenon Demidowicz, Iain Soden and
Margaret Rylatt

Decorated Tiles – in situ

Nave (not illustrated)

At the west-end entrance to the nave a large area of floor survived, and small numbers of decorated tiles lay amongst a wider expanse of plain tile (Fig 13). All were very heavily worn and were of unremarkable design. None of these was removed but recorded *in situ*. No widespread attempt at patterning using these decorated tiles was observed. They date from the second half of the fourteenth century. The following is a concordance of the recorded *in situ* tiles related to the principal published works covering local tiles, namely: Chatwin (1936), Whitcomb (1956), Hobley (1971), Eames (1982), Soden (1995) and Woodfield (forthcoming).

North Range (Plate 1c&d)

In the north claustral range, a little-worn floor composed of encaustic tiles was discovered sandwiched between the collapsed vault of the undercroft beneath and the rubble of the refectory. It had collapsed *en bloc* and its layout was still recognisable since a group of over thirty tiles had come to rest on a former subdividing wall in the undercroft. The fourteenth-century tiles are of local manufacture, almost certainly Stoke, Coventry. The date is arrived at from the armorial tiles which form

the centrepiece of the design, the arms of England after 1340 and the arms of Sir Thomas Beauchamp, Earl of Warwick (1360s). The tiles were laid in repeating squares offset in rows across the room, alternating in fours and nines, touching corner to corner, each separated by a border of plain green tiles.

Decorated Tiles – ex situ (Figs 56-59)

In addition to the above, a large quantity of decorated floor tiles were recovered from *ex situ* contexts throughout the entire site. Whilst many of these were of designs well documented in the local area (catalogued in archive), forty eight were, with respect to the literature consulted, both new to Coventry and also unknown elsewhere. The principal works consulted were as follows: Chatwin (1940), Whitcomb (1956), Hobley (1971), Eames (1980), Walsh & Wright (1983), Woodfield & Griffiths (forthcoming), Lockock (1995), *West Midlands Archaeology* 43 (2000, Fig 11) and Soden (1995).

Of these new designs, sixteen could be described as having a 'geometric' pattern. A further seven were 'heraldic' and eleven were classed as 'script' designs i.e. displaying lettering of various forms. Seven designs depicted animals and seven others were discovered (termed 'miscellaneous') which did not fit readily into any of these simple forms. Most of the tiles were of the two-colour encaustic type although other types, such as impressed, line-impressed, hand-drawn in dark paint on a white slip background and (possibly) incised were also found. Almost half the tiles found belonged to the fourteenth century with most of rest datable to the thirteenth/fourteenth- and fourteenth/fifteenth-century periods. The newly recorded designs are catalogued below (listed according to where they were found) and the designs are illustrated in Figures 56-59.

Chatwin	Whitcomb	Hobley	Eames	Soden	Woodfield
13:5	204			88	23
17:3	227			73	24
23:13				42	91
25:2				2	
25:3					
39:2				11	
41:19				45	94
43:6	122				

Fig 56   Decorated floor tiles

Cathedral Nave

Fig 56

a   SMC99 Context 095 (pit fill, south aisle bay 2). 13th-Century mosaic tile forming a segment of a circle from around a central roundel.

b   SMC99 Context 003 and 151 (roof vault collapse, north aisle bay 7). 13th-Century window tracery design.

c   SMC99 Context 003 (rubble, south aisle bay 7). 13th-Century repeating floral and geometric border design.

d   SMC99 Context 460 (layer, north aisle bay 7). 13th/Early 14th-Century single tile depicting horse with rider jousting.

e   SMC99 Context 003 (rubble). 14th-Century single-tile design depicting a hart (?).

f   SMC99 Context 033 (floor, north aisle bay 6) and CBP99 Context 1005 (rubble, chapter house). 14th-Century single-tile design depicting a lion rampant.

g   SMC99 Context 003 (rubble). 14th-Century single-tile design possibly depicting two leaping figures.

h   SMC99 Context 460 (layer, north aisle bay 7).

13th/Early 14th-century single-tile design depicting the rear half of a beast, possibly a horse or a lion passant.

i   SMC99 Context 019 (roof collapse, south aisle bay 2). 14th-Century impressed script tile; first line possibly Latin NULNE[MO] (nothing, no one. . .), bottom line . . .VG.

j   SMC99 Context 003 (rubble) and CBP00 Context 1672 (fill of cistern west of west range). Crude early 14th-century single-tile design with geometric 'butterfly' shape.

k   SMC99 Context 003 (rubble, south aisle bay 1). 14th/15th-Century tile forming part of a four-tile repeating floral and geometric pattern.

l   SMC99 Context 003 (rubble). Late 14th-century heraldic single-tile design stamped in relief: lion rampant, possibly for Thomas Mowbray Duke of Norfolk (Lord of nearby Caludon Castle until 1397).

m   SMC99 Context 095 (pit fill, south aisle bay 2). 14th-Century geometric tile.

Fig 57

a   CBP00 Context 2201 (demolition rubble, north aisle bay 8). 13th/14th-Century tile, possibly forming the lower part of a leaf pattern.

b   CBP00 Context 2902 (generic grave fill for graves in north aisle bay 6), BP99 Context 103 (grave fill cloister alley) and CBP00 Context 1002 (rubble, north-south undercroft). 15th/16th(?)-Century tile with a hand-drawn design in dark paint on a white slip background: cusped concentric squares enclosing cross.

c   CBP00 Context 2902 (generic grave fill for graves in north aisle bay 6). 15th/16th(?)-Century tile with a hand-drawn design in dark paint on a white slip background, part of a four-tile pattern: quatrefoil on a stalk (possibly part of a floral pattern) enclosed by two concentric circles; rectilinear border with trefoil in spandrel.

Cathedral North Transept

d   JFK00 Context 302a (rubble, north transept of cathedral). Late 14th/early 15th-century line-impressed script tile with gothic lettering, scrolls and a cross, all between two concentric circles: central symmetrical leaf design with leaf pattern in corners; inscription reads WALTERUS JACKYS SONE, probably for 'Walter Jackson'. A fragment of a similar tile was found during excavations on the town wall in Cox Street (Bateman & Redknap 1986, 77, Fig 14).

Cloister

e   CBP99, Context 512 (layer, north cloister alley). 13th/14th-Century tile depicting a lamb facing right.

Fig 57 *Decorated floor tiles*

de Compostela.

l JFK00 Context 1055 (rubble over steps, north-east cloister). 14th-Century script tile, three tiers of lettering:
SEL/[?]
RK/S/[?]
[?]AB(?)/[?]

Fig 58

a JFK00 Context 1059 (rubble over steps, north-east cloister). 13th/14th-Century script tile, three tiers of lettering, probably representing part of The Hail Mary:
AV
RA[?]
[?]OM[?].

b JFK00 Context 1059 (rubble over steps, north-east cloister). 14th/15th-Century tile with a heraldic design in relief; shield with two crosses with polygonal shapes below; Beauchamp (debased), after 1360.

Fig 57b also appears in BP99 Context 103 (grave fill, cloister alley).

Chapter House

c BP99 Context 120 (grave cut, chapter house). 14th/15th-Century quartered tile depicting lion rampant, facing left, within a continuous white border.

Fig 56f also appears in CBP99 Context 1005 (rubble, chapter house).

Undercrofts and Courtyard

d CBP99 Context 1002 (rubble, north-south undercroft). 14th-Century heraldic tile: arms of Clare (debased), Duke of Gloucester; an anachronism, since the Clares no longer held the dukedom at the probable time of manufacture.

e CBP99 Context 1002 (rubble, north-south undercroft). 14th-Century heraldic tile: probable five-shield pattern (interspersed with trefoils) three shields of which are visible and carry, respectively, three circles and a horizontal bar (possibly for Grey), a lion rampant facing right (Thomas Mowbray, Duke of Norfolk) and an engrailed saltire (possibly for Tiptoft or Botetourt).

f CBP99 Context 1002 (rubble, north-south undercroft). 14th-Century; possibly depicting part of a mythical beast.

g CBP00 Context 1003 (rubble, spiral staircase). 14th-Century script tile, possibly part of a four- or nine-tile pattern: gothic lettering ('. . . tinetur') between two concentric circles. It is possibly part of the passive of the verb *'contineo'* (is

f CBP99, Context 703 (layer, cloister garth). 14th/15th-Century tile depicting a five-spoked geometrical wheel design. St Catherine's Wheel?

g CBP99 Context 805 (layer, south cloister alley). 14th-Century script (?) tile with letter design enclosing a leaf pattern; five-petal rosette in corner.

h CBP00 Context 1038 (pit fill, east cloister alley). 13th/14th-Century script tile, three tiers of lettering:
. . . SKI
[?] AR
. . . OLI

i CBP00 Context 1038 (pit fill, east cloister alley). 13th/14th-Century script tile, two (of a possible three) tiers of lettering visible
[?] G [?],
[?] A G [?] [?].

j CBP00 Context 1904 (rubble, south cloister alley). 14th-Century tile: *fleur-de-lys* within a circle; corner trefoil.

k JFK00 Context 1051(rubble, east cloister alley). 14th-Century: possibly an open scallop shell between two vertical inset bands; the scallop shell is symbolic of the pilgrimage to Santiago

enclosed/contained within) and, as such, may relate to a grave.

h   JFK00 Context 1002 (rubble, north-south undercroft). 14th-Century four-tile design: formal three-leaf corner design with a slightly off-diagonal straight band ornamented with four large spots.

i   JFK00 Context 1002 & 1154 (rubble, north-south undercroft). 14th-Century single-tile design: a 'Star of David' within a broken circle; possible eight-petal rosette at tile centre; trefoils and dots between triangular star points and at corners; dots within star points.

j   JFK00 Context 1004 (rubble, north-south undercroft). Heraldic tile, after 1340: arms of England (leopards passant) quartered with the arms of France (*fleur-de-lys*); left-corner leaf motif.

k   JFK00 Context 1004 (rubble, north-south undercroft). Heraldic tile, after 1340: arms of England (leopards passant) quartered with the arms of France (*fleur-de-lys*); top-corner leaf motif: different portion of same design as 35) above.

l   JFK00 Context 1004 (rubble, north-south undercroft). 14th-Century four-tile design: similar to Fig 58h.

m   JFK00 Context 1004 (rubble, north-south undercroft). 14th-Century tile; part of a geometric repeating pattern: halves of eight-petaled rosettes enclosed within concentric circles; circles separated by a bar with a bulbous end.

Fig 59

a   JFK00 Context 1004 (rubble, north-south undercroft). Part of a nine-tile pattern: small *fleur-de-lys* between two concentric circles.

b   JFK00 Context 1061 (rubble, east-west undercroft). 14th-Century line-impressed tile, probably part of a geometric repeating pattern: possibly a six-petal rosette with open centre; two corner concentric quarter-circles.

c   JFK00 Context 1192 (layer, courtyard). 14th-Century tile: possibly a griffin or an eagle.

Fig 57b also appears in CBP00 Context 1002 (rubble, north-south undercroft)

Refectory

d   JFK00 Context 1095 (rubble, refectory undercroft). 13th/14th-Century rectangular script tile with three tiers of Lombardic lettering:
LAM: DEIT:S
ELE:AC:DEBO
LE:SASE:[?]

West range and garderobe

e   CBP99 Context 1602 (rubble west range). 14th-Century tile, may be a part of a multi-tiled design: floral pattern within two concentric circles; possible leaf or part of a heart in corner.

f   CBP99 Context 1602 (rubble west range). 14th/15th-Century tile, design possibly incised, or, more likely, impressed, into the clay: fine fern-like leaves running approximately parallel to each other.

Fig 56j also appears in CBP00 Context 1672 (fill, garderobe cistern)

Unstratified

g   CBP00 Trench 10. 14th/15th-Century tile: cross with tri-lobed arm-ends within a continuous border.

h   CBP00 Trench 10. 13th/14th-Century script tile with only one tier of lettering surviving;
[?] I P G [?].

i   CBP00 Trench 19. 13th/14th-Century script tile with three tiers of lettering:
[?]DA (?)[?]
ESD [?]
ANG [?]

Fig 58   *Decorated floor tiles*

Fig 59   Decorated floor tiles

j   JFK00 Trench 10. 14th/15th-Century tile, possibly part of a repeating pattern: floral/leaf geometrical design.

Plain Tile

Thousands of fragments of green or yellow glazed, undecorated floor tile were recovered from the excavations. They are unremarkable and in the main very heavily worn. They show a common clay source (Stoke, in Coventry) and are of a type associated with those recovered from Charterhouse and Whitefriars.

In the cathedral, these tiles had been laid in blocks, zones and bands to subdivide the overall floor. Some areas survived, as did patches of tile-less floor mortar bedding, criss-crossed by the ridges of set mortar which had extruded and set hard around the tiles when originally laid. Close to the west end, plain tiles had been used to form repeating diamonds within diamonds; each set at different angles to the floor axis.

Only a small sample of the plain tile was retained. The remainder was discarded on site.

The Ceramic Roof Tiles
Margaret Rylatt, Paul Mason & Iain Soden

The Cathedral

A vast quantity of ceramic roof tile was recovered; 5244 fragments from the demolition levels of the nave alone. Of these a small proportion (2%) were fragments of curved ridge tile, most of which had a dark green glaze. Two plain, 'bull-horns' ridge crests were also recovered. No complete tiles were found. Most seem to have had one raised (pulled) hanging nib in the short side with a nail hole in the corners on either side. They had been prepared in a sanded tray, the smooth, upper side being that which was laid face-down against the laths of the roof, the rougher, sanded side being exposed to the elements. This outer side bore signs of mortar used for sealing gaps in the roof against the elements. It is not known how much of the church roof was tiled as opposed to any other roof covering such as lead, but it may be stated that such tile was ubiquitous on the site. Depending upon where in the pitch of a roof any tile came from, any amount of surface area of a tile might be left exposed so it is not possible to calculate the exact area of roof covered by the recovered materials.

If a single complete example found in the north range superstructure collapse is typical (280mm x 70mm) then the 5244 fragments, if representing the same number of complete tiles, would create a roof of no more than 250m², (with no overlapping tiles, which is not possible). A 50% overlap average would halve that to 125m². Each aisle alone, if covered with a near-flat roof, would require at least 270m² of tiled area. The presence of ridge tiles indicates that pitched roofs were present either on the nave or the aisles, requiring even more tiles. If all the recovered tile fragments represented whole examples, they would roof over less than half of one aisle. Clearly a vast number were removed from the site at the Dissolution leaving behind only broken debris.

The Conventual Buildings

From the conventual buildings a small quantity of complete or near complete roof tiles were recovered along with many thousands of broken fragments (only a representative sample of which were retained). It is evident that a number of different sizes were used and varying methods were employed to attach the tiles to the roof battens. This

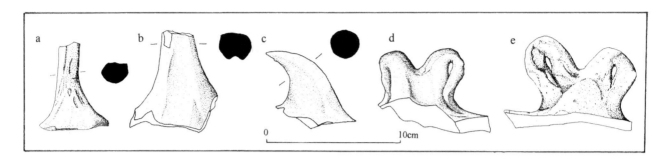

Fig 60   *Roof tiles – ridge crests*

diversity is mirrored in both the range of fabric types and applications of glaze. Fragments, some large, of curved ridge tiles were also found and exhibited a similarly diverse range of characteristics. A small quantity of crests were also found, broken from the main body of the tiles (Fig 60). The main variants of each tile type are as follows:

Flat Tiles (not illustrated)
1. CBP99/00, Context 2102; CRU, Context 003 (rubble, refectory undercroft); JFK00 Context 1152 (rubble, courtyard). Rectangular (280mm x 170mm x 16mm), coarse orange fabric with few inclusions. Has nib placed centrally on short side. No glaze.
2. CBP99/00, Context 1672 (fill, garderobe cistern). Rectangular (? x 170mm x 13mm), coarse orange fabric. Has nib on short side and rectangular nail holes (7mm x 5mm) in each corner. Unglazed.
3. PP01, Context 24032 (fill, latrine). Fragment (8mm thick), mid-grey fabric with occasional quartz and black grits. Evenly applied green glaze.
4. CBP99/00, Context 1602 (rubble, west range). Fragment (24mm thick), coarse orange fabric with frequent quartz grits. Has peg hole (10mm diameter).
5. CBP99/00, Context 701a (post-Dissolution layer, cloister garth) and JFK00, Context 1179 (post-Dissolution layer, north-south undercroft?). Fragment (9mm thick), orange/cream fabric with pale green glaze.
6. JFK00, Context 1252 (rubble, passage – north-east cloister). Fragment (17mm thick), orange fabric with grey core perforated by peg hole (17mm diameter). Has mortar on under-side.
7. JFK00, Context 1061 (rubble, east-west under-croft). Fragment (21mm thick), coarse orange fabric with nib and square nail hole (10mm²) to right.
8. JFK00, Context 1061 (rubble, east-west under-croft). Fragment (15mm thick), coarse orange fabric with circular peg hole in corner (12mm diameter).

Ridge Tiles (not illustrated)
1. CBP99/00, Context 601 (cloister garth); Context 1061 (rubble, east-west undercroft). Curved tile (20mm thick), coarse orange fabric with inclusions of small pebbles. Unglazed. Mortar on underside. Fragments of brown glazed ridge tile of the same fabric and thickness were retrieved from context CBP99/00 1002 (rubble, north-south undercroft).
2. JFK00, Context 1059 (rubble, passage – north-east cloister). Fragment of curved tile (12mm thick), coarse grey/orange fabric. Has thick dark green glaze.

Ridge Crests (Fig 60a-e)
a   JFK00, Context 1294 (layer, courtyard). Lightly glazed 'pinnacle' (7mm tall). Fine orange fabric.
b   CBP99/00, Context 1003 (rubble, spiral staircase); PP01, Context 24024 (post-Dissolution layer, reredorter). Mottled-green glazed 'pinnacle' (65mm+ tall). Coarse orange fabric.
c   JFK00, Context 1188 (layer, courtyard). Dark-brown glazed 'horn' (*c*50mm tall). Coarse orange fabric.
d   JFK00, Context 1192 (layer, courtyard). Looped crest with dark-green mottled glaze. Fine cream/grey fabric.
e   JFK00, Context 1192 (layer, courtyard). Looped crest with light-green glaze. Fine cream/grey fabric.

Anomalous Fragments
1. PP01 U/S (vicinity of mill). A large fragment of a flat tile (? x *c*170mm x 15mm) of orange fabric with a dogs paw print just below the (broken) nib (Fig 61a).
2. Upper half of tile (? x 160mm x 19mm) of orange/brown fabric with central nib. Has an 'L' shaped cut away from left hand corner (as laid) (not illustrated)

In addition to those found *ex-situ*, a number of roof tiles had been used in the monastic period to line the back of the fireplace in the north-south undercroft

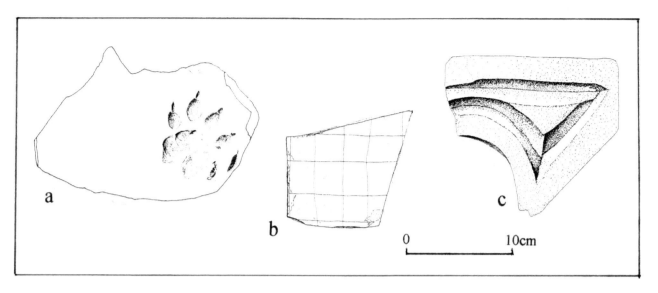

Fig 61   *Anomalous building materials (a) roof tile with dogs paw print (b) slate with incised lines*
(c) glazed brick (from tracery structure?)

(Fig 27). Here ten courses are present, sandwiched between courses of roughly hewn mortared sandstone (above) and brick (below). Most are laid with their short side showing; widths ranging from 160mm-185mm and thickness varying from 13-16mm. The only example laid on its longitudinal axis measures 257mm. All are fire blackened.

The Roof Slate
Margaret Rylatt, Paul Mason & Iain Soden

A total of 361 fragments of Swithland roof slate from Leicestershire were recovered from the nave. Of these the context which produced most was the widespread layer 003, the general Dissolution rubble which stretched over the entire site and which was exposed for at least 200 years. As such it is not possible to decide where any of the slate might have originated. Observation of piers 1 (both arcades) at the west end showed that slate still lay *in situ*, used as spacers between courses of ashlar facing blocks. This practice alone throughout the Early English part of the arcades would account for hundreds of pieces throughout the three dimensions of the structure. Thus the presence of slate is no guide to the possibility that any of the roofs were slate covered.

Slate was also used for spacing in the wall fabric of many of the conventual buildings but on this part of the site perforated *ex situ* fragments were also found, indicating that some of the buildings had incorporated slate into their roofs. The thickness of these slates varied considerably as did the diameter of the nail/peg holes (7mm-19mm). Fragments confidently identified with roofing were recovered in

the vicinity of the north east crossing pier, east cloister alley, refectory undercroft, east-west undercroft and courtyard.

Two anomalous fragments were found. The first is a piece of slate bearing a lightly incised checkerboard pattern – probably a fragment of a crude gaming board (CBP99/00 SF12, Context 1537) (Fig 61b). The other, a perforated fragment of shale, was found close to the site of the reredorter (PP01, Context 24024). It was presumably once part of a roof. This type of shale is not found in the local geology so must have been imported from some distance – the Cotswolds being a possible source.

The Brick
Margaret Rylatt, Paul Mason & Iain Soden

A total of 165 fragments of late medieval hand-made bricks were recovered during the excavation of the nave. The majority derives from deposits dating to the immediate post-Dissolution period which may have come from the fabric of the cathedral itself. The largest number (seventy-one) was recovered from the matrix of the earthen ramp laid down inside the west entrance of the nave, probably in the 1540s (Context 199). None of the bricks are complete, only two full sides at the most surviving. The size range is 112mm-134mm breadth x 42mm-70mm thickness.

A small amount of *ex-situ* brick was also recovered from demolition contexts in the area of the conventual buildings. Once again, no complete examples were found. The size range of those that clearly fall within the late medieval period is 116mm-120mm width x 53mm-64mm thickness.

The only bricks found *in-situ* in a monastic context were those used to line the back of the fire-place in the north-south undercroft (Fig 27). Here there are seven roughly coursed layers bonded with mortar. Their sizes vary as follows: length 256mm-264mm, width 133mm, thickness 60mm-70mm.

In addition to the plain bricks, four large fragments of shaped brick were found (Fig 61c). They were decorated with deeply incised lines and rendered with a thick application of brown glaze. All were found close to water features (the basin in the north-south undercroft and the fill of the garderobe cistern) and may have formed a tracery cladding or framing associated with these features. The have been provisionally assigned a sixteenth-century date (John Cherry, *pers comm*)

The Window Glass (Fig 62a&b)
Margaret Rylatt, Paul Mason & Iain Soden

While there was a widespread occurrence of window glass throughout the excavated areas of the church, much lay within the demolition rubble (SMC99, Context 003) which was long-lived, being picked over for some 200-plus years. Thus the origin of the majority of this glass cannot be traced with any confidence. However, the deposition at the Dissolution of a clay- and stone-ramp over the former western steps, sealed a large, dense scatter of high quality, painted window glass in stunning colours. Along with that from the chapter house (see below), this is arguably the most important assemblage of such material ever to have been excavated in Coventry. This appears to have been the remains of the former nave west window, which was pushed in very soon after the Dissolution. A number of fragments from this assemblage were found to fit together, forming the image of a young woman with flowing locks (see Fig 62a).

Another large assemblage of broken window glass was recovered from the chapter house where it lay scattered over the robbed floor and surviving grave slab at the east end of the building. No attempt has been made to reconstruct the windows using the fragments but individual pieces are clearly decorated with finely detailed floral, foliate and zoomorphic designs (see Fig 62b). A similar assemblage was recovered from the chapter house during the 1960s excavations and had been assigned a date of *c*1310-1330 (Newton in Hobley 1971, 107-11).

The Pottery – conventual Buildings
(Figs 63-69)
Paul Blinkhorn

Introduction

The pottery assemblage comprised 756 sherds with a total weight of 13,677 g. The estimated vessel equivalent (EVE), by summation of surviving rimsherd circumference was 7.94. All the material was medieval or later, with the exception of a single sherd of Romano-British ware and another of early or middle Anglo-Saxon date. The majority of the assemblage dates to the later part of the monastic occupation of the priory (fifteenth to mid-sixteenth century), with the earlier medieval wares generally re-deposited. The later medieval material is of some interest; the majority of the vessels are types which are associated with the serving and consumption of drink, with pottery associated with the cooking, serving and consumption of food entirely absent.

Analytical Methodology

The pottery was initially bulk-sorted and recorded on a computer using DBase IV software. The material from each context was recorded by number and weight of sherds per fabric type, with featureless body sherds of the same fabric counted, weighed and recorded as one database entry. Feature sherds such as rims, bases and lugs were individually recorded, with individual codes used for the various types. Decorated sherds were similarly treated. In the case of the rimsherds, the form, diameter in mm and the percentage remaining of the original complete circumference were all recorded. This figure was summed for each fabric type to obtain the estimated vessel equivalent (EVE).

The terminology used is that defined by the Medieval Pottery Research Group's Guide to the Classification of Medieval Ceramic Forms (MPRG 1998) and to the minimum standards laid out in the Minimum Standards for the Processing, Recording, Analysis and Publication of post-Roman Ceramics (MPRG2001). All the statistical analyses were carried out using a Dbase package written by the author, which interrogated the original or subsidiary databases, with some of the final calculations made with an electronic calculator. Any statistical analyses were carried out to the minimum standards suggested by Orton (1998-9, 135-7).

Fig 62 *Stained and painted window glass (a) nave (b) chapter house*

Fabric

The pottery was recorded using the codes and chronology of the Warwickshire Medieval and Post-Medieval Pottery Type-Series (Ratkai and Soden, Warwickshire Museum in archive), as follows (the numeric codes prefixed by 'F' refer to those used in the databases, tables and appendices):

F205:   WW20 Stamford Ware, 850-1200. 1 sherd, 2g, EVE = 0.

F298:   CS02 Northants Shelly Ware, 1150-1200. 1 sherd, 11g, EVE = 0.06.

F299:   Sq202 Coventry Sandy Ware, 12th-14th century. 9 sherds, 135g, EVE = 0.12.

F300:   Sq203 Coventry Sandy Ware, 12th-14th century. 64 sherds, 2129g, EVE = 0.85.

F301:   Sq232 Cannon Park Ware, 13th century. 5 sherds, 70g, EVE = 0.

F302:   Sq231 Cannon Park Ware (fine), 13th century. 11 sherds, 289g, EVE = 0.10.

F303:   Sq30 Chilvers Coton 'C' Ware, 1300-1500. 222 sherds, 3810g, EVE = 1.68.

F320:   WW01 Chilvers Coton 'A' Ware, 1250-1300. 73 sherds, 698g, EVE = 0.14.

F324:   Sq40 Brill/Boarstall Ware. 13th-16th century. 1 sherd, 1g, EVE = 0.08.

F401:   SLM10 Late Chilvers Coton Ware, 15th century. 70 sherds, 1171g, EVE = 0.26.

F403:   WW02 'Tudor Green' Ware, 1380-1550. 4 sherds, 32g, EVE = 0.61.

F404:   CIST Cistercian Ware, 1475-1550. 199 sherds, 1639g, EVE = 1.64.

F405:   STG04 Raeren Stoneware, 1470-1550. 34 sherds, 786g, EVE = 1.21.

F406:   MP Midland Purple Ware, 15th- mid-17th century. 37 sherds, 1865g, EVE = 0.88.

F407:   (No CTS code) Red Earthenwares, 16th-19th century? 2 sherds, 241g, EVE = 0.

F408:   MY Midland Yellow Ware, 1550-1720. 1 sherd, 2g, EVE = 0.06.

F409:   IMP103 Martincamp Ware, 15th-17th century. 1 sherd, 6g, EVE = 0.05.

F410:   TGE01 Tin-Glazed Earthenware, 16th-18th century. 1 sherd, 3g, EVE = 0.

F425:   SLPW02 Staffordshire Trailed Slipware, 1640-1700. 3 sherds, 48g.

F426:   SLWP04 Staffordshire 'dark on light' Slipware, 1670-1740. 1 sherd, 30g.

F427:   MB02 Late Midland Blackware, 1600-1900. 7 sherds, 692g.

F428:   MANG Staffordshire Manganese Mottled Ware, 1680-1740. 1 sherd, 6g.

F430:   STE03 Staffordshire White Salt-Glazed Stoneware, 1720-1780. 1 sherd, 11g.

F432:   PLW01 Plain Pearlware, 1775-1840. 1 sherd, 4g.

F449:   MO Mocha Ware, 1830-50. 1 sherd, 7g.

F450:   MGW Modern earthenwares, late 18th century (or later). 3 sherds, 5g.

The following were also noted:

F1:   Early/middle Saxon hand-made ware, c450-850. Fine sandy fabric, few visible inclusions, sparse fine organic voids up to 4mm. 1 sherd, 2g, EVE = 0.

F1001:   Romano-British wares. 1 sherd, 12g, EVE = 0.

The range of medieval fabrics from these excavations shows some differences to those noted in other areas of the site. The excavations in the refectory undercroft produced a medieval pottery assemblage which included large quantities of 'Wiltshire Flint-tempered Ware' and London Ware, along with a few sherds of an earlier medieval import, Paffrath Ware (see below). Their absence amongst the assemblages from this part of the site seems likely to be due to chronology; the three wares are all types which had largely fallen from use by the end of the fourteenth century, if not earlier; the majority of the pottery from these excavations dates to the fifteenth century and beyond (see Table 2, below). The range of ware types here is very similar to that excavated from the nave area (see below). That assemblage is similar to

Table 1: Ceramic phase chronology

CP	Defining Wares	Date
CP1	Sq202, Sq203	1100-1200
CP2	Sq231, Sq232	1200-1250
CP3	WW01	1250-1300
CP4	Sq30	1300-1400
CP5	MP, SLM10, WW02	1400-1470
CP6	CIST, STG04	1470-1550
CP7	Redwares	1550-1650
CP8	MB02, SLPW02-4,	1650-1720
CP9	STE03	1720-1790
CP10	MGW, MO	1790+

Table 2: Pottery occurrence per ceramic phase by number and weight (in g) of sherds and EVE

CP	No	Wt	EVE
CP1*	31	653	0.45
CP2	12	1141	0.47
CP3	7	48	0
CP4	82	2075	1.03
CP5	9	217	0.06
CP6	441	6179	4.45
CP7	0	0	0
CP8	161	3110	1.48
CP9	4	186	0
CP10	8	46	0.07
Total	755	13655	7.94

*excluding the Roman sherd

this in that the majority of the pottery dates to the late and post-medieval periods.

Chronology

Each context-specific pottery assemblage was given a ceramic phase ('CP') date, based on the range of major fabrics present, as shown in Table 1.

These dates were then adjusted with reference to the stratigraphic matrix. The pottery occurrence per ceramic phase is shown in Table 2.

The data in Table 2 shows that the majority of the pottery from these excavations dates to the latest period of monastic activity at this site. The CP8 material appears to be largely part of a CP6 midden deposit which was disturbed during stone robbing (see below). The groups are examined in greater detail in the sections discussing in detail the pottery

Table 3: Pottery occurrence per ceramic phase by fabric type, major fabrics only, expressed as a percentage of the phase total, all fabrics

CP	F300	F302	F320	F303	F401	F406	F404	F405	Phase Total
CP1	97.7%	-	-	-	-	-	-	-	653g*
CP2	96.9%	0.4%	-	-	-	-	-	-	1141g
CP3	0	0	95.8%	-	-	-	-	-	48g
CP4	2.5%	8.0%	10.9%	78.0%	-	-	-	-	2075g
CP5			23.5%	11.5%	27.6%	35.5%	-	-	217g
CP6	5.2%	1.4%	5.9%	32.4%	16.4%	18.5%	10.6%	6.4%	6179g
CP7	0	0	0	0	0	0	0	0	0g
CP8	0	1.0%	0.4%	5.1%	3.2%	19.6%	31.5%	12.6%	3110g
CP9	0	0	0	0	0	0	0	0	186g
CP10	0	0	0	15.2%	0	10.9%	0	0	46g
Total	2129g	289g	698g	3810g	1171g	1865g	1639g	786g	13655g

*excluding the Roman sherd
shaded areas = residuality

Table 4: Mean sherd weight per ceramic phase by fabric type, major fabrics only

CP	F300	F302	F320	F303	F401	F406	F404	F405	Phase Total
CP1	22.4g	-	-	-	-	-	-	-	653g*
CP2	138.3g	4.0g	-	-	-	-	-	-	1141g
CP3	0	0	7.7g	-	-	-	-	-	48g
CP4	17.3g	33.2g	10.3g	32.4g	-	-	-	-	2075g
CP5	0	0	12.8g	25.0g	30.0g	77.0g	-	-	217g
CP6	13.4g	29.3g	9.1g	13.0g	16.1g	47.6g	6.8g	20.7g	6179g
CP7	0	0	0	0	0	0	0	0	0g
CP8	0	15.5g	11.1g	10.0g	19.6g	55.5g	9.7g	26.2g	3110g
CP9	0	0	0	0	0	0	0	0	186g
CP10	0	0	0	7.0g	0	5.0g	0	0	46g

*excluding the Roman sherd
shaded areas = residuality

Table 5: Vessel occurrence per ceramic phase, by vessel types, expressed as a percentage of the phase total, all fabrics

CP	Jars	Jugs	Cups/Mugs	Bottle	Costrel	Flask	Lid	Total EVE
CP1	80.9%	19.41%	0	0	0	0	0	0.45
CP2	100%	0	0	0	0	0	0	0.47
CP3	0	0	0	0	0	0	0	0
CP4	0	46.6%	0	0	0	0	53.4%	1.03
CP5	100%	0	0	0	0	0	0	0.06
CP6	17.5%	28.3%	34.8%	1.8%	11.9%	5.6%	0	4.45

from each different excavated structural element of the priory (see below).

The general pattern for the site shows a small degree of residuality, but the amounts in question are not exceptional.

Fragmentation Analysis

The data in Table 4 shows that, by and large, most of the earlier (pre-fifteenth century) material from this site is the result of secondary deposition, or is residual. In most cases, the earlier medieval wares (F300, F302, F320) have a mean sherd weight broadly equal to or greater than that for the deposits in which they are supposedly residual.

The pottery from the CP8 groups, which is mainly disturbed later fifteenth-century material, generally has a mean sherd weight which is comparable with that of the stratified groups, and in most cases is slightly larger. This shows that the strata were not subject to a great deal of attrition; it seems likely that later pottery was introduced to the earlier strata during digging for stone rather than the earlier sherds being dug out and re-deposited.

Vessel Occurrence

The data in Table 5 is largely what one would expect for the earlier medieval phases, the small assemblage sizes notwithstanding. The range of vessels during CP6 is somewhat more significant, and comprises mainly vessels associated with the serving and consumption of liquids, comprising almost entirely jugs, costrels, bottles and flasks in the former category, and mugs and cups in the latter.

It is also striking that pottery types associated with the preparation and consumption of food are all but absent, indicating that the waste from the monastic kitchens was not being disposed of in the areas of the priory which were examined during the course of this project. Vessels such as bowls and skillets are entirely absent from the assemblage. Whilst the latter are not common finds at sites of the period, they have been found in quantity at some religious houses, such as Eynsham Abbey in Oxfordshire

(Blinkhorn in print), but the lack of bowls is more of a surprise; certainly, in this analyst's experience, this is one of the few medieval pottery assemblages of any size which completely lacks such vessels, which were almost universal in the medieval period in England. They were certainly noted in quantity at the Broadgate East excavations (Rylatt and Stokes 1996, Fig 23), so their absence cannot be blamed on the medieval pottery supply to the city. A probable explanation may be the use of other materials such as wood for tableware and iron for cooking vessels. The distribution of the ceramic vessel types will be examined in greater detail in the section of each individual area.

Cross-fits

The following cross-fits were noted:

1188=1189, F404 cup/tyg.
1188=1189, F404 cup/tyg.
1188=1189, F404 cup/tyg.
1188=1192, F404 cup/tyg.
1188=1192, F404 cup/tyg.
1188=1192, F404 mug.
1188=1189=1192, F404 mug.
1189=1190, F405, mug.
1672=1673, F406, ?jug

The Assemblages

Courtyard Area (Site JFK00)

Yard Midden (Fig 63a-e)
The yard area produced a total of 478 sherds with a total weight of 7340g. The EVE was 4.51. The pottery occurrence per ceramic phase is shown in Table 6.

Table 6: Pottery occurrence per ceramic phase, yard area

CP	No	Wt	EVE
CP5	8	140	0.06
CP6	326	4854	3.23
CP8	152	2486	1.48
Total	487	8367	4.77

The majority of the assemblage dates to CP6 and CP8, with the latter phase comprising almost entirely phase CP6 assemblages which were disturbed by later activity. This suggests that the courtyard area was kept clean for most of the life of the priory, until the later fifteenth or earlier sixteenth centuries, and that the pottery which was excavated there was a midden which remained uncleared at the Dissolution. It is these deposits, particularly contexts 1188, 1189, 1190 and 1192 which were the source of most of the pottery associated with drink which was noted above (also see Table 7).

It seems likely that the source of the pottery from this midden was either the dormitory or the infirmary, or perhaps even both. This would perhaps also explain why no pottery types which are directly attributable to the preparation or consumption of

Table 7: Vessel occurrence by type, yard midden deposits, expressed as a percentage of the total per phase by vessel type

CP	Jars	Jugs	Cups/Mug	Flask	Total EVE
CP6	24.4%	37.3%	30.0%	8.3%	3.03
CP8	4.7%	10.1%	85.1%	0	1.48
Total	0.81	1.28	2.17	0.25	4.51

food are present. It would not be expected that monks would eat in their dormitory, although those in the infirmary may have done so. If they were, they were not using pottery to any great degree.

a Context 1192, F404. Bodysherd. Purple fabric with dark brown glaze, moulded prunt with ?zoomorphic decoration outer surface.

b Contexts 1189 and 1190, F405. Rim and upper

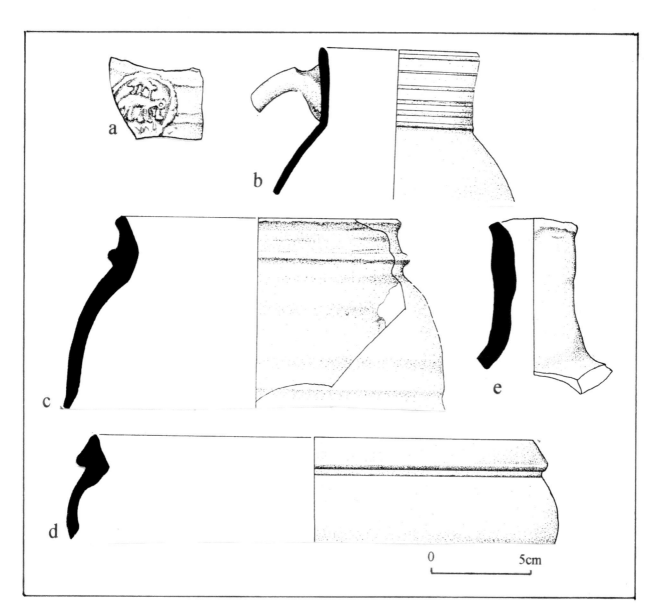

Fig 63 Pottery from yard midden

Table 8: Pottery occurrence per ceramic phase by fabric by weight, major wares only

CP	F300	F302	F320	F303	F401	F403	F404	F405	Phase Total
CP1	66.7%	-	-	-	-	-	-	-	33
CP2	0	100%	-	-	-	-	-	-	4
CP3	0	0	100%	-	-	-	-	-	1
CP4	0	0	0	100%	-	-	-	-	25
CP5	0	0	0	33.3%	61.3%	0	5.3%	-	75
CP6	47.0%	5.0%	2.7%	16.7%	11.5%	4.9%	4.9%	1.9%	515

body of mug. Grey fabric with streaky pale-grey and light-brown outer surface, light brown inner surface.

c Context 1192, F406. Brick-red fabric with purple surfaces.

d Context 1192, F406. Jar rim. Uniform purple fabric with thin purple glaze on the inner surface.

e Context 1192, F303. Long tubular spout. Grey fabric with brown surfaces, dark greenish-brown glazes with copper spotting on outer surface.

Pit Group 1256 (Fig 64a-d)
This feature produced thirty-two sherds with a total weight of 1423g (EVE = 1.08), although the bulk of the assemblage comprised the complete lower part

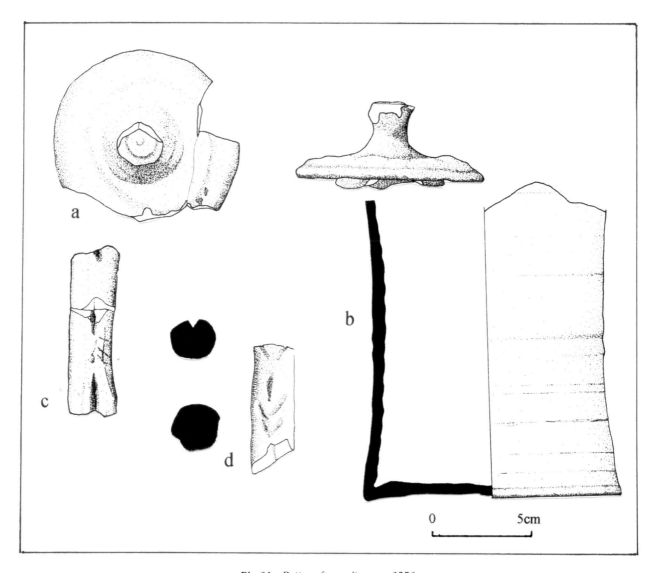

0   5cm

Fig 64   Pottery from pit group 1256

of a Chilvers Coton 'C' Ware jug (886g, Fig 64d). It was discovered in one of the drains which ran into the pit. It is assumed that this found its way into the drain during the backfilling of the pit.

The pit contained a number of deposits (in stratigraphic order), 1257, 1260, 1261 and 1262, which range from CP4 to CP6 in date, with the chronology respecting the stratigraphic order, suggesting that they built up over a period of time. The stratigraphically earliest deposit, 1262, produced only three small sherds of medieval pottery. The other groups all produced small groups of fairly well preserved material although it seems largely the result of secondary deposition, as all the sherds were from different vessels, and no re-fitting was possible. Similarly, there were no cross-fits, suggesting that each deposit was the result of a separate action. Some of the material is shown in Fig 64 below. The medieval material shows little change through the sequence, and comprises largely sherds of F303 with copper-spotted glaze, and fragments of incised and applied decoration in various styles.

a   Context 1261, F303. Lid. Grey fabric with orange-brown surfaces. Upper surface and edges of lower covered in a dull-green glaze streaked with brown.
b   Context 1259, F303. Lower part of jug. Grey fabric with orange-brown surfaces. Glossy green glaze with darker copper-spotting.
c   Context 1261, F303. Jug Handle. Grey fabric with orange brown surfaces. Glossy green glaze with darker copper spotting.
d   Context 1260, F303. Jug handle. Grey fabric with orange-brown surfaces. Glossy green glaze with darker copper spotting.

North-South Undercroft (Fig 65a&b)
This produced a series of contexts which in the main yielded only a handful of sherds. Most were of CP5 or CP6 date, as shown in Table 8.

The data in Table 8 shows that the majority of the pottery from the north-south undercroft dates to the later medieval period, but also that these later deposits contain a considerable amount of residual material, with well over 50% of the CP6 groups comprising medieval wares which had fallen from use by that time. Only four rimsherds were present, two of which were residual medieval jar rims, but the two contemporary rimsherds are from a 'Tudor Green' costrel (Fig 65a) and a Brill/Boarstall bottle. The other contemporary sherds, Cistercian Ware and German Stoneware, are bodysherds from cups and mugs, and a handle from a late Chilvers Coton 'C' Ware jug was also noted (Fig 65b). Thus, as with the pottery from the adjoining courtyard area, the bulk of the later fifteenth-century pottery types are associated with the consumption of drink.

a   Context 1179, F403. Rim, neck and suspension lug from a costrel. White fabric with a pool of bright copper-green glaze around the neck and lug.
b   Context 1179, F401. Jug handle. Brick-red fabric with grey core, splashes of speckled orange-brown glaze on outer surface.

East-West Undercroft (Fig 66a-c)
The pottery assemblage from the east-west undercroft comprised thirty-seven sherds with a total weight of 612g (EVE = 0.25). It is quite different to the material from the adjoining courtyard and north-south undercroft, comprising entirely 'high' medieval (CP2-CP4) material, as shown in Table 9. All but three very small sherds date to CP4. The assemblage comprises mainly single sherds from different vessels, and most are quite small. All are glazed, however, and are likely to be jug sherds. This is perhaps significant, and suggests that although earlier than the material from the courtyard and north-south undercroft, the entire assemblage is, like those groups, from vessels associated with the serving and consumption of drink.

A few feature sherds were noted including the

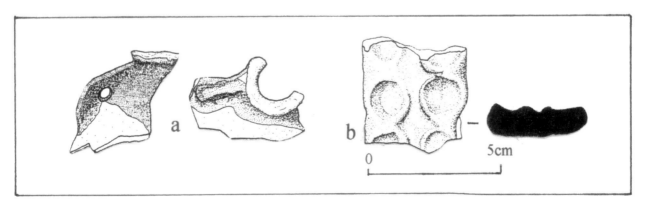

Fig 65   Pottery from north-south undercroft

base of a F302 jug (Fig 66a), the handle of a jug in F303 (Fig 66b), and a large fragment of an anthropomorphic (?) jug in F303 (Fig 66c). The last named is by far the most ornate medieval vessel from the site, and cannot easily be paralleled with the material from the Chilvers Coton kilns, although a vessel with a face-mask and applied tendrils was noted amongst the material from kiln 10c at site 2 (Mayes & Scott 1984, Fig 23:61). It is without parallel amongst the Broadgate East material, although three sherds from an anthropomorphic vessel were noted amongst the material from the refectory undercroft (see below). A complete probable Nuneaton Ware anthropomorphic jug is held by the Herbert Art

Table 9: Pottery occurrence by weight of sherds per fabric type, east-west undercroft

CP	F300	F302	F320	F303	Phase Total
CP2	100%	0	0	0	2
CP3	0	0	100%	0	4
CP4	0	27.4%	37.3%	34.3%	606

Gallery and Museum in Coventry (McCarthy & Brooks 1988, Fig 227) but it is by no means similar to this example.

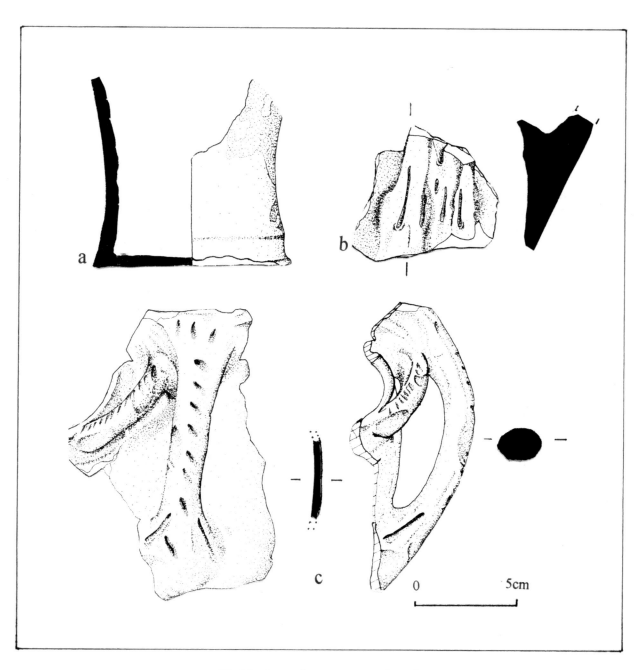

Fig 66 *Pottery from east-west undercroft*

a Context 1129, F302. Jug base. Pale brick-red fabric. Splashes of copper-spotted yellowish-green glaze on the outer surface.

b Context 1129, F303. Jug handle. Light-grey fabric with darker core. Glossy, copper-spotted green glaze on both surfaces.

c Context 1169, F303. Rim, neck and handle from anthropomorphic jug. Grey fabric with pale-orange inner surface. Thick coating of glossy green, copper-streaked glaze on both surfaces. Inner surface is thickly lime-scaled.

Passage – North-East Cloister (Fig 67)

The assemblage comprised twenty-six sherds weighing 206g (EVE = 0.08). All the material was earlier medieval in date. The assemblage from 1303, a layer predating the insertion of the drain, appears to be of twelfth-century date. It only comprises two sherds, one being from the base of a Coventry Sandy Ware unglazed jar, but the other is the only sherd of Stamford Ware from the site. As such pottery had largely fallen from use by 1150, this dating seems secure, and the layer is likely to predate the medieval foundation of the priory. The rest of the material dates to CP4, and is from a drain and its backfill. The sherds are once again all from glazed jugs, with the exception of a sherd of Coventry Sandy Ware, probably from a jar. A bodysherd of Coventry Sandy Ware with applied white slip scales was noted (Fig 67).

Fig 67   Context 1274, F300. Orange fabric, copper-spotted orange-brown glaze on outer surface. Scales and stripes in a white-firing slip which appears yellow under the glaze.

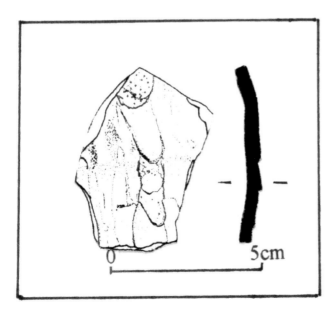

Fig 67 *Pottery from passage – north-east cloister*

Garderobe Cistern (not illustrated)

The assemblage from the back-fill of this feature comprised thirty-five sherds with a total weight of 565g (EVE = 0.37). The two contexts, 1672 and 1673 are both dated to CP6, and a cross-fit was noted. Six sherds of medieval pottery (149g) were present, all from glazed jugs, with the rest of the group comprising Cistercian Ware, Midland Purple and late Chilvers Coton 'C' Ware. All the sherds were from cups or jugs, with the exception of a fragment of a lid in F401.

Foundations of North Nave Wall (not illustrated)

The pottery from the nave wall foundations comprised a single (intrusive) small glazed sherd (4g) in F303.

Inner Precinct (Fig 68a-c)

These layers produced twenty-six sherds with a total weight of 634g (EVE = 0.26). All the pottery was of earlier medieval date, with most dated to CP1. One context, 24082, produced a single sherd of F303 (33g), the other two (24079, 24081) produced only F300, apart from a single sherd (12g) of Romano-British pottery from context 24081. All the rims were from jars (Fig 68a-c), in contrast with the assemblages from the later deposits at the site. All the F300 bodysherds were unglazed, with the exception of three which had a poor quality, dark-green glaze, and are likely to be from the same tripod pitcher, although they did not join.

a Context 24079, F300. Jar rim. Dark grey fabric with reddish-brown surfaces. Some sooting on edge of rim bead.

b Context 24079, F300. Jar rim. Light-grey fabric with darker core, brown surfaces. Even sooting on the rim.

c Context 24079, F300. Jar rim. Uniform dark-grey fabric.

Priory Mill (not illustrated)

The assemblage comprised three sherds with a total weight of 81g. A single sherd of F406 (77g) came from 25135 and dates the fill to CP5, while 25143 produced two small sherds, one of F320 weighing 2g, and the other a early/middle-Saxon sherd. The latter weighed 2g, and was somewhat worn from water-action.

Drains (Fig 69)

The fill of the drain to the west of the kitchen (1801) yielded a large fragment of a Coventry Sandy Ware jar (Fig 69), along with two small fragments of other vessels, one in the same fabric, and the other from the base of a Cannon Park Ware pot. The assemblage

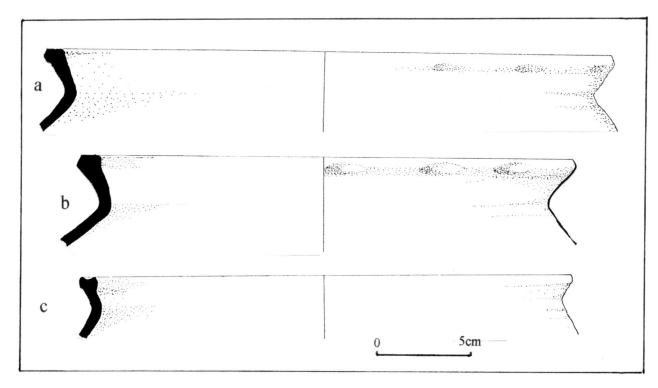

Fig 68   Pottery from inner precinct

is likely to date to CP2. The main drain (Contexts 24048/2811) produced a range of medieval and CP6 wares, along with a single fragment of mid-nineteenth-century Mocha Ware. There were no feature sherds except the base of a Cistercian Ware cup, two fragments of F303 handles and a small jug rim in the same fabric

Fig 69   F300, F1802. Full profile of jar. Uniform dark grey fabric.

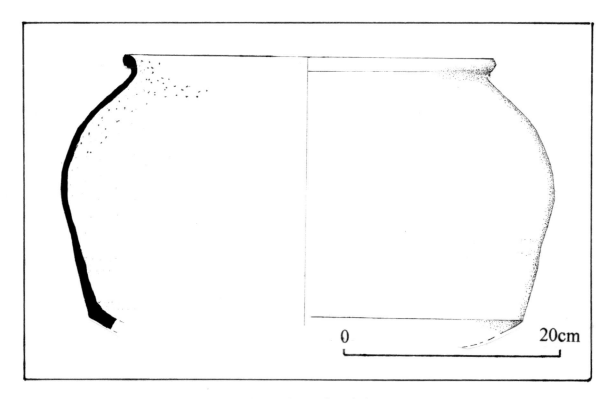

Fig 69   Pottery from drain

The Pottery – North and West Range Undercrofts
Vanessa Clarke and Iain Soden

Quantification

A total of 2014 sherds of pottery, weighing 36.16kg, were recovered from the undercrofts. The method of examination adopted was to record the pottery from each context in terms of its fabric, sherd count and weight.

The pottery spans the date range thirteenth century to nineteenth century. Twenty-one medieval and twelve post-medieval fabrics were represented (not illustrated). The occurrence by number and weight of sherds per context per fabric is shown in Table 1. The fabrics or types have in all cases been related to either the Coventry or Warwickshire Type Series (Rylatt & Stokes 1996; Ratkai & Soden, Warwickshire Museum in archive) in which each type has been assigned a code in addition to its common name (CTS or WTS).

Coventry Sandy Ware: Fabric A1 (CTS).
In all, a total of eleven sherds were recovered, of which ten were residual. The only form to be identified is the cooking pot. One example has a flat-topped, square-rim profile with everted neck (Rylatt & Stokes 1996, Fig 13:24 for similar).

Fabric A3 (CTS):
Two sherds were recovered of which one was a body sherd from a soot-blackened cooking pot, the other, a thumbed handle from a pitcher/jug.

Fabric A4 (CTS):
Only one sherd of this fabric was found, belonging to the base of a soot-blackened cooking pot with sagging base. This dates to the late twelfth/early thirteenth century.

Fabric B (CTS):
Two sherds of this fabric were recovered; both derived from soot-blackened cooking pots.

Coventry Glazed Ware: Fabric D (CTS).
One residual sherd of this ware was found. It had a distinctive splashed olive-green glaze, characterised by thin body coverage and reddish patches where particularly thin. It is decorated with horizontal wavy lines and dates from about *c*1150-1240. The form represented has not been identified but elsewhere these are principally tripod pitchers (Rylatt & Stokes 1996, 41).

Sandy wares with mainly quartz temper: Sq. 22 & 23 (WTS).
A total of forty-six sherds were recovered. These were not easily attributed to any group within the Coventry Type Series, a match being made somewhere between a variation of a Coventry Sandy Ware and an Sq.22 type (refer to the Warwickshire County Type Series). Most are hard-fired with a rough surface. They are glazed with a thin, patchy, light-green or tan glaze. The surfaces are a dull orange or light grey, often exhibiting a reddish bloom, with dull-orange margins and light-grey core. There are a number of flat-base sherds, probably belonging to jugs/pitchers dating to the twelfth or thirteenth century. Of these three represent one vessel.

Cannon Park Type Ware: Fabric E (CTS).
A total of 104 sherds were recovered from site which cannot easily be attributed to any group within the Coventry Type Series, the closest match being made to Cannon Park Ware. They have a moderately hard, brick-orange fabric with a slightly rough surface, moderate-abundant inclusions of fine-medium clear, milky-white-grey sub-angular quartz and an occasional reddish exterior bloom. The glaze is a thin, patchy tan-green colour, probably from a flat-based baluster jug dating to the late thirteenth/early fourteenth century.

Local Redware.
A total of 106 sherds were recovered which did not readily fit with any of the fabric descriptions within the Coventry Type Series. They are of a brick-orange colour throughout, with abundant medium-coarse sub-angular milky-white-grey quartz grains and black pyrite inclusions. A small number have cores in a mid-grey colour and an exterior reddish bloom. The main form identified appears to be that of the baluster jug. A number of simple, everted rims were discovered, along with thumbed bases and a variety of strap and rod handles. The latter can be divided into examples with perforations, central grooves and thumbing at the handle junction. There is little variation between the Sq.22/23 Sandy Ware, Cannon Park 'Type' Ware and Local Redware, suggesting that they may all indeed derive from the same source. The differences exhibited may be due to a fluctuating range of firing temperatures.

Wiltshire Flint Tempered Type Ware: Fabric (WTS).
A total of forty-five sherds were recovered, which again could not be easily attributed to any fabric group within the Coventry Type Series, the closest

Table 1: Pottery occurrence by number and weight of sherds per context

Ware/Fabric:	Sherd Count/Weight in kg:	Contexts containing fabrics:
Coventry Sandy Ware Fabric A1	11/0.2kg.	17, 19, 20, 27/4, 45,
Fabric A4	1/0.03kg.	13
Fabric A3	1/0.03kg.	20
Fabric B	2/0.024kg.	27/7
Coventry Glazed Ware Fabric D	1/0.018kg.	19
Sandy Wares Sq. 23 (W.T.S)	45/1kg.	20, 27, 27/4, 27/6, 58, 66
Sandy Ware Sq.22 (W.T.S.)	1/0.03kg.	20
Cannon-Park Type Ware Fabric E	104/1.4kg.	26, 27, 27/4, 27/5, 27/6, 27/7, 69
Local Redware	110/1.23kg.	20, 26, 27, 27/4, 27/6, 27/7
Wiltshire Flint Tempered Ware	45/1.28kg.	26, 27/6, 57, 66
Nuneaton 'A' Ware Fabric H1	1081/10.86kg.	03, 05, 12, 13, 17, 19, 20, 24, 26, 27, 27/6, 27/7, 30, 41, 045, 49, 65, 66, 69, U/S
Nuneaton 'B' Ware Fabric H3	51/0.67kg.	26, 27/4, 27/6, 27/7, 45
Nuneaton 'C' Ware Fabric SLM 10	9/0.25kg.	26, 27/4
London Ware Fabric	340/13.4kg	U/S, 19, 26, 27/6, 27/7, 33, 66,
Warwick Product	37/0.25kg.	U/S, 05, 27, 27/4, 27/7
Local Buffware	3/0.04kg.	27/6
'Midland' Purple Fabrics N1-3	7/0.18kg.	13, 24, 44
'Midland' Purple Type Ware	2/0.045kg.	
Surrey Whiteware: 'Tudor Green' Type Fabrics J1-3	1/0.02kg.	26
Paffrath Blue-greyware	3/0.07kg.	26/, 27/6
Raeren Stoneware Fabrics I1-10	1/0.008kg.	35
Siegburg Stoneware Fabrics I1-10	8/0.28kg.	04
Cistercian Ware Fabrics K1-4	71/0.58kg.	02, 03, 12, 13, 19, 26, 30, 43, 44
'Midland' Blackware Fabrics 11-5	29/0.62kg.	02, 03, 12, 35
Glazed Red Earthenware Fabrics P1-4	7/0.34kg.	03, 04, 17, 24, 28
Slipware Fabrics O1-4	26/0.6kg.	02, 03, 04, 15, 39
Manganese Mottled Ware Fabric Z	4/0.04	02, 03
Mocha Ware Fabric Z	7 & 1 vessel/0.37kg.	02, 13, 39
Creamware Fabric Z	1/0.29kg.	02
c.19th Industrialised Ware Fabric Z	2/0.41kg.	02
Blue and White Transfer-Printed Ware Fabric Z	10/0.29kg.	02,39
Nottingham Stoneware Fabric Z	1/0.007kg.	02
English Stoneware Fabric Z	1/0.55kg.	39

match being to Wiltshire Flint Tempered Ware, previously found as far north as Warwickshire and Northamptonshire. The type was made in the Wiltshire and Berkshire area. They are of a moderately hard fabric, with orange margins and a mid-grey core. The interior surface varies from light brown to a brick orange with a pinkish-brown exterior. The inclusions range from moderate amounts of sub-rounded quartz to sparse flint. Decoration takes the form of thumbed vertical strips.

Nuneaton Ware: Fabrics H1-H4 (CTS); SLM 10 (WTS)
A total of 1141 sherds were recovered, representing 56.5% of the total assemblage. Three Mayes and Scott fabrics were present: fabrics A, B and C (equivalent to Coventry Types H1 and H3). Nuneaton 'A' was clearly the main fabric with 1081 sherds (approximately a third are dark grey in colour showing evidence of being fired in a reduced atmosphere), followed by Nuneaton 'B' with fifty-one sherds and Nuneaton 'C' fabric with nine sherds. These have been classified into their main vessel forms: jugs, cooking pots and bowls. Jugs in fabric 'A' were the most numerous, typified by a baluster-shaped body, cylindrical neck and simple in-turned rims, thumbed bases which sag – a characteristic of the thirteenth century, simple pouring lips and thumbing at handle junctions (Mayes & Scott 1984, Fig 96:54). They have a thin external light-olive glaze or less frequently, a thick, lustrous copper-green glaze. Four sherds exhibit an olive-green glaze both internally and externally. Decoration is mainly limited to horizontal rilling on the cylindrical necks of jugs. Less common are vertical scales, combed horizontal straight and zigzag lines, applied dark-green vertical strips, perforated holes and thumbed rims. There are also four examples of rim sherds which have crosses carved through their glaze and fabric and three sherds of an anthropomorphic face jug (Mayes & Scott 1984, Fig 46:328 for similar). Handles are normally strap with a slight central groove decorated with diagonal slashing and, rarely, vertical slashing (*ibid*, Fig 99:104; Rylatt & Stokes 1996, Fig 98:84,85&108, Fig 99:107&108 for similar). Cooking pots/bowls appear to be represented by only five body sherds. These have soot-blackened exteriors and an interior speckled yellowish-green glaze. Nuneaton 'B' was represented by non-diagnostic body sherds dating from the thirteenth to fifteenth century. A probable jug with triangular roulette decoration dating to the fifteenth century represented fabric Nuneaton 'C'.

London Type-Ware.
A total of 340 sherds were recovered representing 17.9 % of the total assemblage. The majority of sherds were from baluster-type jugs dating approximately from the 1240's to the 1340's. A pear-shaped or rounded body, with a distinct neck and a slightly constricted and flared base (Pearce, Vince & Jenner 1986) characterises this form. A number of different styles of decoration were recognised. There are examples of 'early' style jugs with white-slip decoration or horizontal lines of applied scales. The most common form of decoration is the 'North French' style, characterised by vessels with a lustrous copper-stained green glaze and applied vertical lines of scales made from thick white slip. There are also frequent examples of sherds with 'ring and dot stamp' decoration (*ibid*, Fig 40:134; Fig 52:186 for similar) and two with anthropomorphic designs.

Warwick Product (?)
A total of ten sherds were recovered which did not fit readily with the fabric descriptions within the Coventry Type Series. They are moderately hard, with dull orange surfaces, mid-grey cores and a smooth, dark-olive-green glaze. The only form represented is a small and shallow, rounded bowl.

Local Buffware.
Only three sherds of this ware were recovered and these did not fit readily with any fabric description within the Coventry Type Series. They are of a very hard fabric with a rough surface texture. The inclusions were moderately abundant, fine-medium sub-angular white-grey quartz. The surfaces were of a buff-pale-orange colour with mid-grey cores. One rim sherd, probably from a cooking pot, had a near-flat top, with square rim profile and everted neck. The second appears to be from a cylindrical neck of a jug/pitcher. The third sherd is from a plain handle.

Midland Purple: Fabrics N1-3 (CTS).
A total of seven sherds were found, only one of which was derived from a pre-Dissolution context. Only one form could be identified, that of a jug with characteristic frilled base (Mayes & Scott 1984, Fig 59:494).

'Midland Purple' Types.
Two non-diagnostic body sherds of proto-stoneware in a grey-olive fabric with a thin mottled green-brown glaze were recovered from site.

Surrey Whitewares: 'Tudor Green' Type: Fabrics J1-3 (CTS).
Only one sherd was recovered which would appear to be from a vessel with a full, bulbous body and three incised grooves at its maximum girth, probably a cup or globular drinking jug.

Paffrath blue-greyware.
A total of two sherds were found and they are both of a highly fired light-grey fabric with grey-blue

surfaces. The form represented has not been identified although earlier research has dated this ware to the fifteenth century (Jennings 1981). It has been previously seen in the form of a ladle at 114-5 Gosford Street, Coventry (Dickinson 1992).

Siegburg Stoneware: Fabrics I1-10 (CTS).
One near-complete vessel was recovered from the sixteenth-century collapse of an internal cellar doorway. The form represented was that of a jug with a frilled base and pronounced rilling around its body, otherwise lacking decoration. The quality of the light-grey fabric of the jug is characteristic of the ware at a date *c*1500. It also exhibits splashes of orange-brown, which is a likely result of ash in the kiln. It is of interest as it contains a substantial copper-alloy residue probably as a result of being used as a crucible after initial breakage, the high-firing temperature of this ware making it ideally suited to such a function.

Raeren Stoneware: Fabrics I1-10 (CTS).
Only one sherd was recovered deriving from a stratified sixteenth-century context. The form represented was a probable globular drinking jug, with exterior salt glaze over a strong brown body and characteristic splayed frilled base.

Cistercian Ware: Fabrics K1-4 (CTS).
A total of seventy-one sherds were recovered representing about 2.5% of the total, of which only one was residual, forty one were from Dissolution collapse contexts and thirty were from the successive build-up of the latest medieval floor layers, internal and external. Cups with one, two or three handles, were most common. The only other identifiable type was a candlestick similar to one found at Broadgate East, Coventry (Rylatt & Stokes 1996, Fig 40:606). The source of this ware is likely to be either Chilvers Coton, Warwickshire or Burslem/Hanley in Staffordshire (Mayes & Scott 1984; Barker 1986).

'Midland' Blackware: Fabrics L1-5 (CTS).
A total of twenty-nine sherds were recovered representing 1.5% of the total, of which seven were residual and eighteen were from loosely stratified post-Dissolution contexts. The remaining four were derived from a stratified sixteenth-century context. They can be sub-divided into two main groups, table-wares in a variety of forms of drinking vessels and later coarse-wares. The main form of the latter was the dish/pancheon but a rarer form was encountered in that of a colander.

Glazed Red Earthenware: Fabrics P1-4 (CTS).
A total of seven sherds were recovered from the site, of which four were from loosely stratified contexts

and four were from a sixteenth-century-stratified context. Vessel forms identified include cooking pots with soot blackening on the external surface and a possible storage jar with a random thin external glaze. This may have been the result of a kiln explosion as small fragments of Cistercian Ware can be identified adhering to the vessel body.

Unglazed Red Earthenware.
Only two sherds of this post-medieval fabric were recovered. Both were non-diagnostic.

Slipware: Fabrics O1-4 (CTS).
A total of twenty-six sherds were found representing 1.4% of the total assemblage recovered, of which four were residual. The main form recovered was the press-moulded dish/plate with trailed, feathered and combed slip-decoration (Rylatt & Stokes 1996, Fig 42:634 for similar). These were likely to have been produced in Burslem or Hanley, Stoke-on-Trent around 1720-40, with the exception of one example with the date in relief from the 1760's. A probable honey-pot, richly marbled or clouded in shades of orange-brown on a yellow background, with a highly glossy, yet blistered glaze was also present. This over-fired example is likely to date to the *c*1680's and is similar to one found at Temple Balsall, Warwickshire (Gooder 1984, Fig 30:233).

Manganese Mottled Ware: Fabric Z (CTS).
A total of four sherds were found, of which two were residual. The only identifiable form is that of a mug, similar to an example from Temple Balsall, Warwickshire (*ibid*, Fig 13:124). A product of Staffordshire between *c*1690-*c*1750.

Creamware: Fabric Z (CTS).
Only one sherd was recovered and this was residual, probably dating to the 1780's. It is from a cup that exhibits a yellowish tinge around its edge, which is diagnostic of early examples, produced in Staffordshire.

'Mocha' Ware: Fabric Z (CTS).
A total of seven sherds and one complete vessel were recovered from site. Among these were two identifiable forms: bowl (one sherd) and cups/mugs (four sherds). The complete vessel belongs to the latter group and is characteristically decorated in yellow with a white horizontal band and a feathery straw-blown pattern in bluish-green. It dates to *c*1830-50. Other sherds of note include that of a mug/cup with horizontal blue and white-banded decoration and a sharply carinated profile.

The origin of these vessels is either Staffordshire or Swadlincote in Derbyshire where kilns have recently been excavated.

Lead-Glazed Earthenwares: Fabric Z (CTS).
A total of four sherds representing mug and cups were retrieved from a nineteenth-century pit.

Nottingham Salt Glazed Stoneware: Fabric Z (CTS).
Only one sherd was recovered from site and this was residual. It is characteristic of its type in possessing a lustrous bronze-like sheen and incised decoration, probably part of a mug, dating from between *c*1750 and 1900.

Other English Stoneware: Fabric Z (CTS).
Only one sherd is present, deriving from a nineteenth-century pit. It is part of pancheon with a thin, brown, speckled salt glaze.

Underglazed Transfer-Printed Ware: Fabric Z (CTS).
A total of ten sherds were found of which four were residual and six were from a nineteenth-century pit. All but three exhibit floral designs in various tones of blue, and are examples of tableware i.e. cups and plates. The remaining sherds represent two English examples of *chinoiserie* and a child's plate with a printed homily in the tondo and the alphabet in relief around the rim.

Nineteenth-Century Industrialised Ware: Fabric Z (CTS).
Two examples of a nineteenth-century factory produced glazed ware were recovered from the assemblage. A source could not be attributed.

Chronology

The pottery from St. Mary's Priory refectory undercroft falls into five main chronological groups:

Group A. Pre-undercroft in origin.
Group B. Floor makeup and structural features e.g. postholes (thirteenth century).
Group C. Pre-Dissolution occupation floors (sixteenth century).
Group D. Originating in the loose stratigraphy of Dissolution contexts (1539-present). It includes material residual from groups A and B.
Group E. The post-medieval assemblage.

In addition to the ceramic material from these groups is the unstratified material from the topsoil across the site. The exceptionally long time allotted to Group D for the 'Dissolution period' can be explained by the fact that during this period the monastic remains stood in a ruinous state where town rubbish accumulated.

Group A
Contexts which predate the undercroft produced relatively large quantities of pottery. The following

types were present: Nuneaton 'A' Ware, London-Type Ware, Sq. 22/23, Local Redwares.

The sealed contexts from which this group derives are not associated with the use of the refectory undercroft but relate to in-filling of gullies before the undercrofts were built (contexts 66 and 69).

The assemblage is dominated by Nuneaton 'A' Ware comprising ninety of 158 sherds. The in-filling of the pre-cellar features therefore cannot date to any earlier than the mid-thirteenth century although they may have been cut at a considerably earlier date.

The recovery of smaller amounts of other wares also suggests a late thirteenth-century date. The regionally imported London Ware diagnostic and non-diagnostic sherds are consistent with this, as are the jug fragments with flared necks identified to the Sq.22/23 fabric.

Group B
Group B is a series of floor make-up layers and structural features associated with the refectory undercroft (27/1, 27/4, 27/5, 27/6, 27/7, 43, 44) producing the largest quantity of sherds from the excavation. The following types were present: Nuneaton 'A' Ware, Nuneaton 'B' Ware, Coventry Sandy Ware-fabric A, London Ware, Sq.22/23, Local Buffware, Cannon Park Ware Type.

Again the assemblage is dominated by Nuneaton 'A' Wares which accounted for 587 of the 872 sherds recovered, providing a *terminus post quem* of *c*1250 for these deposits. The appearance of smaller amounts of other fabrics suggests a date of *c*1250-1300 for the earliest domestic occupation layers and thus probably the construction of the undercroft. The regionally imported London Ware fragments and cooking pot/storage jar in Coventry 'A' fabric, non-diagnostic body sherds in Nuneaton 'B' Ware, Cannon Park Type Wares and base and body sherds in Sq.22/23 fabric are all consistent with this.

Group C
A single domestic occupation layer associated with the undercroft (26) produced the following types: Nuneaton 'A' Ware, Cistercian Ware, Nuneaton 'C' Ware, Wiltshire Flint Tempered Ware.

The assemblage is dominated by Nuneaton 'A' Ware which comprised 165 of the 176 sherds recovered, but a single sherd of Cistercian Ware provides us with a *terminus post quem* for the deposition of this occupation layer. It was sealed by a Dissolution context and therefore must date to between *c*1450 and *c*1539.

Pottery was also recovered from two external, domestic occupation layers (43) and (44), a post-hole (28) and occupation layer (24). The first layer must have been deposited *c*1450-1539 as it also contained a single sherd of Cistercian Ware. The latter two have been dated to the pre-Dissolution sixteenth century due to the presence of sherds of Glazed Red Earthenware and the fact that they are sealed by a Dissolution context.

Group D
The sixteenth-century to post-Dissolution layers (03, 04, 12, 13, 17, 19, 20, and 35) were loosely stratified and are characterised by long deposition. The pottery production range is from *c*1539–*c*1910.

Group E
The latest well-stratified group to be excavated was from a brick-lined pit (39). The pottery ranged from *c*1720-1880. The group contained a range of table and kitchen ware. Another pit (15) was dated from *c*1720 due to the presence of a single Slipware sherd.

The last layers of the site contain a very high proportion of residual pot. This can be seen in acute form when analyzing the pottery recovered from context (02). The digging of the 1930's foundations of the Alhambra pub has brought pottery dating from anything between 1475 to around 1900 up to these later surfaces.

The Development of Pottery Types within the Assemblage
Approximately nine hundred years passed between the appearance in the archaeological record of the earliest and latest pottery types found on this part of the site. This period witnessed the beginnings of different potteries, their peak of production and their end. At any one time there would have been several different production centres supplying Coventry, one of the most prosperous medieval towns in the country. During the period of monastic occupation of the site, the largest fabric groups consisted of locally produced wares: Coventry and Chilvers Coton. Three, hitherto unidentified fabrics were found, their petrology indicating that they too were produced locally using coal-measure clays. The large number of London Ware sherds was unexpected and has certainly not been paralleled in Coventry before. These types of pottery appeared mainly during the thirteenth and fourteenth centuries.

Expansion of the range of vessel types can be seen to have begun during the fifteenth century with traditional cooking pots, storage jars and jugs being supplemented by cups and related small forms i.e. Cistercian Wares. These had died out by the turn of the sixteenth/seventeenth century but their tradition is carried on with the 'Midland' Blackwares. From the last quarter of the seventeenth century, pottery

groups contain slipware. Their use can be seen to carry on throughout the eighteenth century. The general change in the scale of output of English ceramics in the middle decades of the eighteenth century can be recognised within the pottery assemblage, especially with the mass production of earthenwares in the Staffordshire industry.

Discussion and Conclusions

Examination of the thirteenth-century ceramic material has indicated that it is not a primary deposit. The lack of complete vessels points to it being a secondary deposit, having been brought in from the close vicinity to be used as floor make-up. There is some indication as to the origin of this back-fill, as it appears to be the vestiges of household rubbish and mostly comprised of tablewares, jugs and cooking pots.

These types could be used in a variety of ways – serving at table, fetching and keeping water and storage of ingredients. Some derive from the cooking of food. The thirteenth century wares recovered represent a limited range of vessels. This may not only reflect their area of usage but the fact that pottery containers formed only part of the total complement of household vessels.

The high percentage of jugs recovered must partly reflect the fashions in tableware fostered by the growth in the wine trade or simply changes in social customs (McCarthy & Brooks 1988, 110). They may also indicate a storage function nearby.

For the pre-Dissolution period, the dating of the pottery has been partly based upon the recorded stratigraphic relationships between layers. In contrast, for the post-Dissolution period, the ceramic material derives from contexts characterised by loose stratification and long deposition. This is a result of the monastic buildings having fallen into a ruinous state and the precinct functioning as a town 'rubbish tip'. The usefulness of this part of the assemblage is therefore limited. This is also the case for the earlier medieval period as a large percentage of the ceramic assemblage is derived from the thirteenth-century floor make-up layers. The nature of the sherds present would appear to indicate that they were brought in from elsewhere to form the make-up layers and were not occupation debris. It is possible that they did not travel far, possibly from within the monastic precinct. Social or economic conclusions for this part of the assemblage cannot, therefore, be drawn.

The Pottery – The Nave
Vanessa Clarke and Iain Soden

Introduction

A total of 1549 sherds were recovered, weighing 64.8 kg. Most of the deposits encountered in the nave which contained pottery were either long-lived or unsealed. This is particularly so amongst the post-Dissolution and post-medieval contexts. Most result from a period of long deposition as the church remains were left in a ruinous state and the nave was used for rubbish dumping and picked over for stone. Thereafter, the creation of the late eighteenth-century cemetery imported material (002). This has limited the value of widespread analysis. Therefore the analysis has concentrated upon the short sequence of stratified pits within bay 2 of the south aisle and those medieval features which contained pottery. This small amount of stratified pottery forms the basis of analysis and comprises a total of 589 sherds (38% of the total assemblage), weighing 9.73 kg (15% of the total weight) (not illustrated).

Method of analysis

The method of examination adopted was to record the pottery in terms of fabric, sherd count and weight. The identification of fabric was based upon the published Coventry Type series from Broadgate East (Redknap & Perry 1996). Other recourse was made to those publications on Coventry which contain material not in the original type series (for which see Gooder 1984; Soden 1995). In addition there was concordance with definitive publications on particular wares (for which see Hurst & Van Beuningen 1986). Full fabric descriptions and their

Table 1: Quantification by fabric, sherd count and weight (bracketed letters refer to Coventry Type Series after Redknapp and Perry 1996).

WARE	SHERD COUNT/ WEIGHT	CONTEXT
Coventry 'A' Ware (A)	5/0.039kg	(384), (388), (473)
Nuneaton 'A' Ware (H)	19/0.207kg	(095), (092), (063), (336), (361), (388).
Nuneaton 'C' Ware (H)	2/0.016kg	(291),(336)
Cannon Park Ware (E)		
14th-Century Redware (Soden 1995, 85)	5/0.086kg	(063), (066)
'Cistercian' Ware (K)	137 / 0.239kg	(019), (022), (053), (063), (069), (080), (091), (095), (118), (131),(132), (202), (208), (212), (249), (335)
Midland Blackware (L)	208/4.43kg	(004),(022),(019),(063),(066) (069), (080), (082), (090), (091), (092), (095), (118), (131), (199), (202), (208), (212), (249),(377)
Midland Purple (N)	49/0.618kg	(004), (019), (022), (063), (066) (092), (095), (118), (202), (212), (291), (292)
Raeren-Langerwehe Stoneware (I)	8/0.16kg	(069), (095)
Koln-Frechen Stoneware (I)	3/0.16kg	(022), (095)
Siegburg Stoneware (I)	1/0.006kg	(095)
Martincamp: Flasks (Hurst *et al* 1986, 102-4)	44/	(019), (022), (095), (202), (212), (391)
Saintonge Ware (*ibid*, 78ff)	2/ 0.09kg	(019), (063)
Midland Yellow (M)	9/0.63kg	(019), (022), (095)
Manganese Mottled Ware (Gooder 1984, 173-81)	5/0.024kg	(004), (019), (082)
Slipware (O)	3/0.231kg	(004), (095)
Glazed Red Earthenware (P)	44/1.309kg	(019), (063), (066), (069), (080), (092), (095), (131), (196)
Unglazed Red Earthenware (Soden 1995,88)	32/773g	(019), (022), (066), (053), (092), (095), (131), (132)

complete characteristics can be found in these publications.

Occurrence

Coventry 'A' Ware
The few sherds found derive from the rapidly in-filled ditch lying beneath the nave and north aisle of the church (bay 2). They and the ditch predate the church but their fabric is not closely datable other than that they occur throughout the twelfth century. In a further section adjacent to the west range of the cloister, fragments of Coventry 'D' Ware, which flourished in the period c1150-1240, were found. All are cooking-pot sherds.

Nuneaton 'A' Ware
Nuneaton (otherwise Chilvers Coton) Fabric A occurs most commonly in the period 1250-1300 (Mayes & Scott 1984, 40). The fragments represented derive mostly from the fill of a rock-cut grave in the gap between piers 6 and 7 of the south aisle and date its digging to this period (336, 361). The remainder was mostly residual.

Nuneaton 'C' Ware
Two sherds, alone which were undiagnostic body sherds, represent this fabric characteristic of the thirteenth and fourteenth centuries. They help corroborate existing dating of features.

Cannon Park Ware
A few sherds of this local type help confirm a thirteenth-century date for the rock-cut grave between piers 6 and 7 in the south aisle.

Fourteenth-Century Redware
Not always red, and occurring well into the sixteenth century, the few fragments of this local type were all found residual in later contexts dating to the post-Dissolution period.

Cistercian Ware
These sherds represent approximately 25% of the entire stratified assemblage. The main vessel forms were identified as cups with single or multiple handles similar to those discovered at the Broadgate East excavations (Rylatt & Stokes 1996, Figs 40:594:600:601:602). The typical finish of these vessels was a dark-brown glaze. Decoration was rare, represented here by only three sherds, two of which were patterned with near-circular blobs. One unusual form was encountered, that of a cup-salt (Brears Type 18) with applied white-slip decoration in the form of leaves. This key range of cups and small wares originated late in the fifteenth century and over the sixteenth century the form evolved into a variety of blackware and Yellow Ware vessels. The presence of Cistercian Ware in a group normally points to a deposition date between 1475 and 1550 (Crossley 1994, 245) although in Coventry it can occur until about 1580 alongside early Blackware types (Charmian Woodfield, *pers comm*).

Midland Blackware
This formed the largest fabric group recovered. Major differences in this ware are apparent, a characteristic also noted in the Coventry Charterhouse assemblage (Soden 1995, 87). The early blackwares are mainly 'tyg' types and drinking beakers which had supplanted the earlier Cistercian finewares by 1600, possibly earlier (*ibid*, 95). The later forms produced were large storage vessels, dishes and bowls (Gooder 1984, Fig 237), cylindrical pots and pancheons, these date from the later seventeenth through to the early nineteenth centuries.

'Midland Purple'
All the sherds of this type were from Dissolution or post-Dissolution deposits. The comparatively large number of rim sherds recovered for this ware means that a number of distinctive forms could be identified. At least seven sherds represented cisterns/jars characterised by thick bifid rims with scalloped rim tops and external rim beads. All of these rim sherds were similar to vessels discovered on the Town Wall and Charterhouse excavations (Soden 1995; Bateman & Redknap 1986, Fig 13, 31 & 27) and have been dated to the sixteenth/early seventeenth century. One other type of jar was recovered (Rylatt & Stokes 1996, Fig 40:584:585 for similar examples) which can be dated to the early fifteenth century but the two sherds representing it may be residual. There were also two examples of a small bowl (Mayes & Scott 1984, Fig 107:444) dating to the late fourteenth/early fifteenth century and a single example of a wide-mouthed bowl (*ibid*, Fig 86:1). Amongst the non-diagnostic sherds were frequent over-fired examples, showing the fine tolerances necessary in firing this almost proto-stoneware.

German Stoneware
A total of fifteen sherds were found which could be categorised further into three regional groups: 'Koln-Frechen', 'Raeren-Langerwehe' and 'Siegburg'. Six sherds were identified as belonging to the first group, eight to the second and one from the last. The earliest stoneware is represented by two sherds deriving from a 'Raeren-Langerwehe' medium-sized drinking jug dating to the first half of the sixteenth century (similar to one found at Broadgate East: Rylatt & Stokes 1996, Fig 40:590). A Frechen plain wide globular jug (Hurst *et al* 1986, Fig 106, 332) with

a distinctive mottled brown 'Tiger' salt glaze characteristic of this ware was also present, dating to *c*1550-75. The 'Siegburg' stoneware industry is represented by only one small non-diagnostic body sherd decorated with foliage.

French Martincamp Flasks

A total of forty-four sherds were found. Three types can be distinguished, in differing fabrics; the earliest type, in a fine off-white earthenware fabric with a flattened profile, is common from about 1475 to 1550 and is represented by only one sherd. It overlaps with the rounder brown stoneware flask, common throughout the sixteenth century. This in turn overlaps with the last flasks, an orange-red earthenware fabric, common in early seventeenth-century contexts (Hurst *et al* 1986, 103 & Fig 143). This was clearly the main fabric with 38 sherds, all of which derived from fairly immediate post-Dissolution contexts.

French Saintonge Ware

This was represented by only two sherds, one of which comprised the triangular knob and applied stamped face medallion of a Simple Knobs Type I Chafing Dish, dating from *c*1500-*c*1600 (*ibid*, Fig 35:104). These were characterised by low-level handles, often more than three knobs, with simple upright rims and splayed open pedestals. They are the most common type in Britain and have been found on at least fifty other sites (*ibid*) but denote widespread continental links and with it a degree of emergent aspiration to wealth and status.

Midland Yellow Ware

A total of only nine undiagnostic body sherds were found, with the exception of a single example of a handled cup with narrow mouth: a form at the top end of the quality range. As with the Martincamp flasks, all were derived from immediate post-Dissolution contexts. Previous excavations at Whitefriars, Coventry (Woodfield 1963-4) have shown Yellow Wares to have been present by the 1570's and common throughout the seventeenth century.

Manganese Mottled Ware

A total of five sherds of this distinctive Staffordshire product were recovered from the site. All were from loosely stratified post-Dissolution deposits. There was a single example of a fire-blackened cup/tankard dating to *c*1700-30.

Slipware

Only three sherds were found: all are diagnostic rim sherds, the first from a Staffordshire press-moulded joggled-slip plate, *c*1720-40 (Rylatt & Stokes 1996, Fig 42:634), the second and third from Staffordshire press-moulded trailed and combed-slip decorated plates, dating to the early eighteenth century.

Red Earthenware

A total of forty-two 'unglazed' and thirty-two 'glazed' sherds of red earthenware were recovered. These ubiquitous post-medieval coarse-wares are mainly represented by utility wares, particularly the pancheon dated to the seventeenth to nineteenth century (*ibid*, Fig 43:646:649).

Conclusion

There was little pottery which was associated with either the construction or occupation of the cathedral church or the layers pre-dating it. What little there was is useful for corroborative dating alone, this primary requirement being much better provided by the large quantities of architectural stonework, floor tiles, window glass and other finds whose stylistic development is reasonably well-understood. The majority of the pottery present dated to the very early post-medieval period. Over 70% of the assemblage derives from the long-lived and much disturbed layers 002 and 003, which between them span a full 345 years, an unhelpfully loosely dated context. This is an identical deposition pattern to that encountered at Charterhouse (Soden 1995, 94-5), with the Dissolution rubble picked over endlessly and rubbish dumped haphazardly across a wide area. A total of 38% of the assemblage (589 sherds), was well stratified, most deriving from the backfill of a series of grave robbing pits cut into bay 2 of the former south aisle of the church.

While these pits of late sixteenth-century date seem to have been specific in their origin, disturbing the chantry burials in the south aisle, their backfilling seems to have been more general, attracting domestic rubbish from unknown quarters. It is this very lack of provenance, in that the refuse cannot be attributed to any domestic plot fronting Trinity Churchyard or Great Butcher Row, that severely limits the potential of these groups. As such they are vastly inferior to similarly dated and altogether better provenanced material already published from Broadgate (Redknap & Perry 1996).

The Animal Bone
Dr Philip L Armitage

Introduction

Species and Numbers of Bones
A total of 2,247 animal bone elements/fragments were submitted for identification and analysis. This

material included small mammal and fish bones recovered from the residues of sieved soil/bulk samples as well as hand-collected bones. By employing standard archaeozoological methodological procedures, 1,088 of the bone elements/fragments (48.4% of the total) are identified to species and anatomy; representing thirteen mammal, nine bird, and thirteen fish species (see below). Compared with other archaeological sites examined by the author, St. Mary's Priory produced a disproportionately high amount of unidentifiable bone specimens (1,159 = 51.6% of the total) (Table 2 in archive). This situation arises from the exceptionally high numbers of very small, pulverised bone fragments recovered from the sieved samples and the presence in these of quantities of broken fish spines/rays that lack diagnostic features required for determining species. The amount of unidentified material is further inflated by the over 500 highly-fragmented/splintered pieces of bird long bone shafts (*cf* domestic fowl sized) from the trample layer (Context 1179) in the north-south undercroft.

The species identified are listed as follows:

Mammals:
    cattle *Bos* (domestic)
    sheep *Ovis* (domestic)
    pig *Sus* (domestic)
    cat *Felis* (domestic)
    rabbit *Oryctolagus cuniculus*
    brown hare *Lepus* **cf.** *capensis*
    fallow deer *Dama dama*
    oe deer *Capreolus capreolus*
    black rat *Rattus rattus*
    house mouse *Mus musculus*
    water shrew *Neomys fodiens*
    common shrew *Sorex araneus*
    field vole *Microtus agrestis*

Birds:
    domestic goose *Anser anser* (domestic)
    domestic fowl *Gallus gallus* (domestic)
    partridge *Perdix perdix*
    domestic duck *Anas platyrhynchos* (domestic)
    teal *Anas crecca*
    mute swan *Cygnus olor*
    oodcock *Scolopax rusticola*
    magpie *Pica pica*
    blackbird *Turdus merula*

Fishes:
    cod *Gadus morhua*
    whiting *Merlangius merlangus*
    haddock *Melangogrammus aeglefinus*
    herring *Clupea harengus*
    plaice *Pleuronectes platessa*

conger eel *Conger conger*
salmon *Salmo salar*
freshwater eel *Anguilla anguilla*
pike *Esox lucius*
perch *Perca fluviatilis*
roach *Rutilus rutilus*
tench *Tinca tinca*
dace *Leuciscus leuciscus*

Grouping the Contexts for the Purposes of Analysis
For the purposes of the assessment of the animal bone samples from the St. Mary's Priory site, the elements/fragments from the different contexts were grouped as indicated below according to the ceramic chronological phasing, with phase 6 divided into two sub-phases to allow for separate consideration of the material from the late monastic period and that assigned to the late monastic/post-Dissolution period. Assigning Context 1179 proved problematical owing to the apparent anomaly between the faunal and pottery evidence. From the viewpoint of the faunal composition the bone assemblage appears to be priory food debris (especially as regards the wide variety of freshwater fish – see discussion on monastic diet, below); and arguably the context should be included in the Phase 6.1 grouping. On the basis of the pottery dating and stratigraphic position at the site, however, context 1179 is interpreted as a post-Dissolution trample layer [i.e. falls within the Phase 6.2 grouping]. Following advice from the site director, the bones from context 1179 were included with the Phase 6.2 assemblages.

Phase	Designation/period	Ceramic date range
1	early monastic	AD 1100 – 1200
2	monastic	AD 1200 – 1250
3	monastic	AD 1250 – 1300
4	mid to late monastic	AD 1300 – 1400
5	late monastic	AD 1400 – 1470
6.1	late monastic to Dissolution	AD 1470 – *c*1539
6.2	late monastic/post-Dissolution	AD 1470 – 1550
8	post-medieval	AD 1650 – 1720

General Observations on the Bone Assemblages

Spatial Pattern in the Bone Deposits
Over the site, the following contexts yielded note-worthy concentrations of animal bone:

1179 [Phase 6.2]: trample layer in north-south undercroft; high density of bird and fish bones. Post-Dissolution.

1257, 1260, 1261, 1262 & 1264 [Phases 4-6]: back fill deposits of the stone-lined pit 1256 in the court-yard; high density of food bone waste. Monastic.

1296 [Phase 6.2]: fill of drain 1195 in the north-south undercroft; concentration of fish bones (food debris). Possibly post-Dissolution.

1398 [Phase 2]: earliest occupation layer in east-west undercroft; high density of fish bones (food debris – predominately herring vertebrae). Monastic

1673 [Phase 6.2]: fill of garderobe cistern off west range; large quantity of food bone waste. Probably post-Dissolution

25143 [Phase 3]: back-fill deposit of the timber-lined wheel pit; large quantity of food bone waste. Possibly post-Dissolution.

Preservation & post-depositional modification
Overall, the state of preservation of the bone elements from all phases is fair to good; with only moderate levels of bones exhibiting evidence of sub-aerial weathering/erosion or biological degradation (recorded in 2.4% of the identified mammal and bird bones). It would appear, therefore, that most of the food refuse had been buried (become incorporated into the archaeological deposits) soon after being discarded and that only a relatively small proportion of such waste had been left scattered on open ground for any length of time. Rapid burial/covering of the bulk of the food waste had denied feral dogs, cats and other animals (e.g. rats) any opportunity of scavenging and feeding off this debris; as evidenced by the generally low to moderate incidence over the site of gnawed/chewed bone elements (all phases) (see Table 4 in archive). The exception is seen in the bone assemblage from Context 1192, a late monastic [Phase 6.1] levelling-up layer in the courtyard; in which there is a relatively high incidence of weathered/abraded bones (recorded in 10.5% of the mammal bones) as well as evidence of dog gnawing (noted on 3.2% of the mammal bones) and rat gnawing on a lamb radius. It is suggested on the basis of the above observations, that the bones in 1192 may represent residual/re-deposited organic debris imported in the soil used for levelling.

Apart from the large quantity of splintered/pulverised bones from Context 1179 [Phase 6.2], already mentioned above, high frequencies of bone fragments also came from sieved samples taken from the following contexts: 1262<2> [Phase 4] bulk fill of the stone-lined pit in the courtyard, and 1297<7> [Phase 6.2] fill of drain 1195 in the north-south undercroft

Burnt Bone
For the site (all phases) the incidence of burnt bone is 3.5% of the combined total of the mammal, bird and fish bones. By far the highest concentration of burnt bone fragments came from Phase 4 context 1262<6> a back-fill deposit of the stone-lined pit (1256) in the courtyard (see Table 5 in archive). Some of the bones from 1262 (particularly the calcined specimens) may represent food waste that had been purposely burnt as a routine hygienic measure carried out prior to disposal and burial. However, as the larger proportion appears only to have been charred (incompletely combusted) it may be suggested that the burning had instead been entirely incidental arising from the casual throwing of pieces of unwanted kitchen and table waste into cooking fires – the assemblage perhaps comprising rakings from the fireplace of the kitchen attached to the priory refectory.

Apart from an isolated sheep rib and four very small mammalian bone fragments, all of which are burnt/calcined (from Phase 6.2 contexts 1149 & 1150, layers in hearth 1148 (in the north-south undercroft)), and two burnt mammal bone fragments in the black burned layer (believed to be a post-Dissolution squatter fire), in the east-west undercroft (Phase 6.2 context 1389<8>) there is no other concordance between the distributions of the burnt bones from the site and those contexts associated with burning. This situation is illustrated with reference to Phase 6.2 context 1189, interpreted as a post-Dissolution burnt layer in the yard, but in which none of the fifty-one mammal and two bird bones recovered from this layer shows any evidence of burning. The bone assemblage from Phase 6.2 Context 1126, also interpreted as a post-Dissolution burnt layer, likewise shows no evidence of burning (even slight charring/scorching). The remaining burnt bones from the site appear to have been randomly distributed with no discernible pattern.

Masticated Fish Vertebrae
Deposits in the east-west undercroft yielded examples of fish vertebrae showing the effects of crushing caused by mastication: noted in three of the ten freshwater eel vertebrae and two of the thirty-six herring vertebrae from Phase 2 Context 1398<10> (earliest occupation layer), and in two of the three freshwater eel vertebrae from Phase 6.2 Context 1389<8> (post-Dissolution squatter fire layer). Similarly deformed fish bones are documented from a tenth-century latrine pit at 16-22 Coppergate, York; where they were interpreted as the skeletal remains

of fish that had been chewed, ingested and voided in human faeces (see Wheeler and Jones 1989, 74-75).

Descriptions of the Species Represented

Ageing and Sexing of the Major Domesticates/Meat-Yielding Species

Ages at time of death/slaughter in the cattle, sheep and pigs from the mid- to late monastic and late monastic/post-Dissolution deposits are established using epiphyseal fusion in the long bones and from the dental eruption/wear stages in the mandibles (criteria of Silver 1971 and Getty 1975) (see Tables 15-20 in archive).

In the cattle, several animals had been killed as calves and most of the remaining animals slaughtered at ages between one and a half and three and a half years. This kill-off pattern indicates that the veal and beef supplied to the priory came from a thriving and well-established cattle economy, able to provide a solid surplus of young animals in their prime and exploited as a meat source well before they had made any significant contribution towards stock replacement or had served as plough/draught animals. It is of interest that the pattern at St. Mary's, Coventry, is mirrored at the medieval Collegiate (Bedern) site at York, where the notably high numbers of calves (represented in the excavated bone assemblage) was interpreted as the by-product of a dairy herd and the elderly cattle as worn-out milk cows (see Bond & O'Connor 1999, 364). Some support for a similar interpretation of the evidence at St. Mary's is provided by the identification (using the criteria of Grigson 1982) of an adult female innominate bone from a late monastic/post-Dissolution occupation layer in the yard (Context 1190); perhaps representing a culled breeding/milch cow.

In the sheep, animals were apparently being slaughtered as neonates/young lambs or at ages between one and a half and three and a half years. Such animals provided succulent, prime-quality meat and as in the case of the cattle, their inclusion in the priory's dietary regime reflects a well-established sheep economy in the rural hinterland, able to supply animals surplus to maintaining the core breeding stock and those kept into old age as wool producers. Less privileged members of medieval society (the peasantry) had to accept the tougher, inferior meat provided by elderly sheep culled from the wool flocks. Horn cores of an adult ram and an adult ewe are identified (using the criteria of Armitage 1977) among the sheep bones from context 1673 (fill of the garderobe cistern) [Phase 6.2]. These were most probably introduced from the town after the Dissolution.

Pigs were either very young (neonates/sucking pigs) [with examples from both Phases 1 and 6.2] or between one and three years of age. An upper canine tooth from context 1189 [Phase 6.2] is identified as female, and a lower canine tooth from context 1300 [also Phase 6.2] identified as male (using the criteria of Mayer and Brisbin 1988).

Other Domestic Food Species

Rabbits: From the relatively small size of the rabbit bones these appear to have been reared in warrens.

Poultry: Anatomical distributions of the domestic fowl and goose bones by phase are summarised in Tables 12 and 13 (in archive). Using the criteria of West (1982 and 1985a) the unspurred domestic fowl tarsometarsal bone from Context 1304 [Phase 4] is recognised as female (hen) and the much larger and more robust specimen with a spur scar from Context 1296<7> [Phase 6.2] is identified as a castrate (capon). Comparisons made of the measurements taken of the domestic fowl bones from St. Mary's Priory against their modern counterparts reveal that most of the medieval birds compare in size with modern bantams and only a very few would have been of similar size to the much larger laying and boiling fowl commonplace today.

Game Species and Wild Birds

Fallow deer is represented by three bone elements from two of the contexts excavated in the courtyard area (1192 & 1256) [both Phase 6.1]. The only roe deer bone found, a piece of the shaft of a metatarsus, also came from the yard area (Context 1192) [Phase 6.1]. This same context produced three hare bone elements: one mandible and two radii. A tibia from Context 1672 (fill of the monastic cistern [Phase 6.2]), is also identified as hare.

Exploitation of a variety of wild birds in the rural hinterland as a source of food for the priory is reflected in the bone assemblages (see Tables 7 & 14 in archive). Among these species are woodcock (represented in Context 1296 (fill of drain 1195 in the north-south undercroft) by four bone elements from a single bird) and magpie (represented in Context 1192 (levelling up layer in the courtyard) by two bone elements also from a single bird). Interpretation of the magpie bones as food debris is based on the knowledge that other monastic houses included this bird in their diet, as for example at Waltham Abbey, Essex (referenced by Fitter 1945, 48).

Feral Cats

Evidence for the presence in the post-Dissolution ruins [Phase 6.2] of feral cats is provided by two bone elements from Contexts 1061 (north-south undercroft) and 1126 (east-west undercroft).

Small Wild Mammalian Fauna

Evidence of the presence at St. Mary's Priory of the ubiquitous black rat that infested medieval Britain is provided by four bone elements: a sub adult femur from context 1156 (back-fill of a foundation trench in the north-south undercroft) [Phase 6.1]; a cervical vertebra from 1296<7> (layer located in a niche below the spiral staircase in the north-south under-croft) [Phase 6.2]; and one lower incisor tooth and a metapodial bone, both from 1673<2> (back-fill deposit in the garderobe cistern) [Phase 6.2]. Context 1296<7> also produced evidence for the presence of house mouse (in the form of an immature ulna) and water shrew (represented by a mandible). An immature common shrew is represented by a tibia in the assemblage from Context 1673<2> (fill of the garderobe cistern) [Phase 6.2], and from the same deposit came the skeletal remains of two field voles (comprising two mandibles, one humerus, one innominate, two femora, and one tibia).

Sizes in the Fish

From measurements taken from selected fish bone elements, total lengths were calculated as shown in Table 21 (in archive). The Total Length (TL) of the cod dentary from 1302 (fill of drain 1253 west of north-south undercroft) was estimated at 55.1cm; a value which falls into the smaller size-range (55 to 65cm) documented by Wheeler (1977, 408) for the cod bones from medieval deposits at Kings Lynn, interpreted by him as the product of an inshore rather than a distant-water fishery. Modern size ranges (published in Newdick 1988) (shown in parenthesis below) of the freshwater fish species represented in the St. Mary's Priory bone assemblages may be used to evaluate how large or small were the fishes consumed at this site. The large cleithrum of a freshwater eel from 1179 (trample layer in north-south undercroft) comes from a fish of TL 59cm, and was probably therefore female (males are much smaller and usually about 40 cm long, while females are rarely less than 50cm and often between 80 to 100cm long). With reference to the cyprinid species at St. Mary's Priory, it is seen that the two roaches from Context 1179 of TL 24.7 and 27.3cm both fall within the length range given in Newdick (15 to 39cm) but the tench from Context 1396 (black organic layer in the east-west undercroft) of TL 12.3cm is noticeably much smaller than the adult size-range for this species (20 to 30cm). Perhaps the St. Mary's Priory specimen is an immature fish. The perch of TL 30cm (represented in Context 1179 by a right articular) falls within the uppermost end of the average range for this species (20 to 30cm).

Interpretation and Discussion

Site Environment

Monastic Occupation

The earliest occupation layers yielded only modest quantities of discarded kitchen/table bone debris (compared with the significantly greater amounts in post-Dissolution contexts), which seems to indicate a reasonably efficient regime of removal of unwanted refuse from the priory. Despite these standards of cleanliness, rodent vermin such as rats also appear to have co-inhabited the buildings with the humans and would have posed serious potential health risks as "reservoirs" of murine typhus and bubonic plague.

In the Post-Dissolution Period

In her assessment of the sixteenth-century bone assemblages from the excavations of the Cathedral Church of St. Mary's, Lloyd (see below) interpreted five articulated skeletons in the south aisle as the remains of a pack of scavenging feral dogs living in the post-Dissolution ruins. Cat bones from the same location were likewise interpreted as evidence for the presence of feral cats. No dog bones are identified in the assemblages examined by the present author, but the kitten ulna from the east-west undercroft [Phase 6.2] supports the scenario for the presence in the ruins of an established feral population of cats, which presumably subsisted on the rats and mice infesting the abandoned buildings. The presence of bones of a common shrew and two field voles in the garderobe cistern and the mandible of a water shrew in the fill of the drain in the north-south undercroft, indicates the surrounding area immediately outside the building precincts had, in the post-Dissolution period, become overgrown and a suitable habitat for small wild mammalian fauna. Indirect evidence (masticated fish bones) indicating human faeces had been voided in the east-west undercroft, supports the suggestion that squatters may have occupied the ruins in the post-Dissolution period.

Food Consumed at St Mary's Priory with a Comparison with Other Monastic Sites

Early Monastic Period [Phases 1, 2 & 3]

Evidence at St. Mary's Priory of the early monastic diet is extremely limited but apparently herring was the prime food fish (probably obtained in preserved form). Other monastic archaeological assemblages dating from the early/High Medieval Period (eleventh to thirteenth century) reviewed by Locker (2001) show similar high percentages of herring; such as at Westminster Abbey, London, St. Mary's Clerkenwall, London (kitchen deposit) and Eynsham Abbey, Oxford.

Mid to Late Monastic Period [Phases 4, 5 & 6.1]

Analysis of the food bones excavated from the mid- to late monastic contexts at St. Mary's Priory reveals a diet that extended beyond 'solid sufficiency' to one of indulgence and extravagance. Beef and veal comprised the bulk of the flesh-meat consumed, with mutton and lamb of secondary importance and pork and sucking piglets making a lesser contribution (see Table 22 in archive). Rabbits and hares also featured in the diet, together with the occasional haunch of venison. Goose and domestic fowl appear to have been regularly eaten, with swans, partridges and a variety of small wild birds served as pittances at special feast days. Although located inland away from the coastal fisheries, St. Mary's Priory does seem to have been supplied with some marine fish, probably in preserved form (stockfish, salted cod, red & white herrings, salted conger eel) but by far the greatest proportion of fish consumed were fresh-water species. The priory would have relied heavily for its supplies of roach, tench, pike and perch on the stocks of such species kept in millponds and artificial ponds (stews). In summary, the apparent richness and variety in the meat, poultry and fish consumed at St. Mary's Priory fits very well into what is known concerning the typical medieval monastic diet which Harvey (1995, 34) categorised as a *'form of upper-class diet, the equivalent within the cloister of the diet of the nobility, gentry or urban élites outside'*.

With respect to the evidence showing greater proportions of beef than mutton were consumed at St. Mary's Priory, this is a common feature of many other Midland monasteries, as reviewed by Gilchrist (1995) who documented a similar profile for St. Anne's Charterhouse, Coventry.

Editorial Note

In addition to the animal bone studied by Dr Armitage, Rowena Lloyd of Northamptonshire Archaeology examined two further assemblages. The reports made as a result of these studies can be found in the archive. The following are summaries based upon her findings:

Animal Bone from Monastic contexts in the Refectory and North Range Undercrofts

602 fragments were identified to species; 426 of mammal and 176 of bird. Fish bones were also noted as present in many of the contexts but were not quantified. The interpretation of the assemblage mirrored that of the above i.e. that the occupants of the priory were eating high-status food such as beef,

mutton and pork together with goose, domestic fowl, duck, pheasant, grey heron, and woodcock. A bias of female domestic fowl over male was noted and interpreted as evidence for egg production. Extensive evidence for butchery was found throughout the assemblage and included split vertebrae bearing testament to the practice of longitudinal halving of carcasses. Attention was drawn to the richer diet enjoyed by the monastic community in relation to that of the average citizen. This is evidenced by comparisons made with assemblages recovered from excavations of secular sites in Coventry such as at Much Park Street (Cram in Wright 1986).

Animal Bone from Post-Dissolution (Sixteenth-Century) Contexts in the Cathedral Nave

1382 fragments were identified to species, 1350 of mammal and thirty-two of bird. Small amounts of fish bones were also noted as present in some of the contexts but were not quantified. Cattle bone was most commonly encountered, with large quantities of sheep also present. The remains of five crushed but articulated dogs were recovered and interpreted as being the remains of scavengers living on the site (see Fig 16b). Lesser quantities of pig, cat, horse, rabbit and red deer were identified. Birds were represented by the following species: domestic fowl, domestic goose, pheasant, mute swan and crow. Many of the mammal and bird bones bore butchery marks and is thought that the assemblage is largely the product of butchery and table waste being dumped on the site from both household and commercial sources.

The Charred and Waterlogged Plant Remains
Wendy J Carruthers

Introduction

Environmental soil samples were taken from a variety of pits, occupation layers, drains etc during the excavation of the conventual buildings. A water-logged soil sample was also taken from the wheel pit of the Priory Mill, to the north of the main buildings.

Methods

The soil samples were processed by Phoenix Initiative staff using standard methods of floatation (dry contexts) and wet-sieving (wheel pit). A minimum mesh size of 500 microns was used to retain the flots (dry contexts) and finest residue (wheel pit).

The flots and residues from seven dry contexts

Table 1: The Charred Plant Remains from St Mary's Priory, Coventry

Sample no.	10	6	2	7	2	8
Context	1398	1262	1673	1296	1149	1389
Feature	Occ. Layer	Pit 1256	Cistern 1665	Drain 1195	Hearth 1148	Burnt layer
TAXA phase	1200-1250	1300-1400	1470-1550	1470-1550	Post-Dissn.	Post-Dissn.
Grain:						
Triticum sp. (free-threshing wheat grain)		205				
Avena sp. (wild/cultivated oat grain)		12				
Avena / Bromus sp. (oat/chess grain)		7			2	
Hordeum sp. (hulled barley grain)		4				
Secale cereale L. (rye grain)		260			1	
Indeterminate cereals		329				13
Chaff:						
Triticum aestivum-type (bread wheat type rachis frag.)		4				
T. turgidum-type (rivet-type wheat rachis frag.)		7				
Triticum sp. (free-threshing wheat rachis frag.)		13				
Avena sativa L. (cultivated oat pedicel)		1				
Secale cereale L. (rye rachis frag.)		56				
Cereal-sized culm nodes		11			2	
Weeds etc.:						
Ranunculus acris/bulbosus/repens (buttercup achene) DG		1				
Ficus carica L. (fig seed) *	1#	2#				
Corylus avellana L. (hazelnut shell frags) HSW*		5				1
cf. *Alnus glutinosa* (L.) Gaertn. (cf. Alder catkin frag) HSWB		2				
Agrostemma githago (corn cockle)		1				
Rumex sp. (dock achene) CDG	1#	4			1	
Rubus sect. *Glandulosus* Wimmer & Grab. (bramble seed) HSW*		1#, 2			1#	
Rubus cf. *idaeus* (cf. raspberry seed)		1#				
Prunus domestica ssp. *insititia* (damson stone) HS*		1				
Vicia/Lathyrus (small seeded vetch/tare)	4	8			6	1
Bupleurum rotundifolium L. (thorow-wax mericarp) Ac		3				
Lithospermum arvense L. (field gromwell nutlet) AD		1				
Stachys sylvatica L. (hedge woundwort nutlet) DHW		1#, 1				
Sambucus nigra L. (uncharred elder seeds) HSW*	2#	2#	48#	12#	2#	
Chrysanthemum segetum L. (corn marigold achene) Ada					1	
Centaurea cyanus L. (cornflower achene) AD		2				
Centaurea sp. (cf. cornflower achene frag.) AD		3				
Anthemis cotula L. (stinking chamomile achene) Adh		3				
Carex sp. (sedge nutlet) GdMB	1#					
Bromus sect. *Bromus* (chess caryopsis)		13				
Charcoal present	++	++++	+++	+++	+++	++
Fish bones & scales present	+			+		+
TOTAL:	9	966	48	12	16	15
Sample volume (litres):	4	10	1.5	6	7	5
Frags per litre:	2.3	96.6	32	2	2.3	3

KEY:

Plant remains were charred apart from # = uncharred

+ = present; ++ = several; +++ = frequent; ++++ = numerous

Habitats: A = Arable; B = bankside, along rivers, ditches etc.; C = cultivated; D = disturbed, wasteground; E = heath; G = grassland; H = hedgerow; M = marsh, bog; P = ponds, ditches, slow-flowing rivers; S = scrub; W = woodland; Wo = open woodland, woodland margins & clearings; Y = waysides

a = acid soils; c = calcareous / basic soils; d = dry soils; h = heavy soils; n = nutrient-rich; o = open; s = sandy; w = wet/damp soils

Table 2: Waterlogged & Charred Plant Remains from St Mary's Priory Mill, Coventry, PP01

Taxa	Priory Mill, wheel pit <6> 25143
Economic plants	
Triticum sp. (indeterminate wheat grain)	[1]
Avena sp.(oat grain)	[1]
Indeterminate cereal fragment	[3]
Linum usitatissimum L. (cultivated flax seed) *	34
Linum usitatissimum L. (cultivated flax capsule frag.) *	11
Cannabis sativa L. (hemp seed)*	2
Arable/cultivated ground weeds	
Agrostemma githago L. (corn cockle seed & seed coat frag.) A	2
Anthemis cotula L. (stinking chamomile achene) Adhw	2
Fallopia convolvulus (L.) A.Love (black-bindweed achene) AD	6
Lapsana comunis L. (nipplewort) CDH	1
Scleranthus annuus L. (annual knawel achene) Cos	1
Spergula arvensis L. (corn spurrey) Aa	5
Grasslands, including damp soils	
Carex sp(p). (sedge nut) GwM	7
Cirsium / Carduus sp. (thistle achene) DGMWo	1
Filipendula ulmaria (L.) Maxim. (meadowsweet achene) Gw	1
Lychnis flos-cuculi L. (ragged robin) Gw	5
Montia fontana ssp. *chondrosperma* (Fenzl)Walters GwB	2
Poaceae NFI (grass caryopses) CDG	1
Potentilla sp. (cinquefoil achene) EG	1
Ranunculus repens/acris/bulbosus (buttercup achene) DG	55
Rumex conglomeratus Murray (clustered dock achene & perianth) GP	1
R. acetosella (sheep's sorrel) Gea	1
Stellaria graminea L. (lesser stitchwort seed) Gd	1
Plants bordering streams, ditches and ponds & other damp places	
Apium nodiflorum (L.) Lag. (fool's water-cress mericarp) MP	3
Caltha palustris L. (marsh-marigold) BMP	1
Conium maculatum L. (hemlock mericarp frag.) BD	2
Glyceria sp. (sweet-grass caryopsis) BP	4
Mentha sp. (mint nutlet) BGPw	1
Polygonum hydropiper (L.)Spach (water-pepper nutlet) MPw	4
General weeds of cultivated and disturbed soils	
Aethusa cynapium L. (fool's parsley mericarp) CD	2
Atriplex patula/prostrata (orache seed) CDn	2
Chenopodium album L. (fat-hen seed) CDn	12
Galeopsis tetrahit L. (common hemp nettle nutlet) AD	8
Persicaria maculosa Gray (redshank nutlet) Cdo	12
P. lapathifolia (L.) Gray (pale persicaria nutlet) Cdow	15
Polygonum aviculare L. (knotgrass achene) CD	3
Raphanus raphanistrum L. (wild radish mericarp) CD	2
Rumex sp. (dock achene) CDG	39
Stellaria media (L.) Villars (common chickweed seed) CD	1
Urtica dioica L. (common nettle achene) Dwon	48
Urtica urens L. (small nettle achene) CDn	2
Woods, Scrub, Hedgerows - includes some edible fruits	
Ajuga reptans L. (bugle nutlet) GdW	1
Alnus glutinosa (L.) Gaertn. (alder fruit) HSWB	1
Alnus glutinosa (L.) Gaertn. (alder female catkins) HSWB	6
Corylus avellana L. (hazelnuts, whole) HSW*	4
Corylus avellana L. (hazelnut shell frags) HSW*	152
Crataegus monogyna L. Jacq. (hawthorn seed) HSW*	2
Ilex aquilfolium L. (holly seed) HSW	1
Malus sylvestris (L.)Mill. (crab apple seed) HSW*	1
Moehringia trinervia (L.) Clairv. (three-nerved sandwort) HW	1
Prunus spinosa L. (sloe fruit stone) HSW*	4
Quercus sp. (acorn cup frag.) HSW	1
Rubus sect. *Glandulosus* Wimmer & Grab. (bramble seed) HSW*	11
Sambucus nigra L. (elder seed) DHSW*	30
Solanum dulcamara L. (bittersweet seed) HWD	5
Stachys sylvatica L. (hedge woundwort nutlet) DHW	1
TOTAL	[5] 522

KEY:
Plant remains were waterlogged apart from [ ] = charred
Habitats: A = Arable; B = bankside, along rivers, ditches etc; C = cultivated; D = disturbed, wasteground; E = heath;
G = grassland; H = hedgerow; M = marsh, bog; P = ponds, ditches, slow-flowing rivers; S = scrub; W = woodland;
Wo = open woodland, woodland margins & clearings; Y = waysides
a = acid soils; c = calcareous / basic soils; d = dry soils; h = heavy soils; n = nutrient-rich; o = open; s = sandy;
w = wet/damp soils; * = introduced cultivated species

from the priory and the waterlogged residues from the wheel pit were sent to the author for analysis. The dry flots were coarse sieved to remove the large charcoal (2mm) and both fractions were fully sorted under a dissecting microscope. The residues were scanned to check for mineralised remains, and as a check on the recovery of charred material. Although some charcoal was still present in many of the residues, full sorting was not considered to be necessary. No mineralised concretions or plant remains were noted in the residues.

Two samples from the wheel pit were sent to the author; one that had been machine floated and one that had been fine-sieved to 500 microns. Full analysis was undertaken on a 25% sub-sample of the fine-sieved sample. Sub-sampling was necessary because context was an extremely rich, organic deposit, and it would have taken too long to analyse the entire residue. The machine floated sample was rapidly checked by eye for further large plant remains, such as fruit stones and grain. Since no new taxa were observed during the scanning (although lots of hazelnuts and nutshell fragments were present), these results were omitted from Table 2.

Results

The results of the analysis are presented in Tables 1 (charred samples) and 2 (waterlogged remains from the priory wheel pit). The nomenclature and much of the habitat information follow Stace (1987).

Discussion

Most of the samples from dry contexts produced very few charred plant macrofossils, although charcoal was often present in large quantities. In the case of sample 2 (post-Dissolution) from the garderobe cistern, a lot of the charcoal consisted of well-preserved roundwood.

The few poorly-preserved charred plant remains in five of the six dry samples provide very little information about the arable economy of the priory, since they comprised just a few cereal grains and weed seeds which may not all be monastic in origin. However, the presence of fish bones and scales, and a few uncharred edible fruit seeds such as fig, (*Ficus carica*), bramble (*Rubus* sect *Glandulosus*) and elderberry (*Sambucus nigra*) suggest that sewage may have been seeping into some of the contexts. Most of these samples were from the area of the undercroft, although they span several phases of occupation and the post-Dissolution phase. It is possible that the uncharred seeds were intrusive, but because all of the taxa represented possess thick, resistant seed coats it is quite likely that they had survived for many centuries. The remains may have become

partially mineralised if they had a faecal origin (Green 1979; Carruthers 2000). However, apart from the survival of fish remains, no further signs of mineralisation were found in the flots or residues, so concentrated cess remains were not preserved in these samples.

Fill of Pit 1256 – One charred sample, from the primary fill of the stone-lined pit (1262) in the yard, did produce large quantities of well-preserved charred plant remains. The main components of this sample were wheat and rye grains, in almost equal quantities. Chaff fragments were relatively frequent, but these consisted primarily of rye rachis fragments which are small and thin enough to pass through even the finest crop-cleaning sieve. There were remarkably few weed contaminants present, suggesting that the crop cleaning had been thorough, or perhaps that crop husbandry methods were efficient. The ratio of grain to chaff to weed seeds was 16:2:1, suggesting that the assemblage represented a fairly clean sample of wheat and rye grain.

Wheat and rye were commonly grown together as 'maslin' during the middle ages (Pretty 1989). They are both free-threshing cereals, making the processing of maslin straightforward. When ground together to make flour, they can be made into a dark bread. Mixed crops were commonly grown during the medieval period in order to reduce the chance of total crop failure, and to help to smother weeds. Productivity may not have been increased by this method, but stability of production and sustainability were possibly more important at this time (*ibid*).

A further point of interest is that two types of free-threshing wheat were being grown with the rye; both bread-type wheat (*Triticum aestivum*-type) and rivet-type wheat (*T. turgidum*-type). Although the grains of these two taxa cannot safely be differentiated (Jacomet 1987), enough well-preserved rachis fragments were recovered to demonstrate that both crops were being grown (see criteria described by Moffett, 1991). These two types of wheat have different growth habits and different culinary properties, which would seem to make growing them as a maslin disadvantageous. Bread wheat has a high gluten content and so makes the lightest bread. Rivet wheat is more commonly used for biscuits, but it also grows on a long straw that is ideal for thatching. Since rye straw was also favoured for thatching, a maslin of these two cereals begins to make more sense.

Since identification criteria were established for rivet-type wheat (*ibid*), the occurrence of this crop is increasingly being recorded from medieval sites across southern and central England (*ibid*). Many of the records date back to the twelfth to fourteenth centuries, although a few possible late Saxon records are beginning to be made. Rivet wheat continued to be grown in Britain into the post-medieval period. Bread-type wheat and rye are both frequent in Saxon and later deposits, although rye is often more frequent on poor soils that are unsuitable for wheat.

It is possible that the assemblage from fill 1262 was made up of waste from a number of episodes of dumping, but considering its uniformity and lack of weed contaminants this seems unlikely. The two other cereal crops represented, cultivated oats (*Avena sativa*) and hulled barley (*Hordeum* sp.), were present in very small numbers, so they are likely to represent volunteer plants growing from previous years' crops amongst the maslin. Since only one oat chaff fragment (pedicel) could be identified to species level, it is also possible that some of the oats were the common weed, wild oats.

Although the deposit had probably been burnt and deposited within a short space of time, it is possible that originally it had been made up of maslins derived from different farms. Admittedly, the evidence for this is slim, consisting of just a few weed seeds. However, the two weed taxa concerned, thorow-wax (*Bupleurum rotundifolium*) and corn marigold (*Chrysanthemum segetum*) are indicative of two different types of soil, the former arable weed preferring calcareous or other high pH soils, whilst the latter usually grows on moderately acidic soils (Hill *et al* 1999). This could suggest that crops had been brought in from different sources to supply the priory with food.

Other arable weeds represented are typical of the medieval period, including corn cockle (*Agrostemma githago*), cornflower (*Centaurea cyanus*) and stinking chamomile (*Anthemis cotula*), a weed of heavy, damp clay soils. The presence of a single charred damson (*Prunus domestica* ssp. *insititia*) stone and a few fragments of hazelnut shell (*Corylus avellana*) demonstrate that a few other types of burnt food waste were also deposited in the pit.

There is no obvious reason why this deposit of maslin had been burnt and dumped in pit 1256. There were no signs of spoilage, such as sprouting or insect damage. The crop may have become charred by accident, whilst it was being dried prior to milling, perhaps.

Priory Mill Wheel Pit – Organic silts recovered from the timber-lined wheel pit of the mill were examined by Prof. D Keen (University of Coventry Geography Department). He suggested that the silts had been deposited while the mill was in use, rather than post-abandonment. The findings from the plant macrofossils, as outlined below, agree with this interpretation.

The principal components of this highly organic deposit were small wood and charcoal fragments, mixed with frequent hazelnuts and hazelnut shell fragments. Because several of the nuts were whole, it is likely that hazel trees overhung the millstream for some of its length. No doubt workers at the mill enjoyed the benefits of this readily available food source, judging from the large numbers of nutshell fragments recovered. However, in general, food remains were scarce in this deposit. Several other remains from trees, shrubs and herbs of shady places were present, such as oak (*Quercus* sp.; acorn cup fragment), holly (*Ilex aquifolium*) and three-nerved sandwort (*Moehringia trinervia*). Apart from the hazel remains, none of these other taxa were numerous, and leaves and twigs were not frequent in the sample. Therefore, it is unlikely that the banks were heavily wooded, but some woods, scrub or hedgerow probably existed nearby.

The other most dominant groups were the weeds of disturbed ground and grassland taxa. Weeds of disturbed, nutrient-rich soils such as nettles and docks were not especially numerous, as is sometimes the case in wasteground situations. Buttercup achenes were frequent, and a number of plants of damp grasslands such as ragged robin (*Lychnis flos-cuculi*) and meadowsweet (*Filipendula ulmaria*) were represented. The presence of seeds from these two tall-growing taxa suggests that at least some areas were protected from grazing animals, perhaps being cut for hay in late summer.

Aquatic plants were not well represented, apart from a few bankside and emergent plants such as marsh marigold (*Caltha palustris*), flote grass (*Glyceria* sp.) and water-pepper (*Polygonum hydropiper*). These plants can withstand moderate rates of water flow, indicating that the stream was in use when the remains were deposited. No plants of stagnant water were recorded, and caddis-fly larvae cases were present, indicating fairly fresh, flowing water.

Of particular interest is the recovery of seeds and capsule fragments from cultivated flax (*Linum usitatissimum*), and seeds of hemp (*Cannabis sativa*). Flax remains are commonly recovered from Saxon and medieval streams and rivers, as the method of fibre production – retting – requires long periods of soaking bundles of plants in order to rot off the soft tissues. As this is a smelly process, flowing water is preferable, and by-laws were passed to prevent retting from taking place in public watercourses (Pretty, 1989). Hemp seeds are less commonly found, although Godwin (1967) cites place-name evidence for hemp growing in Norfolk during the fourteenth century. Hemp would also need to be retted in order to extract its coarse, bast fibres. Both plants also have medicinal properties, but the recovery of flax capsule fragments and the presence of the remains in a millstream suggests that fibre production was taking place.

Similar evidence for textile working was recovered from the millstream of Bordesley Abbey, near Redditch, dating from the later twelfth to fourteenth/fifteenth centuries (Carruthers, 1993). In this case, however, in addition to flax and hemp retting, there was evidence that the power of the mill had been used for fulling, since Fuller's teasel remains were frequent. Metalworking was also being carried out at the Bordesley Abbey mills, and a number of workshops were excavated (Astill, 1993). Flax and hemp retting were also probably taking place at Reading Abbey wharf, since seeds and flax capsule fragments were recovered from the waterfront sediments (Carruthers, 1997). The Abbey millstream joined the River Kennet close to the area excavated at the Abbey wharf, so it is uncertain whether retting was taking place in the millstream or the River Kennet.

Only a few charred cereals and waterlogged weeds of arable fields were recovered from the sediments, so there is little evidence that cereal processing was taking place nearby. If cereals were being brought to the mill for grinding into flour, spillage into the wheel pit was not taking place. Neither were weed contaminants being picked out of the crop and being deposited in the stream, to any great extent. The few arable weed seeds present were similar to those from the charred grain sample from pit 1256, with the addition of two weeds of acidic, sandy soils; annual knawel (*Scleranthus annuus*) and corn spurrey (*Spergula arvensis*).

The general picture painted by this well-preserved assemblage is of an operational mill stream flowing through grassland with some hazel scrub, woods or hedgerows nearby. It is likely that the area around the stream was well managed and not over-grazed or trampled. Sewage and cereal processing waste were not being deposited in the stream, although flax and probably hemp retting was taking place in the flowing water. If the water-flow was sufficient and the industry was not too intensive, this may not have led to too much nutrient-enrichment and pollution.

The Coins and Tokens (not illustrated)
Iain Soden

Of the coins and tokens recovered from stratified contexts, fourteen could be identified. One was gold, the remainder silver or copper alloy. Many others were found but were heavily worn, aspects of both sides and legends being at best indistinct. A large proportion of those from the mill site were poorly stratified and so heavily encrusted with extraneous materials that cleaning was felt to be an unwarranted use of resources.

Those identified were as follows:

1. CRU00 SF5, Context 13 (superstructure collapse, refectory undercroft). Silver Groat (four pence) of Edward III (1327-77). Issued 1361-9.
2. RWF01 SF15, Context 26006 (post-medieval deposit, west range). Copper-alloy Farthing of Victoria (1837-1901). Issued 1886.
3. JFK00 SF12, Context 1305 (monastic layer, north-south undercroft). Silver Cut Halfpenny (short cross type) of Henry III (1216-72). Issued 1216-47.
4. JFK00 SF13, Context 1179 (post-Dissolution layer, north-south undercroft). Silver broken Penny (long cross type). Issued after 1247.
5. JFK00 SF15, Context 1272 (pit fill, courtyard). Silver Cut Halfpenny (long cross type with continuous legend) of Henry III (1216-72). Obverse: legend HEN[RICUS] REX. Reverse: legend [A]NGLIE[TERCI]. Issued 1247-72. It is not known whether the royal bust holds a sceptre or not.
6. JFK00 SF16, Context 1256 (pit fill, courtyard). Silver Farthing of Edward I (1272-1307). Legend illegible.
7. JFK00 SF17, Context 1115 (post-Dissolution layer, east-west undercroft). Silver Penny of Edward III (1327-77). First coinage issued 1327-35. Obverse: legend EDWARDUS REX ANG. Reverse: legend [CIVI]TAS [LON]DON.
8. JFK00 SF146, Context 1304 (rubble deposit, steps from cloister). Residual Roman copper alloy coin, probably House of Constantine (307-37).
9. JFK00 SF197, Context 1398 (monastic layer, east-west undercroft). Silver Cut Halfpenny of long cross type. Issued post-1247; otherwise illegible.
10. PP01 SF1, Context 25136 (layer, mill). Gold coin of Alfred the Great (871-99). Issued 886 to commemorate Alfred's taking of London from the Danes. Obverse: blank or worn away, milling only discernible. Reverse: monogram of LONDINIA, possibly double struck, worn, milled. Probably an official (if ineptly struck) Alfredian issue, since, while the period gave rise to many Norse copies of Alfred's coins, it seems perverse that they should wish to copy one commemorating Alfred's success and their own loss of London (North 1960, Vol 1, 88).
11. PP01 SF41, Context 25078 (fill, mill tail race). Copper-alloy Halfpenny of George I (1714-27). Issued 1723.
12. PP01 SF185, Context 25042 (layer, mill). Silver Halfpenny of Edward III (1327-77). Individual coinage not discernible. Obverse: legend EDW[ARDUS REX AN]. Reverse: legend [CIV]ITAS LON[D]ON.
13. PP01 SF190, Context 25040 (layer, mill).

Copper-alloy coin (token) with continuous legend. Obverse: E.R. with cinquefoils within tondo. Legend EDWARD REVELL. Reverse: St George, mounted, killing dragon. Legend IN LUTTERWORTH. Edward Revell was working from the George Inn in Lutterworth during the mid-17th century (Dyson 1913, 88). Such tokens were issued to combat the dearth of regal small change during the Commonwealth following the execution of Charles I but later banned by Charles II in 1672 when new coinage was sufficiently in circulation.

14. PP01 SF194, Context 25050 (layer, mill). Silver Shilling of Philip and Mary 1554-8). Obverse: Regnal busts facing each other with single crown above. Legend PHILIP Z MARIA D G REX Z REGINA. Reverse: Crowned shield of Spain quartered with England. Numerals X and II on either side of crown. Legend POSUIMUS DEUM ADIUTOREM NOSTRUM.

The Metal Objects (Fig 70)
Margaret Rylatt, Paul Mason & Iain Soden

A large assemblage of metal objects was recovered which included: **iron** nails, fittings, chain links, chisels and keys; **copper alloy** buttons, buckles, studs, clasps, lace chapes, pins, hinges, brackets, fittings and off cuts; **lead** strips from the windows and amorphous lead blobs.

Noteworthy items from the Northamptonshire Archaeology excavations in the cathedral (SMC99) included a fragment of face mail, a small knife and silver plated coffin furniture from the post-medieval graveyard. They have not been illustrated but can be found in the archive. From the priory excavations the more interesting objects are illustrated as follows:

a   CRU00 SF13, Context 03, (superstructure rubble, refectory undercroft). Rectangular copper-alloy buckle with angular cross-section. 16th century.

b   CRU00 SF17, Context 19 (superstructure rubble). Copper-alloy spectacle buckle. The type is late 15th century in date. A similar example was recovered at the Charterhouse, Coventry (Soden 1995, 133-4).

c   JFK00 SF21, Context 1109 (demolition rubble, chapter house). Buckle

d   CRU00 SF40, Context 27 (monastic floor layer). Copper-alloy buckle. Medieval

e   CBP99/00 SF3, Context 2902(grave fill, bay 6 nave). Buckle.

f   JFK00 SF139, Context 1192 (monastic levelling layer). Strap end.

g   JFK00 SF137, Context 1192 (monastic levelling layer, courtyard). Decorative dress fitment.

h   BP99 SF39, Context 409 (demolition rubble). Copper-alloy tweezers

i   CBP99/00 SF1, Context 1005 (monastic floor layer). Copper alloy strap end.

j   JFK00 SF136, Context 1198 (pit fill). Copper-alloy (book?) mount (Hirst *et al* 1983, 204).

k   JFK00 SF6, Context 1002 (demolition rubble, north-south undercroft). Bronze enamelled book mount.

l   JFK00 SF14, Context 1179 (post-Dissolution layer, north-south undercroft). Copper-alloy mount.

m   JFK00 SF135, Context 1179 (post-Dissolution layer, north-south undercroft). Stud for corner of book binding.

n   CBP99/00 SF48, Context 1048 (Demolition rubble, east cloister alley). Bronze pin with decorative head.

o   CBP99/00 SF17, Context 1650 (ditch fill). Bronze pin.

p   JFK00 SF22, Context 1109 (demolition rubble, chapter house). Copper-alloy key?

q   CBP99/00 SF 2, Context 1004 (demolition rubble, north-south undercroft). Lead cloth seal (three others were found on the mill site but are not illustrated).

r   CRU00 SF31, Context 20 (vaulted ceiling collapse). Lead parchment pricker. Medieval.

The Worked Bone (Fig 71)
Margaret Rylatt, Paul Mason & Iain Soden

Bone objects, including a knife handle and bead, were recovered from the cathedral excavation and can be found in the archive. From the priory the following items are of particular interest:

a   CRU00 SF6, Context 03 (superstructure rubble). Worked-bone knife handle with fragment of iron tang inside. 16th century.

b   CRU00 SF23, Context 26 (monastic floor layer). Fragment of worked-bone whistle or other musical wind instrument. Medieval.

c   PP01, Context 25040 (post-medieval layer). Bone skate?

d   CBP99/00 SF3, Context 2013 (demolition rubble). Bone needle.

e   JFK00, Context 1262<6> (monastic pit fill). Perforated and incised bone. Button bone?

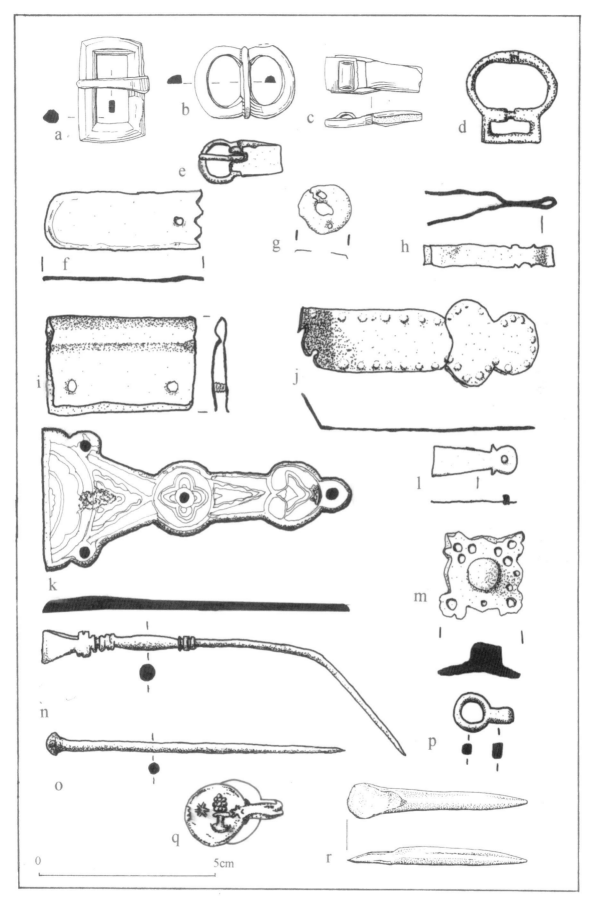

Fig 70   *Copper alloy and lead objects*

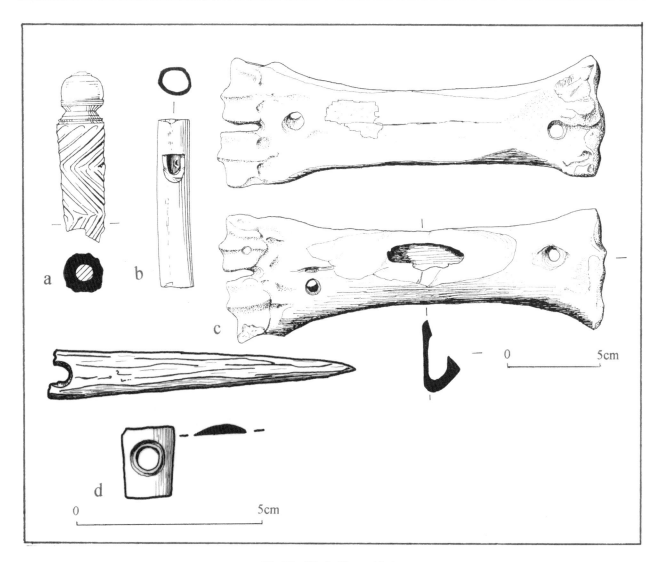

Fig 71 *Worked bone objects*

The Stone/Flint Objects (Fig 72)
Margaret Rylatt, Paul Mason & Iain Soden

A small assemblage of objects manufactured from stone was recovered. A stone mould for casting copper-alloy objects was recovered from the cathedral excavations and can be found in archive. Of the remainder, the following are of particular interest:

a   CRU00 SF24, Context 26 (monastic floor layer). Worked green sandstone inkwell. Medieval. Twelve sandstone inkwells of the l550s were recovered from the resonance passage excavations at Whitefriars, Coventry (Woodfield 1981, 116-8).

b   JFK00 SF74, Context 1305 (monastic levelling layer). Whetstone/Strikestone.

c   CBP99/00 SF1, Context 1904 (demolition rubble). Whetstone.

d   JFK00 SF11, Context 1305 (monastic levelling layer). Flint.

Vessel Glass (not illustrated)
Margaret Rylatt & Paul Mason

Small assemblages of fragmented vessel glass were recovered from demolition contexts throughout the site. Of these very few appeared to derive from the medieval period. A larger assemblage of broken material was recovered from the post-medieval fill of the tail race of the mill (PP01, 25078) which included a number of bases and rims from a range of small bottles and vials. A representative sample of these are retained in archive.

The only noteworthy vessel fragments were recovered from the late monastic/early post-Dissolution layers below the rubble in the courtyard

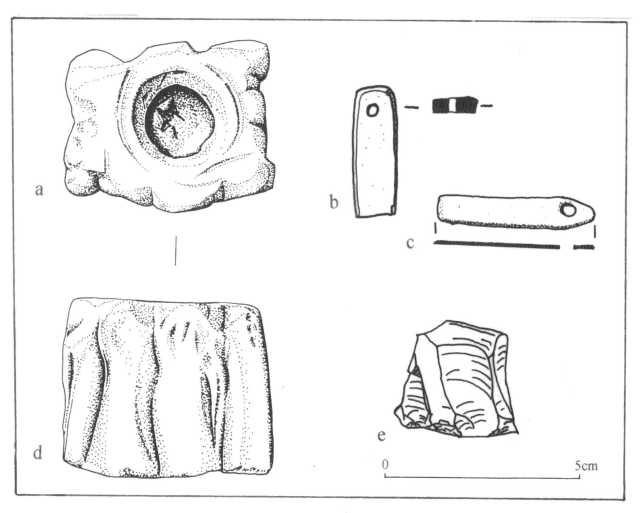

Fig 72 *Stone and flint objects*

(JFK00 1188/1189). Here a number of fragments of decayed, light green glass were found – some of which were convex base sherds from small vessels. Similar fragments were found during excavations at Bordesley Abbey (Hirst *et al* 1983, Fig 65:GLV4-6) and at Whitefriars, Coventry (Woodfield 1981, Fig 12:22) where they were interpreted as being the bases from glass urinals (*ibid*, 108). Glass rim fragments recovered from the priory excavations of the 1960's were also identified as urinals (Harden in Hobley 1971, 121, Fig 17:1,3,4). They too were manufactured from a thin, green glass.

The analysis of urine samples, collected in glass urinals, was an important diagnostic tool for the medieval doctor (Rowling 1968, 178, Fig 82). As the fragments were found in the courtyard, in close proximity to the infirmary, identification as sherds from urinals seems sound.

The Wooden Objects (not illustrated)
Margaret Rylatt & Paul Mason

A few objects crafted from wood survived in waterlogged deposits associated with the Priory Mill. They were retrieved from post-medieval contexts and are not thought to have originated from monastic period. The most interesting artefacts include a gaming piece and a wooden ball.

The Leather Work (not illustrated)
Margaret Rylatt & Paul Mason

A small assemblage of nineteenth-century leather shoe-soles was retrieved from post-medieval, waterlogged deposits associated with the Priory Mill.

The Human Bone
T Anderson MA (with contributions from
J Andrews BDS BSc FRSM)

The detailed catalogue of the skeletal material, including all metric and non-metric data, remains as unpublished archive. This is a summary of the age, sex, stature, pathology and oral health (examined by Dr J Andrews) of the skeletal sample.

The Articulated Skeletons (see APPENDIX 3)

CBP99/00 Context 1913: Underlying South Cloister Arcade
Represented by rather fragmented bones. Most of the left side was not recovered. The cranial vault had been deformed in the ground by soil pressure and the facial region was also damaged. Cranial and pelvic morphology, as well as metrics all support a diagnosis of a male (Appendix A in archive). Available aging criteria suggest a young adult of 27-32 years (Appendix A in archive).

Stature, based on right leg bones, was assessed as 1.707m (5' 7¼") (Trotter & Gleser 1958). Pathology was restricted to vertebral degeneration (Appendix A in archive). Oral health was poor. A very large palatal cyst indicates the presence of chronic infection. In life, the first molar was probably represented by broken down root fragments. Two mandibular teeth, a second right premolar and left first molar, had been lost during life. Two adjacent tooth crowns (the left maxillary premolars) had been totally destroyed by caries, possibly secondary to trauma. Three molars displayed occlusal cavities. Although common today, such cavities are quite rare in archaeological material due to the higher attrition rate and coarser diet (Corbett & Moore 1976; Moore & Corbett 1971, 1973, 1975). In this late Anglo-Saxon individual dental attrition does indeed give a younger age than other methods (Appendix A in archive). A soft food diet may indicate an invalid who was unable to eat normal food or possibly a rich person with access to high-quality refined food.

Apparently, this burial has disturbed earlier graves. A minimum of two other individuals are indicated by duplicated bones in the grave fill. One, represented by an incomplete mandible, appears to be a young adult female (Appendix A in archive). Three animal bones were also mixed into this soil.

CBP99/00 Context 2908: Cathedral North Aisle (bay 6)
Practically complete with only the feet unavailable. The frontal region of the skull displays recent serious damage. Most of the bones are solid, although the spine is very fragmented. Cranial and pelvic morphology, as well as metrics support a diagnosis of a female (Appendix A in archive). Available aging criteria provide a wide age range, but, on balance, an age of 27-32 years is suggested (Appendix A in archive).

Stature, based on arm and leg bones, was assessed as 1.574m (5' 2") (Trotter & Gleser 1958). No pathology was noted. Fusion of the manubrium and corpus of the sternum should be considered as an anatomical variant. The fusion occurs due to the non-development of a fibrous lamina during the fetal period (Scheuer & Black 2000, 227-229).

No scars of parturition were present; however, marked development (although not true extension of) the pubic tubercle, may be evidence that this female had given birth to children during her life (Bergfelder & Herrmann 1980; Cox 2000). This, if correct, may explain the 'elderly' appearance of the pubic symphysis.

Oral health was very good; disease was confined to carious destruction of an upper left second premolar. Such localised destruction suggests that the tooth was broken during life. A single tooth, the left central maxillary incisor, displays an abnormally short root. The root, 7mm in length, is 6.3mm shorter than the normal lateral incisor root. The right upper incisors were not available for examination.

In modern day material, some 1.3% of the population are thought to be affected by short root abnormality (Apajalahti *et al* 2002). Most frequently (70%), the maxillary incisors are involved and a significant female bias has been reported (*ibid*). Short root anomaly may be found in conjunction with absence of other teeth and mal-positioned canines (*ibid*)

Apparently this burial disturbed an earlier grave. Three skull fragments, including two fragments of frontal bone, were found in the grave fill.

SMC99 Context 424 Skeleton 1708: South Aisle Bay 1-2 (tomb)
A practically complete skeleton. All the bones are solid and well preserved, except for the ribs and the upper spine which were incomplete and eroded. Grave-fill contained a single animal bone bagged with the left foot. The anterior aspect of both femoral necks display bright green staining, suggesting that they had been in close proximity to a copper/bronze object.

Cranial and pelvic morphology as well as bone size (articular surfaces) all clearly indicate a male individual (Bass 1987; Ferembach *et al* 1980). The lack of dental attrition; the sharpness of the cranial sutures as well as the pubic symphysis suggest a young adult (25-30 years) (Bass, 1987; Ferembach et al 1980). Stature, based on femoral and fibular lengths, was calculated as 1.759m (5' 9½") (Trotter & Gleser, 1958).

Spinal degeneration was confined to linear defects

(a mild form of Schmorls' Nodes?) on the inferior surface of thoracic vertebrae (TV 7-9) and both superior and inferior surfaces of TV 10. The only other evidence of pathology was a small benign dense bone swelling on the medial surface of the right tibia. The benign overgrowth (26mm in length and 6mm wide) is located just proximal to the mid-shaft and there are fine striae posterior to the lesion. It may represent evidence of previous injury.

A single caries cavity was noted on the occlusal surface of the second left mandibular molar. Deposits of calculus were widespread on the lingual surface of the mandibular teeth. The left second mandibular premolar was rotated 45° mesio-buccally. Both mandibular third molars were congenitally absent.

SMC99 Skeleton 1713: North Aisle (buried with 1714)
A reasonably complete skeleton, missing the right radius; all three left arm bones and most of the left ribs. Both hands were incompletely preserved and the left calcaneus and talus were not recovered. The shaft and distal left fibula were bagged with SK 1714. Grave-fill contained four animal bones and bones of a child and an adult: three child skull fragments and a right femur missing its distal end. The latter was estimated to be c200mm in length which suggests an age of 4-6 years (Ferembach *et al* 1980). Adult bones included a fragmented fifth lumbar vertebra, R. lunate and a proximal phalanx, a right femoral head and femoral fragments. The lunate displays clear eburnation on the radial surface, evidence of osteo-arthritis of the wrist.

Cranial and pelvic morphology as well as bone size (articular surfaces) indicate a male individual (Bass 1987; Ferembach *et al* 1980). Dental attrition; the degree of cranial sutures closure as well as the pubic symphysis suggest an adult (30-40 years) (Bass 1987; Ferembach *et al* 1980). Stature, based on femoral and tibial lengths, was calculated as 1.668m (5′ 5¾″) (Trotter & Gleser, 1958). This individual was extremely long-headed (69.5mm). The absence of a right costo-vertebral facet suggests that a twelfth rib was absent. The fifth lumbar vertebra was fused to the sacrum, a congenital variation known as sacralisation.

Spinal degeneration was confined to localised osteo-arthritis (costo-transverse facets of TV 10); minor osteophytic outgrowths of the mid-thoracic (TV 5-9) and lumbar vertebrae (LV 2,3,5) and Schmorls' Nodes (TV 11). Other evidence of pathology included a very minor swelling of the right tenth rib, 30mm from the costal end. This may represent a very well healed costal fracture. The individual also displayed ossification of the thyroid and marked costal cartilage ossification.

Oral health was extremely poor. Eleven teeth had been lost during life. Five teeth displayed carious cavities, four of which were extensive and one had completely destroyed a molar crown. Most teeth presented with deposits of calculus with the labial/buccal and palatal/lingual surfaces most frequently involved. Periodontal disease, based on quality of alveolar bone, was very poor (Kerr 1989).

SMC99 Skeleton 1714: North Aisle (buried with 1713)
A well-preserved, complete skeleton; apart from the ribs, which are damaged and most of the spine which is eroded. Grave-fill contained miscellaneous adult bones; twelfth thoracic (with osteo-arthritis of both costo-vertebral joints; inferior Schmorls' Node), first and second lumbar vertebrae (latter with inferior Schmorls' Node), a right humerus missing its distal portion (female by size of head 42.0mm), R. scapular with osteo-arthritis of the acromial joint, four rib fragments, L. metacarpal II & III, R. ilium (female by width of the sciatic notch) and R. talus (female by maximum length 49.4mm).

Cranial and pelvic morphology as well as bone size (articular surfaces) clearly indicate a male individual (Bass 1987; Ferembach *et al* 1980). Although the cranial sutures are clearly visible (under 30-35 years?); the marked dental attrition of the available teeth and the pubic symphysis morphology indicate an elderly person (40-50 years) (Bass 1987; Ferembach *et al* 1980). Stature, based on femoral and tibial lengths, was calculated as 1.686m (5′ 6½″) (Trotter & Gleser 1958). This individual was broad-headed (83.3).

Spinal degeneration included osteo-arthritis of the upper vertebrae (CV 1-5; TV 3) as well as costo-vertebral (TV1 & 12) and costo-transverse (TV 10) involvement. Widespread large osteophytic outgrowths were demonstrable, involving the lower spine (TV 7-12; LV 2-5), three vertebrae (TV 7-9) were solidly fused by the exuberant outgrowths. Both sides of the sacrum had originally been fused to the pelvis (bilateral sacro-ilitis). Widespread ossification of the posterior longitudinal ligament (TV 6-9) was also noted. The individual also displayed ossification of the thyroid and cricoid cartilage as well as marked costal cartilage ossification. The manubrium was fused to the sternal corpus. The first lumbar vertebra presents with a rib fused to the left side of the body.

Numerous pathologies were noted, including osteo-arthritis, trauma and infection. Osteo-arthritis involved the temporo-mandibular joint; both shoulders and both sterno-clavicular joints as well as both wrists and the left foot. The former presented as localised pitting and roughening anterior to the left articular eminence. Both distal ulnae as well as the left trapezium/scaphoid articulation display eburnation, the latter being quite marked. In the left foot, a sesamoid and the first metatarso-phalangeal joint (the big toe) presents with marked eburnation.

Five mid-left ribs (4-8? or 5-9?) each display well healed fractures at their weakest points, the costal angle. Bone infection, a bilateral lower leg minor osteitic reaction was noted. In addition, localised swelling and increased vascularity at the centre of the frontal bone appears to represent a chronic cranial infection. The latter is restricted to the outer table and is roughly triangular. It commences 20mm anterior to the bregma with a width of 35mm and extends (45mm) towards the brow ridges and narrows to 10mm in width.

Minor osteophytic lipping at the shoulders (glenoids) and the elbow (ulnae olecranons) may be related to degeneration. In addition, widespread bilateral osteophytic outgrowths were noted on the humeri (lesser tuberosities), pelvis (posterior iliac crests, ischial tuberosities), femora (greater tuberosities), patellae (ligamentum patellae) and feet (tendo calcaneus). These findings, in conjunction with the spinal changes: bilateral sacro-ilitis and marked vertebral osteophytes, indicate that the individual was suffering from Diffuse Idiopathic Skeletal Hyperostosis (DISH).

In clinical medicine this is an uncommon condition which is most frequent in elderly males and may be associated with obesity and diabetes (Huskisson & Dudley Hart 1987, 35). In archaeological material, it appears to be frequent on monastic sites (Mays 1991; Waldron 1987). It has been suggested that this bias may be related to the presence of many well-nourished monks (Waldron 1987), or related to high status burials (Conheeney 1997, 228; Rogers 2000). Indeed, Giso, the last Saxon Bishop of Wells Cathedral, suffered from DISH (Rogers *et al* 1981). However, it must be remembered that monastic sites, containing many elderly males, the target population for the disease, would be expected to display the highest frequencies of DISH (Stroud 1993, 213).

Oral health was extremely poor. Seventeen teeth had been lost during life. Only four teeth were recovered, three (a right maxillary lateral incisor, right first and a left second premolar) were worn down to stumps with no crown remaining. The right third maxillary displayed a large buccal carious cavity. Periodontal disease, based on quality of alveolar bone, was very poor (Kerr1989).

SMC 99 Skeleton 1715: North Arcade (below pier 6 foundation)
An incomplete skeleton missing the right arm and most of the mid-lower spine and ribs, both hands and part of the pelvis. Grave-fill contained six animal bones and a hand bone (fifth right metacarpal) of a 3-6 year old child.

Cranial morphology as well as bone size (articular surfaces) indicate a male individual (Bass 1987;

Ferembach *et al* 1980). Dental attrition suggests an elderly adult (over 40 years. Stature, based on femoral lengths, was calculated as 1.698m (5' 7") (Trotter & Gleser, 1958). This individual was long-headed (72.3).

Spinal degeneration included osteoarthritis (right first costo-vertebral facet), osteophytic fusion of a mid-lower thoracic fragment and marked intervertebral osteochondrosis of the cervical (CV 4-7) spine. Other evidence of pathology osteo-arthritis of the left elbow and bilateral spondylolysis of the fourth lumbar vertebra (the fifth was normal). Spondylolysis is the term given to separation of a vertebral arch from its body. The modern day incidence is reported to be 3-7% (Resnick & Niwayama 1981, 2253). Formerly, it was considered to be a congenital defect but it is now realised that very few cases develop before the age of five years (Hensinger 1989). The favoured interpretation of the defect is a stress or fatigue fracture that fails to heal (Adams 1990, 191). However, it is possible that a genetic weakness may predispose to the condition (Hensinger 1989).

A small, smooth cystic cavitation just above the inferior border of the posterior left mandible (location of the internal maxillary artery) may be evidence for an asymptomatic minor vascular problem. The left mandibular first premolar had been lost during life, possibly due to trauma or a clumsy extraction, as an area of buccal bone had also been lost. Two teeth were carious and most displayed minor deposits of calculus. The root of the upper right first premolar was dilacerated (abnormally bent) evidence of trauma during child-hood while the tooth was developing. Two mandibular teeth (a right first premolar and a left canine) both display a single hypoplastic defect. Localised presentation may indicate trauma rather than systemic childhood disease. Three teeth, both lower second premolars and the left upper third molar, were congenitally absent. Periodontal disease, based on quality of alveolar bone, was poor, especially in the posterior maxillae (Kerr 1989).

CBP99/00 Context 814: South Cloister Alley
Represented by spine, ribs and upper arms. Available metrics indicate that the remains are male. No definite age criteria were available. However, the marked costal cartilage ossification suggests an older adult. Stature, based on mean humeral length, was assessed as 171m (5' 7.5") (Trotter & Glesser 1958). Pathology was restricted to bilateral acromio-clavicular osteo-arthritis and vertebral degeneration.

CBP99/00 Context 926: South Cloister Alley
Represented by skull, one arm bone, lower spine and left pelvis and lower legs. Cranial and pelvic

morphology are indicative of a male. Available ageing criteria indicate a mature individual of 50-60 years. All the teeth, except the right maxillary canine and lateral incisor, were lost many years before death. The canine, the only recovered tooth, was worn down to a root.

Stature, based on mean tibial length, was assessed as 1.703m (5' 7¼") (Trotter & Glesser 1958). Both right and left temporal mandibular joints (TMJ), left hp and right ankle (distal tibia) displayed arthritic degeneration. The vertebrae display minor osteophytic lipping. The arch of the fifth lumbar vertebra was recovered as a separate element, a condition known as spondylolsis.

In modern material, TMJ OA is not a very common finding, a prevalence of 8% has been recorded (Toller 1973). Its is well known that *ante-mortem* loss of teeth, especially the molars, will result in an increased strain on the TMJ (Carlsson *et al* 1979). The tibio-talar joint is very rarely affected by osteo-arthritis today (Doyle 1986, 868). Quite possibly previous injury to the ankle has led to this atypical presentation, so-called secondary osteo-arthritis.

Disarticulated Skeletal Remains

The following is a summary of noteworthy/ anomalous cases only. For a complete inventory of the dis-articulated human remains, see archive.

SMC99 Context 468: Mid-late Saxon Remains Beneath North Arcade of Later Cathedral.
Consists of an incomplete cranial vault, a fragmented right temporal and an incomplete sphenoidal corpus. The morphology of the fontal bone indicates male and the sharpness of the available suture suggest a young adult (Ferembach *et al* 1980). In association with these bones there were two ribs; one of a child and the other from an animal.

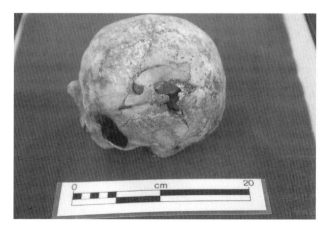

Fig 73 Skull bearing healed weapon injury

SMC 99 Context 291: South Aisle Bay 2 (chapel)
Pathology: male 30-40 years old with a healed weapon injury to the left parietal. The injury exhibits evidence of blade injury; depression fracture; missing cranial bone and cracking, radiating from the edges of the injury (Fig 73).

A smooth-edged linear defect, 90mm in length, runs from the frontal bone (14mm anterior to the coronal suture), 15mm superior to the temporal squama and extending to 70mm anterior to the lambdoid suture. A wide 'V' shaped cleft with a crack extending to the lambdoid suture is visible. The lateral view indicates that a large triangular fragment of bone inferior to the blade injury is missing. The area of missing bone is 16mm deep and 11mm wide, tapering to a point posterior to the temporal bone. A crack, curving posteriorly and extending to the temporal suture, just superior to the mastoid process, extends from the base of the missing bone.

At its highest point, 40mm superior to the blade defect, there is a smooth-edged arc-shaped defect, evidence of a depressed healed fracture. The fracture some 55mm in length runs from the coronal suture, posteriorly. The anterior external surface between the curved fracture and the blade injury displays a definite flattening. In addition, there is a large area of bone missing between it and the blade injury. The superior edge of the defect and internal areas of the skull display small white concretions which are post-mortem and are related to burial conditions. Internally, two sinuous cracks are visible. One (*c*15mm in length) corresponds to the highest portion of the arc of the depressed fracture. The other, bounded by the coronal suture, runs *c*10mm anteriorly from the suture. Otherwise, the internal surface of the skull appears to be normal.

An intact portion of bone, running some 55mm in length from the coronal suture, is present between the two injuries. The inferior border of this bone is solidly united to the blade injury. The middle and posterior portion of the superior surface displays an extension of new bone with multiple small foramina, fused to the lower edge of the flattened depressed bone. A roughly circular area (diameter 12mm) of absent bone is visible just posterior to the coronal suture.

The linear nature of the lower defect is evidence of a blade injury. The 'rounding off' and the smooth edges of the defect as well as new bone formation is clear evidence that healing has taken place and the injuries were not fatal. The nature of the linear defect suggests that two blows may have been delivered. One from an assailant facing the victim: wielding a blade sweeping downwards cutting into the left side of the skull vault. This injury is represented by the horizontal healed smooth-edged defect, directly behind the frontal bone and above the temporal bone. A second blow, downwards and administered from behind has caused the depressed fracture and flattening of the left parietal as well as the posterior linear defect, cracking and triangular area of missing bone.

Both blows have resulted in quite a wide linear defect suggesting that the weapon was a heavy sword or an axe. The extensive cracking, seen laterally and posteriorly to linear defects, as well as a triangular area of missing bone, also favour a heavy sword or axe injury. The greatest flattening and maximum depression, as well as internal cracking, occurs at the anterior portion of the depressed fracture. This supports the view that the blow was administered from behind, the greater momentum of the blade being the further from the assailant has caused the greater injury anteriorly.

There is no evidence that he was wearing a metal helm which might have buckled and caused even more serious cranial injury. However, the use of sword or axe, as well as the location of the injury, strongly suggests a battle victim rather than one of a minor brawl or dispute (Courville 1965). The fact that he has survived without any evident infection suggests that perhaps he was injured in the early stage of the battle while the weapons were still relatively clean. Then, staggering around, with blood pouring from the serious injury, it is possible that a second blow from behind felled him. No longer a threat, he would be left for dead. After the battle he was found to be still alive and was rescued by his comrades or by camp followers.

Other examples of medieval blade injuries with evidence of healing are known from Chelmsford, Ipswich, Norwich and York (Brothwell & Browne 1994, Fig 162c & 164; Boylston 2000; Dawes & Magilton 1980, 56, Plates VIIId-e; Mays 1991, 46-48; Stirland 1996). High frequencies appear to occur in urban centres. At St Helen's, York, four males presented with evidence of sword injuries, all showing some evidence of healing (Dawes & Magilton 1980, 56). At Jewbury, also in York, two females and a male displayed healed weapon injuries and two males apparently suffered fatal blade trauma (Brothwell & Browne 1994). At Ipswich, three adult males display weapon injuries, including a healed blade injury (4cm in length) in a similar location to the present example (Mays 1991, 46-48).

The cemetery of St Margaret in Combusto, Norwich, which was used to bury parishioners and hanged felons, contains ten cases of cranial trauma; eight show evidence of healing (Stirland 1996). The most extensive healed injury, in a similar location to our specimen, occurred in an adult male (*ibid*). A large linear defect with evidence of depression extends across the left side of the skull and circular

penetrating wounds are also demonstrable (*ibid*, Fig 4).

In the present case, based on the fact that cranial bone remodels slowly, it appears that the victim has survived for many years. As the estimated age at death was 30-40 years, it is possible that he survived for up to twenty years. As such, complications such as severe internal bleeding or meningitis, which would cause death within a few days, had been avoided (Courville & Kade 1964). A clean glancing blow without deep internal penetration would be less serious than a deep, penetrative puncture wound or blunt trauma with severe depression and comminution of bone fragments, the latter being more likely to result in neurological deficit. However, the force of the blows, leading to depression of the bone and internal cracking of the skull, may have caused episodes of Jacksonian epilepsy (Dr Ian Hodgins, *pers comm*), a condition in which, initially, localised loss of sensation and convulsions occur. The symptoms may spread and involve one side of the body or become generalised with subsequent loss of consciousness.

There is no evidence that surgical intervention occurred in the present case. A bone reaction in the vicinity of a sword cut has been interpreted as possible evidence for attempted cranial surgery at Jewbury (Brothwell & Browne 1994, 485). Theoderic an Italian surgeon, writing in the thirteenth century describes surgical operation for cranial fracture:

> . . . *having stopped up the ears of the patient with cotton in order that he should not be bothered by the sound of scraping or perforation or by the hammer blow, if any fragment of bone has been separated, let it be removed; if it should be about to separate, let it be scraped off, or, if it should be convenient, let the removal of bone be done as gently as possible with a hammer and iron instruments, with the physician using all possible ingenuity* (Campbell & Colton 1955, 124).

Roger of Parma's Surgery (1180) was translated into Anglo-Norman prose in thirteenth-century England (Hunt 1992, xiii). It displays removal of cranial bone by combined use of surgical trephination and chiselling, secondary to cranial fissure (Hunt 1992, 14-15). Guy de Chauliac, a fourteenth-century French surgeon to the Papal household at Avignon, follows Theoderic's view that before surgery the patient's ears should be stopped up with wool or cotton (Ogden 1971, 249). His work, translated into Middle English in the fifteenth century, also indicates that even if the bone is solid it can be removed by making numerous trephinations around the edge (Ogden 1971, 249). However, he does state that almost all English medical men prefer conservative treatment, consolidating the injury by binding it (*ibid*, 238).

An area of bone is certainly absent. However, there is no evidence of surgical cut marks or trephinations. Even leading Italian surgeons regarded herbal remedies and prayer to God as preferable to surgery (Campbell & Colton 1955, 110-114). Theoderic (*ibid*, 118, 122, 124) and later Bertapaglia, in the fifteenth century, advocate removal of bone if it is driven into the skull (Ladenheim 1989, 57, 63). Certainly, prior to the understanding of asepsis, any surgery would be more likely to be fatal than beneficial. As such, coupled with the fact that we are dealing with a blade injury, it appears that the bone was detached by the trauma rather than removed surgically.

SMC 99 Context 291: South Aisle Bay 2 (chapel)
Anatomical Variant: A damaged, additional cervical rib was fused to the first right thoracic rib. This is an example of cranial shifting of the cervico-thoracic border (Barnes 1994, Fig 3.31). It is an uncommon finding; in a study of 559 skeletons lumbar ribs (caudal shifting) were found to be eight times more frequent than cervical (Lanier 1944). The fusion of

the supernumerary element has led to the formation of a bone with two distinct heads, a so-called bicipital rib. A large radiographic sample (n40,000) revealed an incidence of 0.115% (n46) for bicipital ribs (Etter, 1944). More recent surveys are in agreement with this finding (Moore *et al* 1988; Singh 1973). British archaeological examples of bicipital ribs are known from Bronze Age Kent (Anderson forthcoming), Anglo-Saxon Brackmills (Anderson in press?), medieval York (Stroud 1993, Table 37) and post-medieval London (Black & Scheuer 1997).

There is evidence that cervical ribs contain a genetic component and are familial (Purves & Wedin 1950; Weston 1956). It is well known that they may give rise to neurological and vascular problems (Barnes 1994, 101; Brannon 1963; Gladstone & Wakeley 1932). Large ribs, as here (Barnes class IV), may cause displacement and compression of the subclavian artery, which may affect the blood supply to the upper limb, leading to discolouration of the skin (cyanosis) as well as coldness of the hand (Black & Scheuer 1997). In extreme cases limb asymmetry may be demonstrable (Finnegan 1976) and digital gangrene may develop.

7 Summary and Discussion

Pre-conquest Occupation

The documented Saxon church and monastery endowed by Leofric and Godiva and the enigma of the Osburga tradition are subjects which have provoked debate for as long as the origins of the city have been discussed. The first real opportunity to formulate an archaeological approach to these issues was presented in the 1960s when the site was subjected to excavation on a significant scale. A principal objective of these earlier excavations was to uncover evidence of late Saxon occupation; an objective unfulfilled. The Phoenix Initiative scheme has enabled excavation on a much larger scale producing evidence that the site was indeed occupied in this period. However, whilst the evidence is hugely significant, it remains difficult to interpret.

Skeletal material, recovered from both *in situ* and *ex situ* contexts, has been radiocarbon-dated to the late ninth and tenth centuries, thus pre-dating the dedication of the reliably-documented monastic house in 1043. As such it forms the earliest evidence for the occupation of both the site and of the city of Coventry. Disarticulated human bones present in the grave fill of the tenth-century burial would appear to indicate that it disturbed an earlier grave on the site. The east-west orientation of the grave is indicative of a Christian burial.

Whilst burial over an extended period of time is suggestive of nearby occupation, unequivocal evidence for a pre-Conquest structure remains limited. Based upon the excavated evidence, the stone-built features located beneath the north aisle of the medieval cathedral and the adjacent south cloister arcade could both be vestiges of the late Saxon monastic house. In both instances the remains are sandwiched stratigraphically between pre-Conquest human remains and the fabric of the medieval architecture. Neither, however, can be clearly identified with a specific architectural feature, although the remains below the nave do incorporate part of a distinctive arc of stonework. In both cases their construction could conceivably date from the early medieval period.

More convincing evidence for an early structure somewhere in the vicinity was the discovery of a block of Anglo-Saxon architectural stonework found *ex situ* north of the cloister. This incorporates a semi-circular arch, perhaps part of a small aperture or even part of a narrow arcade as found in the upper tower of All Saint's Church, Earls Barton (Audouy *et al*, 1995, Fig 4). It is decorated with a cross, suggesting that it was once part of an ecclesiastical building and is stylistically consistent with what one might expect of the early monastic house of Godiva's time. It is only the second architectural fragment found in the city to be dated to this period, the other being part of a tenth-century door jamb found close by in Palmer Lane (Hobley 1971, Plate 37).

Other pre-Conquest finds were all found in residual contexts; a sherd of Romano-British pottery and one of early to mid-Saxon date, a gold coin of Alfred the Great and a silver coin of the House of Constantine. All are of intrinsic interest but could easily have been imported onto the site and do little to illuminate the nature of early settlement, be it ecclesiastical or secular.

The pre-Conquest finds from the site are a significant addition to the otherwise limited evidence for late Saxon occupation in Coventry. The pre-existing evidence is largely comprised of spot finds – not evidence of settlement. The exception is a small assemblage of building materials – all of which were found close to the site of the priory. One of these is the aforementioned tenth-century door jamb found within 100m of the priory to the west in Palmer Lane. Over thirty complete Saxon floor and wall tiles have also been recovered from excavations in Broadgate to the south-east (Rylatt & Stokes 1996, 100) and from the site now occupied by Pool Meadow bus station to the north of the conventual buildings. All of these finds could quite conceivably have been part of a late Saxon foundation.

A holistic examination of the evidence leaves little doubt that the site was occupied in the pre-Conquest period and that this most likely took the form of ecclesiastical buildings. The extent, appearance and exact location of these remain unclear. This, perhaps, is not surprising given that the hillside upon which they presumably lay was subsequently extensively terraced to accommodate the medieval cathedral and monastic house. Any earlier structures occupying this space would presumably been demolished and archaeological evidence of their existence at best severely limited, at worst removed. Documentary sources indicate that the early monastery was damaged on three separate occasions; firstly by Peter, Bishop of Chester in the late eleventh century, secondly during the siege of the Earl's castle in 1143 and thirdly by Bishop de Nonant who is said to have destroyed the conventual buildings in 1189. In light of this the search for indisputable evidence for the late Saxon church and house may be in vain – at least unless the opportunity arises to examine the east end of the Romanesque cathedral in the future.

The Construction of the Medieval Cathedral and Priory

The construction of the cathedral was evidently well underway by the early part of the twelfth century, beginning with the chancel and progressing westwards. The earliest diagnostic architectural features identified as a result of the excavations are the bases of the Romanesque crossing piers and the most easterly of the north aisle piers, dated to the period c1115-1140. It is assumed that much of the east end was completed by this date, work having started shortly after Bishop Robert de Limesey moved his See to Coventry in 1102. The west front, visible since it was uncovered during the renovations of the Blue Coat school in 1856-7, has long been assigned a date of c1220. This is borne out by the evidence retrieved from the western-most bay of the nave. It would therefore be reasonable to consider a period of construction, from inception to full completion, of c125 years and exhibiting a stylistic change from Romanesque to Early English Gothic.

The archaeology, coupled with documentary evidence, indicates that the building programme was far from seamless and suffered repeated interruption and occasional setback. Work was halted in the mid-twelfth century when the site was fortified and apparently used as part of a siege work. The ditch found running below the foundations of pier 2 of the unfinished north arcade provides, for the first time, physical corroboration for the fortification of the cathedral. Only the eastern portion of the nave was completed at the time. When peace returned, work resumed but alterations to the foundations of five piers of the north arcade indicate problems with setting out, ostensibly caused by the broken nature of the ground upon which they stood. Further interruption was probably brought about when Bishop de Nonant expelled the monks in 1189,

though demolitions undertaken at this time are recorded as afflicting the conventual buildings rather than the cathedral itself.

Establishing what exactly Nonant demolished is problematic. Before the start of the excavations it was assumed that the conventual buildings would have been built in concert with the cathedral with work beginning in the early to mid-twelfth century. The architectural evidence does not, however, bear this out as the earliest *in situ* features found are of the same style and date as the west front of the cathedral i.e. c1220. Only a handful of loose architectural stones of a Romanesque style were recovered from the site of the conventual buildings and most of these are of uncertain provenance. Whilst it remains a possibility that 'plain' elements of the main walls were built earlier, there is an unquestionable lack of clear evidence for a universal Romanesque building programme in the claustral ranges.

Of all the conventual buildings examined, only the dormitory undercroft appears to have retained visible Romanesque fabric at the time of the Dissolution. A fragment of a multi-scalloped capital characteristic of late Romanesque architecture was found in the 1960s and matches with *in situ* piers recorded on the site of the dormitory undercroft in the late nineteenth century (Hobley 1971, 20, fig 20, plate 27). A large proportion of the loose Romanesque fragments recovered during the Phoenix Initiative excavations were found in the neighbouring undercrofts to the south and could easily have originated from the dormitory undercroft. It is interesting to note that the south wall of the dormitory is built on a slightly different alignment to those of the undercrofts, perhaps reflecting an earlier building plan.

Other than the dormitory undercroft, the only other building that exhibits possible Romanesque fabric is the chapter house and here only at foundation level. The excavations of the 1960's appear to have revealed a semi-circular foundation running below its polygonal east end; possibly the relic of an earlier curved apse – a trait of the Romanesque period (Morris 1994, 42-44).

Given the chequered history of the monastic house in the twelfth century it is possible that a few buildings in the Romanesque style briefly co-existed with what was, in essence, the late Saxon foundation. The archaeology of the cathedral indicates that the terracing of the site was done in stages dictated by the pace of the building work. With work on the cathedral taking precedence over the monastic house, terracing and demolitions of pre-existing buildings could have taken place quite late on in the twelfth century. The scale of Nonant's demolitions is not known but would presumably have slighted existing buildings and set back the completion of others. What is clear is that by the early thirteenth century, a degree of architectural uniformity had been achieved with the Early English Gothic being the predominant style.

An Architectural Canon

Despite the problems which appear to have beset the construction of the cathedral and monastic house, together with the changes in architectural styles that spanned the period, the excavations have provided evidence that a degree of site planning may have been implemented. A mathematical formula, chiefly the medieval architects favourite tool of 'one to the square root of two' or 1:1.41, was used (with some degree of tolerance) to set out some of the main elements of the complex (see Gallacher (1994) for a full, recent exposition of this formula).

The following juxtaposition of figures shows how this relationship occurs on the excavated areas of church and cloister.

Garth diagonal (32m/105ft):west range and cloister including wall widths (45m/147½ft) = **1:1.41**

Nave length (59m/193½ft):cloister and west range internal measurement (41m/134½) = **1:1.43**

Cloister diagonal (42m/138ft):nave length (59m/193½ft) = **1:1.40**

The original Romanesque bay-division (centre to centre) was 6.2m/20ft.

If a 3:4:5 right-angled triangle had formed the nave bay layout (set out on pier centres) then the formula of $a^2+b^2=c^2$ would mean that the measurements ought to be:

- Bay division 6.2m/20ft
- Nave width 9.2m/30ft
- Diagonal 10.9m/36ft

In fact the true figures on the ground are:

- Bay division 6.2m/20ft
- Nave width 11m/36ft
- Diagonal 12.5m/41ft

This means that the hypotenuse of this basic 3:4:5 triangle for laying out has been stretched by a ratio of **1:1.41**.

Furthermore, the following areas of proportional correlation have been noted

Church width = chapter house length = Garth (north-south) side (21m/69ft)

Garth diagonal = north cloister alley length (32m/105ft)

North transept width (15.5m/51ft) is half the south cloister alley length (31m/102ft)

North cloister alley length (32m/105ft) is half the distance of west end of cathedral to centre point of crossing (64m/210ft)

If the overall plan of the cathedral and cloister were laid out to a formula intended for the Romanesque style of the twelfth century it would imply that Early English architectural elements, such as the west end of the cathedral, were merely late completions built in pre-ordained positions. This is contrary to the previous assumption that the west end as it survives is an extension to an earlier plan. The excavations have proven that this was not the case; there never was an earlier west end lying one or two bays east of its eventual position. The Romanesque building programme would, therefore, have simply stopped at pier 2; possibly as a result of the intervention of Bishop Nonant in 1189. When construction resumed it may have adhered to the Romanesque planning module but utilised a new architectural order.

The extent to which overall planning was implemented becomes less clear when the conventual buildings are considered. As has been discussed above, there is a high degree of ambiguity surrounding the nature and extent of the Romanesque monastic house. Excavations have shown that the medieval claustral ranges were probably not completed until the early thirteenth century. This date mirrors that of the cathedral's west end and, similarly, may indicate a late completion built according to the Romanesque plan.

There is, however, an alternative explanation for the proportional relationship observed between elements of the cathedral and claustral ranges. The figures could conceivably have arisen from the conventual buildings being 'surveyed off' completed parts of the cathedral and not as a result of a pre-ordained universal plan. This too would result in a close degree of correlation between key measurements. Given the lack of archaeological evidence for a complete Romanesque house and the historical accounts of destruction being visited upon the priory throughout the twelfth century this interpretation must be given consideration.

Structural Development

As has been discussed, the construction of both cathedral and conventual buildings appears to have been completed by the early/mid-thirteenth century. Early English Gothic appears to have been the principal architectural style of the monastic house at this time with the Romanesque evident in only the cathedral and possibly the chapter house and dormitory. From such beginnings, the cathedral and priory were subjected to a virtually unrelenting series of re-orderings, demolitions and re-buildings.

By 1300 changes had been made to the configuration of buildings north of the chapter house. By 1330 a new chapter house had been built and this was soon followed by a major campaign of works in the refectory and its undercroft. The fourteenth century also saw alterations made to the cathedral crossing, with a possible tower re-build taking place in the first half of the century, followed by the replacement of its vault. A programme of refenestration in the Perpendicular style appears to have begun in the cathedral by the end of the century.

The cloister was modernised in the Perpendicular style with the introduction of elaborate tracery for a glazed arcade and blind arcade cladding for the surrounding walls. This was begun at end of the fourteenth century or in the early fifteenth century. It was around this time that the chevet chapels of the cathedral's east end are thought to have been added (Morris 1994, 31-34).

The pace of modernisation appears to have decreased somewhat by the middle of the fifteenth century and from that point onwards, until the Dissolution, the character of the structural alterations changed. The complete assemblage of architectural stones indicates that no works of major significance took place within this period. Partitioning of internal space within the undercrofts was, however, widespread.

Catalysts for Development

The question of what provided the impetus for architectural change is a difficult one to answer through archaeology alone. The possibilities are diverse and include reforms to the Benedictine Order, Episcopal pressure, ambitions of an individual prior, prevailing architectural style, patronage, competition and catastrophe. Each could have contributed towards structural expansion, contraction or alteration and operated either in isolation or in combination with another. For a concordance of historical and archaeological evidence, highlighting the difficulties in associating architectural change with documented events see Appendix 2.

Function of Rooms & Buildings

Apart from the obvious areas of the cathedral, cloister and chapter house it has been very difficult to identify the function of individual rooms through archaeological excavation alone. Other than the walls of the chapter house and a small room in the west range all the other claustral buildings were represented only by their rubble-filled undercrofts. Thus the identification of the cloister-level buildings has largely been based upon comparison with other Benedictine houses and supported by diagnostic architectural stones found in the rubble. As such, a number of areas of uncertainty remain open to interpretation; most notably the group of buildings located north of the chapter house.

The north-south undercroft in this location was the only room found with a fireplace, a characteristic which has led to the suggestion that this may have been a monastic warming room. There was no evidence, in the form of architectural stonework in the demolition rubble, to suggest that another fireplace was present in the room above. In fact, the configuration, appearance and function of the rooms above both this and the adjoining east-west undercroft remain unknown. The possibility that the room over the north-south undercroft was a wing of the neighbouring dormitory has been considered, although no parallels for this arrangement have been found. Parlours, common rooms, muniment rooms and libraries are alternative suggestions.

Another area of uncertainty concerns the location of the main storage area or *cellarium*, usually found at ground floor level of the west range. Stonework indicative of a building of unexpectedly high status was found filling the northern undercroft of the west range and the door jambs for the ground floor structure were of a quality commensurate with those of the west end of the cathedral and the doorway connecting the nave to the cloister. This evidence is difficult to reconcile with a simple storage area and it is suggested that the Prior's lodging may well have occupied the west range's ground floor at cloister level and possibly a first floor above. Associated chambers, maybe for guest accommodation may also have been present. The undercrofts below the west range probably had a storage capacity but it is unlikely that bulky items were constantly manhandled down the steep flight of steps needed to gain access to them. For this reason, it is thought that the traditional cellarer's range probably lay below the refectory, a location more easily accessible from ground level to the north and near to the kitchen.

The building identified as the kitchen in Hobley's excavation report is somewhat smaller than would be expected for a house of this size but it remains a possibility that another kitchen, perhaps for the preparation of meat dishes lay elsewhere. Meat kitchens are commonly found attached to infirmaries and this arrangement cannot be ruled out at St Mary's where a number of separate rooms appear to have been present in the vicinity of the infirmary.

Cathedral Access and Use of Internal Space

In addition to the great west door of the cathedral a further four points of entry were located. An entrance contemporary with the original Romanesque build was found in the cathedral's south wall opening into bay 6 of the south aisle. This doorway was subsequently blocked and the southern entrance moved westward into bay 3 of the south aisle. The blocking of Romanesque entrances could be associated with the siege-work of 1143; indeed any entrance in the south wall would have faced the besieged castle. The 'new' entrance in bay 3 opposes the north door of Holy Trinity Church which was built in the second half of the thirteenth century. This may have been an important factor as documentary sources indicate that the south door was used for processions. The dating of these alterations is unclear. Architectural stonework found below the steps from the 'new' doorway into bay 3 has been dated to no earlier than *c*1325. This provides a *terminus post quem* for the steps but does not help to date the construction of the 'new' doorway.

A small doorway was located in the west end, opening into bay 1 of the north aisle. This may have provided the clergy with a more convenient day to day entrance to the cathedral rather than having to repeatedly open the great west door. Another doorway gave access to the cloister from bay 5 of the north aisle. This was presumably used only by the monastic community and kept locked at times of public ceremony.

Whilst there was some evidence for a sandstone-flagged floor in the earliest part of the nave (in the vicinity of north aisle pier 8), there was little trace of the original floor elsewhere. A very worn tiled floor of the fourteenth century appears to have covered most of the nave at the time of the Dissolution. Sections of this floor were arranged to form a processional route. It is evident that two parallel lines of coloured tiles once ran longitudinally down the centre of the nave leading from the foot of the steps at the west entrance towards the altar.

The extensive robbing of the nave left little to indicate the former presence of monuments. Burials were, however, commonly found below the arches of the aisle arcades; slots found in the base of pier 6 of the south arcade may betray the presence of a tomb in this location. A large monument may also have been located in bay 8 of the north arcade. A number of chantry chapels are recorded in documentary sources. One of them was located in bay 2 of the south aisle where its collapsed vault was found overlying the remains of a wall monument and a number of robbed graves. It is suggested that this may be the Copstone Chantry of 1291 mentioned by Dugdale (*Dugdale Warks*. 165). The locations of the other chantries remain unknown.

Subsistence and Economy

Faunal and botanical evidence has helped to identify some of the produce the monastic community was consuming. As would be expected for a priory of St Mary's status, the monks were provided with a comparatively rich diet. In divergence from the Rule of St Benedict, meats from domesticated livestock were consumed in large quantities and, to a lesser extent, game and wild birds. Fish also featured significantly in their diet with freshwater species being more widely consumed than marine; perhaps unsurprising given the ample stocks available from their own local sources such the River Sherbourne, Pool Meadow and the Swanswell Pool and also outlying estates. Grains from different types of wheat suitable for bread and biscuit making were found along with rye. Arable crops were evidently supplemented by a range of fruits, nuts and edible seeds.

Many of these resources could have been supplied directly from the priory's immediate hinterland. In addition to owning a significant portion of the city, St Mary's controlled large tracts of land in the locality including various countryside estates and a number of manors. At least one game park, at Whitmore, just outside the city, belonged to the priory from at least *c*1380 (Iain Soden, *pers comm*). Tithes were also extracted from the many parishes ceded to it. Much of the fruit consumed could have been grown in the orchards which were attached to the priory site. The environmental evidence indicates well-established farming economies with solid surpluses of young animals and efficient methods of crop husbandry.

Late Monastic Decline

Archaeological evidence taken from across the site indicates that the priory was experiencing a period of general decline for some time before the Dissolution. As previously mentioned, there appears to have been little improvement to the fabric of the buildings after the mid-fifteenth century. Certain elements of their fabric, such as the tiled floor of the nave, appear to have been very worn by 1539. In other places, such as the courtyard, alterations appear to have been undertaken with little regard for aesthetics and it is also possible that some of the undercrofts had ceased to be used by this time.

This trend was mirrored by a general economic deterioration in the City which also began in the mid-fifteenth century. The woollen-cloth trade, vital to the city's prosperity since the late twelfth century, had begun to decline. By 1523 Coventry is recorded as having 565 empty houses, a reflection of the extent of the economic down-turn (Rylatt 1977, 18).

In the final months of monastic occupation, the psychological effect of the impending Dissolution can only be imagined. The lesser houses had already been suppressed and a new, possibly complicit Prior had been appointed in March 1538 (Scarisbrick 1994, 163; Lambert 1971, 76). Finances would have been tight at the time as the whole of the new Prior's first-year's income was owed to the Crown as a 'first fruit' – a measure introduced in the wake of the Act of Supremacy of 1534. An ensuing wave of despair may have led to a lapse in the disciplined monastic lifestyle. Food waste present in the final occupation layers of some of the undercrofts could be an indication of a relaxation in cleanliness. The pottery assemblages from these layers also contained a large number of sherds from drinking vessels – perhaps an indication that the monks were taking solace in the bottle!

The Dissolution

The monastery was surrendered on the 15th January 1539 and whilst easily-portable, valuable commodities were quickly removed or hidden from the authorities, it is clear from both the excavated evidence and documentary sources that dismantling on a large scale did not begin immediately. Where the initial slighting of the conventual buildings was evident, the robbing of floor tiles was the first detectable act of the Dissolution. The removal of lead from windows and presumably the roofs, conduits and pipes also appears to have been undertaken at an early stage. Evidence for on-site smelting, and possibly casting, was found in the north-south undercroft north of the chapter house. This room was most probably chosen because of its fireplace, which also appears to have been used to burn books and manuscripts. Stratigraphic evidence suggests that these activities were all undertaken immediately after the monastic community had been expelled.

Efforts to save the cathedral may have resulted in a lesser degree of initial exploitation. In July 1539 the city recorder (town clerk) wrote to Cromwell imploring him to stop the officials who had come to Coventry to oversee its demolition (Scarisbrick 1994, 165). His efforts were apparently successful because when, in 1545, the site of the priory was sold to agents of John Hales, the fabric of the cathedral and monastic house was reserved for the Crown. Previous commentaries have interpreted this as evidence for the relatively intact state of the

buildings some six years after the Dissolution – a conclusion supported by archaeological evidence for squatters occupying some of the abandoned buildings prior to wholesale demolition. This may have occurred despite the best efforts of the authorities to secure the buildings against trespass (*ibid*, 160-1).

The windows of the nave, and possibly the chapter house, may have been smashed during acts of wanton vandalism. Also in the nave there was evidence of grave robbing, although this could have taken place after the majority of the cathedral had been dismantled. These activities were, however, short-lived and after the site had been sold to Hales it would appear that the buildings were rapidly dismantled.

This process was well organised and executed in a reasonably controlled manner with dismantling evidently favoured over wholesale demolition. Only in a couple of instances was structural collapse evident, be it controlled or accidental. This resulted in deep, inaccessible deposits of rubble. A more considered approach was generally taken with stones suitable for re-use systematically removed from the site – very few ashlar blocks were found in post-Dissolution contexts. The earthen ramp over the steps in the west end of the cathedral and the cart ruts cut in the nave floor are indicative of one of the routes used to export the stone. The cloister garth appears to have been used as a yard where stone was collected and prepared for re-use.

Following the initial programme of destruction, stone continued to be removed from the site for some time. After the death of John Hales in 1572 the Corporation acquired the land and documentary sources indicate that the sale of stone was still providing revenue at this time (Demidowicz 2000, 9-11). In 1581, a survey of the Corporation's property was made and the buildings standing on the priory site were listed as a dye house, the priory mill and a gate house and there was also stone from the church and a 'steeple' (*ibid*, 11). Ruinous buildings were, however, omitted from the survey, most notable of which in 1581 were the towers of the west end. The south-west tower was evidently standing in 1654 and the north-west tower had been converted into Dr Bryan's dwelling by the mid-1650's and was later incorporated into Blue Coat School in the 1850's (*ibid*, 24-26).

By the end of the sixteenth century parts of the site, principally the nave, were being used for rubbish disposal and in the early seventeenth century it is recorded that animals were being fed amongst the rubble (Reader 1823, 140). The pottery assemblage recovered from the rubble suggests that the nave continued to be picked over for stone well into the seventeenth century.

Themes For Future Research

Areas of Archaeological Potential

Much of the remaining unexplored archaeology of the site lies in pockets east of Hill Top. However, many of these areas are unlikely to be made available for research in the near future. The positions of the quire and presbytery lie partially below 7-11 Priory Row; Grade II listed buildings. A detailed survey of their cellars would be required to assess the potential of remains below. Hill Top, the pedestrian route linking Priory Row and Fairfax Street, runs over the transepts, the chapter house apse and the intersection of the infirmary with the undercrofts and courtyard. Exploration below the surface would be of great value but complicated by the tangle of services and sewers which follow its route. Furthermore, excavations would need to be deep – a difficult undertaking in the prevailing narrow confines. Elsewhere, any opportunity to re-visit the cloister garth and the cathedral forecourt may serve to clarify residual ambiguities.

The early origins of the site are still far from clear. For this reason any opportunity for exploration in the vicinity of the pre-cathedral remains should be seized. Away from the priory buildings themselves, if future development should affect the site of Holy Trinity Church, excavation strategy should be focused upon the earliest detectable phase of occupation in addition to exploring the church's complicated development.

The supply of water to the site is an issue which could be greater illuminated by a combination of excavation and documentary research, as is the extent of the priory precinct. Medieval land-use in and around the priory, especially north of the River Sherbourne could also be studied through systematic environmental sampling of available sites.

Historical Research

A general re-appraisal of the key historical sources would be of great value, particularly for clarifying the earliest events in Coventry's history. St Osburga's links with the city are persistent, but as yet unfounded, and any concerted effort to ascertain documented facts concerning her life would be of merit.

As mentioned above, documentary research into land ownership in the vicinity of the priory may shed light upon the extent of the precinct and land usage in the surrounding area. Knowledge of the monastic water supply could also be broadened through documentary research.

Archived Material

Certain archived materials have not received the attention warranted by their significance and are worthy of future research. A full appraisal of the architectural stonework is required if the full potential of this resource is to be realised for a wider academic community beyond the purely archaeological. Also worthy of particular attention are the large assemblages of stained and painted glass fragments recovered from the west end of the cathedral and the chapter house. Those from the chapter house should be studied in conjunction with the many hundreds of fragments recovered from the same location during the excavations of the 1960s.

Much of the material excavated from post-Dissolution contexts across the site, largely omitted from the finds reports, might benefit from further analysis. A number of post-medieval structures were excavated and recorded during the archaeological programme but do not appear in this report. They include the post-seventeenth-century Priory Mill, the boiler room for the nineteenth-century Ribbon Factory, parts of the Factory itself and another boiler room for a Victorian vinery. The field records for these interesting vestiges of industrial archaeology are part of the Priory Archive.

Osteological analysis of a sample of 100 skeletons excavated from Holy Trinity's eighteenth/nineteenth-century graveyard is being undertaken by Dr Jenny Wakely and colleagues from the University of Leicester. An interim report (in archive) has outlined a number of fascinating pathologies which include trauma, infection, disease and early examples of post-mortems. When completed, it is hoped the study will provide an invaluable corpus of information regarding the lives and deaths of the populace of eighteenth/nineteenth-century Coventry.

Glossary

Annulet – a ring around a circular pier or shaft

Apse – the semicircular or polygonal end to a chancel or chapel

Arcade – a series of arches supported by piers or columns

Aumbry – a cupboard within a wall, usually for sacred vessels

Capital – the head of a column or pier

Chapter House – the building attached to a cathedral, collegiate church or religious house in which the chapter meets

Chamfer – the narrow, flat surface formed when the corner of a block of stone or timber is cut away

Chantry – a chapel, often attached or screened off inside a church, endowed for the celebration of masses principally for the peace of the founder's soul

Chevet French – term for the east end of a church with chancel, ambulatory and radiating chapels

Claustral – like, or characteristic of a cloister

Conventual – belonging to, or characteristic of a convent

Corbel – a projecting block of stone of timber to support a feature above

Corrodian – a lay person maintained by a monastic house at the behest of a third party, usually the Crown.

Decorated – Architectural style prevalent *c*1280-1360

Early English – Architectural style prevalent c1170-1280

Fother – a late medieval measure of weight used largely for the quantification of lead

Gable – the head of a wall at the end of a pitched roof, usually triangular

Groin Vault – a ceiling formed by four curving triangular stone surfaces produced by the intersection of two barrel-vaults at right angles

Hoodmould – moulding projecting above and outlining an arch, doorway or window

Jamb – the sides of a window or door frame

Lavatorium – a structure with basins or troughs for the washing of hands

Lierne – a small, decorative vault-rib connecting other ribs but not linked directly to any of the **springers**

Mullions – the vertical members dividing the lights of windows or screen openings

Patera – a round or oval ornament in shallow relief

Perpendicular – Architectural style prevalent *c*1360-1540

Piscina – a stone basin used for washing sacred vessels

Reredorter – a building containing the monastic latrines

Quadripartite – as groin vault but with four sections divided by ribs springing from each corner of the bay

Refenestration – the rearrangement of a building's window design

Respond – a half column or pier attached to a wall at the end of an arcade

Retting – the action of moistening or soaking to promote bacterial action in order to promote the separation of fibres from woody tissue by beating

Romanesque – Architectural style prevalent *c*1070-1170, also known as **Norman**

Sacristan – the person who has charge of the contents of a church, also known as **sacrist** or **sexton**

Shaft – vertical member of round or polygonal section

Spandrel – the roughly triangular space between an arch and its rectangular frame or between adjacent arches

Springer – the first stone of an arch or vaulting rib above the level from which it rises from its support

Squint – an aperture pierced through a wall, usually to allow a view of an altar

Stew – a fishpond or artificial tank for holding fish

Stoup – a receptacle to contain holy water, often in the form of a deeply-dished stone set in a niche or on a pillar near a doorway

Tracery – the open stonework used in the upper part of gothic windows or carved in relief (blind) in vaults, arcades etc

Tierceron – extra, decorative rib springing from the corners of a vault bay

Undercroft – an underground chamber often with a vaulted ceiling

Vault – a ceiling of stone

Appendices

Appendix 2 – Concordance of Events

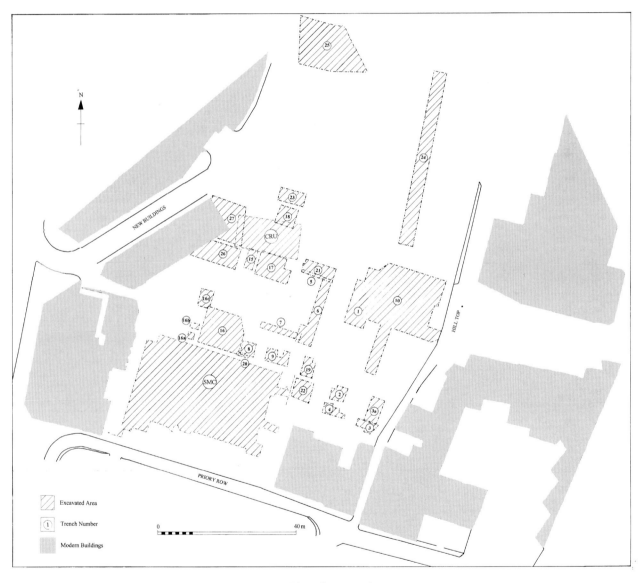

Fig 74   *Plan of excavated areas*

Appendix 2 – Concordance of Events

DATE RANGE	ARCHAEOLOGICAL/ARCHITECTURAL DEVELOPMENT	HISTORICAL EVENTS	PRIORATE
pre-1000	*c*870 radiocarbon date for skull fragment below pier 6	Osburga mentioned in works of Aldhelm,	
	886 issue date of coin of Alfred the Great found *ex situ*	Bishop of Sherbourne d.709	
	900-1000 radiocarbon date for burial 1913 below cloister		
1000-49		1016 tradition of sacking of Osburga's	1045 Leofwine
		nunnery	(Abbot)
		1043 consecration of abbey church	
1050-99		1057 death of Leofric	Leofric (Abbot)
		1066 Norman invasion	c 1070-94 Leofwine II
		1067 death of Godiva	(Abbot)
		Peter, Bishop of Chester destroys	Burwyng?
		monks houses sometime between 1072	Herwey?
		and 1085 (Glover & Gibson 1979, 110-113)	Leasstan?
1100-49	*c*1115-40 cathedral crossing built	1102 St Mary's Church gains cathedral status	Owyne?
		1113 Holy Trinity Chapel first mentioned	Stanulph?
		(*VCH warks.* 2, 321)	Richard?
		1143 cathedral used as siege-work	1139 German
		1144-48 St Michael's Chapel first mentioned	1144 Lawrence
		(*VCH warks.* 2, 346)	
1150-99	1150+ ditch below north aisle pier 2 filled in	1189-98 Nonant ejects monks and installs	1183 Moyses
	*c*1160 earliest date for construction of north aisle pier 6	canons	1199 Joybert
	c1160 earliest date for construction of north aisle vault in		
	bays 6,7&8		
1200-49	1225+ west end of cathedral completed	1234 Greyfriars founded	1216 Geoffrey
	1220-60 earliest in situ evidence for cloister	1248 Priory in danger of dispersal (Lambert	1235 Roger de Walton
	1230-60 tierceron vault at north end of west range	1971, 62)	1248 William de Brithwaulton
	earliest evidence for refectory undercroft		
	earliest evidence for undercroft north of chapter house		
1250-99	construction of 2nd undercroft north of chapter house	1257 Holy Trinity destroyed by fire - rebuild	1281 Thomas de Pavy
	1291 constuction of Copstone's chantry in nave	begins (*VCH Warks*. 8, 326)	1294 Henry de Leicester
		1267 Priory in danger of dispersal (Lambert	
		1971, 64)	
		1291 Copstone's chantry founded (Dugdale *Warks*.)	
1300-49	1300-30 chapter house re-built	1342 Whitefriars founded	1322 Henry Irreys
	cathedral central crossing tower re-built?	1349 Black Death	1342 William Irreys
	third terrace re-inforced		1349 William de Dunstable
	refectory undercroft re-vaulted		
	drain inserted into north-east corner of cloister		
1350-99	1360-70 Apocalypse painting in chapter house	1355 Tripartite Indenture	1361 William de Greneburgh
	nave and refectory floors tiled	1359 '*great winds blew down steeples*'	1390 James de Horton
	cathedral crossing/north transept re-vaulted?	(Burbidge 1952, 215)	1396 Roger Cotton
	cloister refurbished?	1360's plague	1398 Richard Crosby
	cathedral refenestrated?	1382 '*this year was an earthquake*'	
	chevet chapels added to east end of cathedral?	(Burbidge 1952, 216)	
		1385 Charterhouse founded	
		1386 'Great Plague of Coventry' (Iain Soden	
		pers comm)	
1400-49	1432-56 mill timbers replaced	1404 Lack-learning Parliament held at St Marys	1437 Richard Nottingham
	partitioning of undercrofts?	1423 Parliament held at St Mary's (Lambert 1971)	
		1426 '*September 28...began a terrific earthquake*'	
		(Burbidge 1952, 219)	
1450-99		St Michael's church completed by 1450	1443 John Shotteswell
		1450/1 King Henry VI visits priory (*VCH Warks*.	1461 Thomas Deram
		2, 57; Lambert 1971, 71)	1481 Richard Coventry
		1456/7 King Henry VI visits priory (Burbidge 1952,	
		220; Lambert 1971, 71)	
		1459 Diabolical Parliament	
		1461 Parliament in residence at Coventry	
		1461 Prior requests town wall to be diverted	
		around priory property	
		1464 King Edward IV visits priory (*VCH Warks*.	
		2, 57)	
		1474 '*a great flood*' (Burbidge 1952, 222)	
		1479 '*pestilence kills 3300*' (Burbidge 1952, 222)	
1500-49	raising of courtyard level?	1487 King Henry VII visits priory (Lambert 1971, 77)	1500 William Polesworth
		1511 King Henry VII visits priory (Lambert 1971, 77)	1516 John Impingham
		1519 '*a very wet summer*' (Burbidge 1952, 225)	1517 John Webbe
		1526 Princess Mary visits Priory (Lambert 1971, 77)	1527 Thomas Wyford
		Jan 15th 1539 Priory Dissolved	1538 Thomas Camswell
		1545 site sold into private hands	

Appendix 3

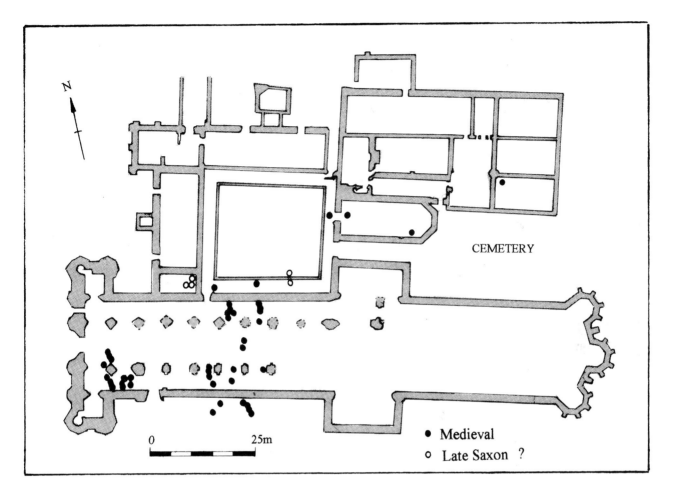

Fig 75 *Locations of late Saxon and medieval graves*

References

1. Primary Sources

Coventry Archives (CA)

Borough Archive
BA/A/1/2/3
BA/B/1/23/1
BA/B/A/25/7
BA/B/A/28/1
BA/B/5/2
BA/D/A/23/9
BA/H/C/17/2,338-9

Private Accessions
PA56/99/1
PA56/99/3
PA56/108
PA56/108/14-15
PA56/108/24-25
PA56/108/32
PA56/108/40
PA56/108/70
PA56/108/71-72
PA96/12/1
PA90/19
TC/L/1/77

Lichfield Record Office (LRO)

B/C/11

Public Record Office (PRO) [Now The National Archives]

Exchequer
E164/21
E303/16

Warwick Record Office (WRO)

County Records
CR1709/206/1
CR1709/206/6-7

2. Published Primary Sources

Clover H & Gibson M 1979, *The Letters of Lanfranc, Archbishop of Canterbury*, Clarendon, Oxford

Coss P R 1980, 'The Langley Cartulary', *Dugdale Society Publication* 32

Coss P R (ed) 1986, *The Early Records of Medieval Coventry*, Oxford University Press

Coventry Herald, 2nd May 1845

Dysinger L (trans) 1996, *The Rule of Saint Benedict*, Source, California

Harris M D 1907-12 (trans), *The Coventry Leet Book 1420-1555*, Dugdale Society Publication

Hughes J B (ed) 2001, *The Register of Bishop Walter de Langton 1296-1321* (1), Canterbury and York Society

Letters and Papers Foreign and Domestic, of Henry VIII, X, I, 1335 (51)

Letters and Papers Foreign and Domestic, of Henry VIII, XX, 1, 1335(51)

Savage H E (ed) 1924, *The Great Register of Lichfield Cathedral, known as Magnum Registrum Album*, William Salt Archaeological Society

3. Published Secondary Sources

Adams J C 1990, *Outline of Orthopaedics,* Churchill Livingstone, Edinburgh

Alcock N W 1990, 'The Catesbys in Coventry: a medieval estate and its archives', *Midland History* 15, pp 1-36

Anderson T (forthcoming), 'A Bronze Age Multiple Grave from Monkton, Thanet, Kent' in *Archaeologia Cantiana*

Armitage P L & West B 1985, 'Faunal evidence from a late medieval garden well of the Greyfriars, London', *Transactions of the London and Middlesex Archaeological Society* 36, pp 107-136

Astill G G 1993, 'A Medieval Industrial Complex & Its Landscape: the Metalworking Watermills & Workshops of Bordesley Abbey', *CBA Research Report* 92, pp 204-212

Audouy M, Dix B & Parsons D 1995, 'The Tower of All Saints' Church, Earls Barton, Northamptonshire: its construction and context', *The Archaeological Journal* 152, pp 73-94

Babington C, Manning T & Stewart S 1999, *Our Painted Past. Wall Paintings of English Heritage*, English Heritage, London

Bainbridge D & Genoves S T 1956, 'A Study of the Sex Differences in the Scapula', *Journal of the Royal Anthropological Institute* 86, pp 109-134

Barnes E 1994, *Developmental Defects of the Axial Skeleton in Paleopathology*, University Press of Colorado, Colorado

Barone R 1976, *Anatomie Comparee des Mammiferes Domestiques,* Vigot Freres Editeurs 1, Paris

Bass W M 1987, *Human Osteology: A Laboratory and Field Manual of the Human Skeleton*, Missouri Archaeological Society, Special Publication 2 (3rd edn), Columbia

Black S & Scheuer L 1997, 'The Ontogenetic Development of the Cervical Rib', *International Journal of Osteoarchaeology* 7, pp 2-10

Binski P 1995, *Westminster Abbey and the Plantagenets – Kingship and the representation of power 1200-1400*, Yale University Press, New Haven & London

Boessneck J 1969, 'Osteological Differences Between Sheep (Ovies aries Linne) and Goat (Capra hircus Linne)', in Brothwell D & Higgs E (eds) 1969, *Science in Archaeology,* pp 331-58

Bond J M & O'Connor T P 1999, 'Bones from Medieval Deposits at 16-22 Coppergate and Other Sites in York', *The Archaeology of York* 15/5, York Archaeological Trust & CBA, York

Bond J 2001, 'Production and Consumption of Food and Drink in the Medieval Monastery', in Keevill G, Aston M & Hall T (eds) 2001, *Monastic Archaeology*, Oxbow, Oxford, pp 54-87

Bond J 2001, 'Monastic Water Management in Great Britain: A Review', in Keevill G, Aston M & Hall T (eds), *Monastic Archaeology*, Oxbow, Oxford, pp 88-136

Bourdillon J M 1980, 'Town Life and Animal Husbandry in the Southampton Area as Suggested by the Excavated Bones', *Proceedings of the Hampshire Field Club Archaeology Society* 36, pp 181-91

Boylston A 2000, 'Evidence for Weapon Related Trauma in British Archaeological Samples', in Cox M & Mays S (eds) 2000, *Human Osteology in Archaeology and Forensic Science*, Greenwich Medical Media, London, pp 357-380

Brannon E W 1963, 'Cervical Rib Syndrome', *Journal of Bone and Joint Surgery* 45A, pp 977-998

Brothwell D R 1981, *Digging Up Bones*, (3rd edn), British Museum (Natural History), London

Brothwell D R & Browne S 1994, 'Pathology', in Lilley J M, Stroud G, Brothwell D R & Williamson M H 1994, *The Jewish Burial Ground at Jewbury*, York Archaeological Trust, York, pp 457-494

Burbidge F B 1952, *Old Coventry and Lady Godiva*, Cornish Brothers Ltd, Birmingham

Campbell E & Colton J 1955, *The Surgery of Theoderic*, Appelton-Century-Crofts Inc, New York

Carruthers W 1993, 'The valley environment: the evidence of the plant remains', in Astill G G 1993, *A Medieval Industrial Complex & Its Landscape: the Metalworking Watermills & Workshops of Bordesley Abbey*, CBA Research Report 92, pp 204-212

Chamberlain A 1999, 'Teaching Surgery and Breaking the Law', *British Archaeology* 48, pp 6-7

Chaplin R E 1966, 'The Animal Remains from the Well Street Site, Coventry', in Gooder E 1966, 'The walls of Coventry', *Transactions of the Birmingham and Warwickshire Archaeological Society* 81, pp 88-138

Chatwin P 1936, 'The Medieval Patterned Tiles of Warwickshire', *Transactions of the Birmingham and Warwickshire Archaeological Society* 60, pp 1-41

Cherry B 1978, 'Romanesque Architecture in Eastern England', *British Archaeological Association Journal* 131, pp 1-29

Cocke T, Findlay D, Halsey R & Williamson E 1996, *Recording a Church: An Illustrated Glossary*, Practical Handbook in Archaeology 7, CBA, York

Cohen A & Serjeantson D 1996, *A Manual to the Identification of Bird Bones from Archaeological Sites*

Conheeney J 1997, 'The Human Bone', in Thomas C, Sloane B & Philpotts C 1997, *Excavations at the Priory and Hospital of St Mary Spital, London*, MoLAS Monograph 1, London, pp 218-231

Coppack G 1990, *Abbeys and Priories*, Batsford, London

Cornwall I W 1974, *Bones for the Archaeologist*, J M Dent & Sons, London

Courville C B 1965, 'War Wounds of the Cranium in the Middle Ages as Disclosed in the Skeletal Material from the Battle of Wisby (1361 AD)', *Bulletin of the Los Angeles Neurological Society* 30, pp 27-33

Courville C B & Kade H 1965, 'Split Fractures Produced by Edged Weapons and their Accompanying Brain Wounds', *Bulletin of the Los Angeles Neurological Society* 29, pp 32-39

Cram L 1986, 'Mammal and Bird Remains', in Wright S 1986, 'Much Park St., Coventry: the development of a medieval street – Excavations 1970-1974', *Transactions of the Birmingham and Warwickshire Archaeological Society* 92, pp 106-108

Crossley D 1990, *Post-Medieval Archaeology in Britain*, Leicester University Press

Davidson C & Alexander J 1985, *The Early Art of Coventry, Stratford-upon-Avon, Warwick and Lesser Sites in Warwickshire. A Subject of List of Extant and Lost Art. Including Items Relevant to Early Drama*, Medieval Institute Publications: EDAM Reference Series 4, Western Michigan University, Kalamazoo

Dawes J D & Magilton J R 1980, 'The Cemetery of St Helen-on-the-Walls, Aldwark', *The Archaeology of York* 12/1, London

Demidowicz G (ed) 1994, *Coventry's First Cathedral*, Paul Watkins, Stamford

Demidowicz G 2000, *A History of the Blue Coat School and the Lych Gate Cottages, Coventry*, Phoenix Initiative, Coventry

Desse J, Desse-Berset N & Rocheteau M 1987, 'Contribution a l'osteometrie de la Perche (*Perca fluviatilis* Linne, 1758)', *Fiches D'Ostéologie Animale Pour L'Archaéologie* 1, Centre de Recherches Archéologiques – CNRS, France

Dickinson J C 1961, *Monastic Life in Medieval England*, Adam & Charles Black, London

Dobson R B 1990, 'Urban Decline in Late Medieval England', in Holt R & Rosser G (eds) 1990, *The Medieval Town: A Reader in English Urban History 1200-1540*, Longman, pp 265-286

von den Driesch A 1976, *A Guide to the Measurement of Animal Bones from Archaeological Sites*, Peabody Museum Bulletin 1

Dugdale W 1656 (1730 revision), *The Antiquities of Warwickshire*

Dugdale W, *Monasticon Anglicanum*

Dutra F 1944, 'Identification of Person and Determination of Cause of Death from Skeletal Remains', *Archives of Pathology* 38, pp 339-349

Dwight T 1905, 'The Size of the Auricular Surfaces of the Long Bones as Characteristics of Sex: an Anthropological Study', *American Journal of Anatomy* 4, pp 19-51

Dyson A S 1913, *History of Lutterworth*

Eames E 1980, *Medieval Lead-Glazed Earthernware Tiles*, British Museums Publications 1-2, London

Eames E 1992, *English Tilers*, British Museum Press, London

Etter L E 1944, 'Osseous abnormalities of the thoracic cage seen in forty thousand consecutive chest photoroentgenograms', *American Journal of Roentgenology* 51, pp 359-363

Fawcett E 1938, 'The Sexing of the Human Sacrum', *Journal of Anatomy* 72, p 633

Ferembach D, Schwidetzky I & Stloukal M 1980, 'Recommendations for age and sex diagnoses of skeletons', *Journal of Human Evolution* 9, pp 517-549

Fernie E 1993, *An Architectural History of Norwich Cathedral*, Oxford

Finnegan M 1976, 'Cervical ribs related to disuse atrophy in an archaic skeleton (490 BC): a preliminary report', *Paleopathology Newsletter* 15, pp 8-10

Fiorato V, Boylston A & Knüsel C 2001, *Blood Red Roses: The Archaeology of a Mass Grave from the Battle of Towton AD 1461*, Oxbow Monograph, Oxford

Fitter R S R 1945, *London's Natural History*, Collins, London

French T 1995, *York Minster: the great east window, Corpus Vitrearum Medii Aevi*, Summary Catalogue 2, Oxford University Press for the British Academy, Oxford

Fretton W G 1876, 'The Benedictine Monastery and Cathedral of Coventry', *Transactions of the Archaeological Section of the Birmingham and Midland Institute*

Gallacher D B 1994, 'The planning of Augustinian Monasteries in Scotland', in Locock M P (ed), *Meaningful Architecture: Social Interpretations of Buildings*, Worldwide Archaeology Series 9, pp 167-87.

Getty R 1975, *Sisson and Grossman's The Anatomy of the Domestic Animals 1&2'*, (5th edn), W B Saunders Company, Philadelphia

Gilchrist R & Mytum H (eds) 1993, *Advances in Monastic Archaeology*, BAR: British Series 227, Oxford

Gilchrist R 1995, 'Animal Bones', in Soden I 1995, *Excavations at St. Anne's Charterhouse, Coventry, 1968-87*, Coventry Museums Monograph 4, pp 78-80

Gill M 1999, 'The role of images in monastic education: the evidence from wall paintings in late medieval England', in Ferzoco G & Muessig C 1999, *Medieval Monastic Education*, Continuum for Leicester University Press, London & New York

Gill M & Morris R K 2001, 'A Wall Painting of the Apocalypse in Coventry Rediscovered', *The Burlington Magazine* 143/1181, pp 467-473

Gimpel J 1980, *The Cathedral Builders*

Gladstone R J & Wakeley C P G 1932, 'Cervical ribs and rudimentary first thoracic ribs considered from the clinical and etiological standpoints', *Journal of Anatomy* 66, pp 334-370

Godwin H 1967, 'The ancient cultivation of hemp', *Antiquity* 41, pp 42-137

Gooder E 1984, 'The finds from the Old Hall, Temple Balsall, Warwickshire', *Post-Medieval Archaeology* 18, pp 149-249

Green F 1979, 'Phosphate Mineralisation of Seeds from Archaeological Sites', *Journal of Archaeological Science* 6, pp 279-284

Greene J P 2001, 'Strategies for Future Research and Site Investigation', in Keevill G, Aston M & Hall T (eds) 2001, *Monastic Archaeology*, Oxbow, Oxford, pp 4-8

Grigson C 1982, 'Sex and age determination of some bones and teeth of domestic cattle: a review of the literature', in Wilson B, Grigson C & Payne S (eds) 1982, *Ageing and Sexing Animal Bones from Archaeological Sites*, BAR British Series 10, pp 7-23

Harley L S 1974, 'A typology of brick', *Journal of the British Archaeological Association*

Harvey J 1974, *Cathedrals of England and Wales*, Batsford, London

Harvey B 1995, *Living and Dying in England 1100–1540*, Oxford, Clarendon Press

Hensinger R N 1989, 'Spondylolysis and spondylolisthesis in children and adolescents', *Journal of Bone and Joint Surgery* 71A, pp 1098-110

Hill M O, Mountford J O, Roy D B & Bunce R G H 1999, *Ellenberg's Indicator Values for British plants*, ECOFACT 2: Technical Annex, HMSO

Hirst S M, Walsh D A & Wright S M 1983, *Bordesley Abbey II*, BAR British Series 3

Hobley B 1971, 'Excavations at the Cathedral and Benedictine Priory of St Mary, Coventry', *Transactions of the Birmingham and Warwickshire Archaeological Society* 84, 45-139.

Holmes J M 1981, 'Report on the animal bones from the resonance chambers of the Whitefriars church, Coventry', in Woodfield C 1981, 'Finds from the Free Grammar School at the Whitefriars church, Coventry, c1545-1557/8', *Post-medieval Archaeology* 15, pp 126-53

Howe E 2001, 'Divine kingship and dynastic display: The altar wall murals of St Stephen's Chapel, Westminster', *Antiquaries Journal* 81, pp 259-303.

Hunt T 1992, *The Medieval Surgery*, The Boydell Press, Woodbridge

Hurst J G, Neal D S & Van Beuningen 1986, *Pottery produced and traded in north-west Europe 1350-1650*, Rotterdam Papers VI. Museum Boymans van Beuningen.

Huskisson E C & Dudley Hart F 1987, *Joint Disease: All the Arthropathies*, Wright, Bristol

Ingram R W (ed) 1981, *Coventry*, Manchester University Press for University of Toronto Press, Toronto, Buffalo, London

Jacomet S 1987, *Prehistorische Getreidefunde*, Botanisches Institut der Universitat Abteilung Pflanzensystematik und Geobotanik, Basel

Jit I, Jhingan V & Kulharni M 1980, 'Sexing the Human Sternum', *American Journal of Physical Anthropology* 53, pp 217-224

Kauffmann, C M 1968, *An Altarpiece of the Apocalypse*, HMSO, London

Keevill G, Aston M & Hall T (eds) 2001, *Monastic Archaeology*, Oxbow, Oxford

Kerr N W 1989, 'A method of assessing periodontal status in archaeologically derived skeletal material', *Journal of Paleopathology* 2, pp 67-78

Ladenheim J C (trans) 1989, *Leonard of Bertapaglia: On Nerve Injuries and Skull Fractures*, Futura Publishing Company Inc, New York

Lambert M W 1971, 'The History of the Benedictine Priory of St Mary, Coventry' in Hobley B 1971, 'Excavations at the Cathedral and Benedictine Priory of St Mary, Coventry', *Transactions of the Birmingham and Warwickshire Archaeological Society* 84, pp 50-78

Lanier R R 1944, 'Length of first, twelfth and accessory ribs in American whites and negroes; their relationship to certain vertebral variations', *American Journal of Physical Anthropology* 2, pp 137-146

Lewis S 1995, *Reading Images. Narrative Discourse and Reception in the Thirteenth-Century Illuminated Apocalypse*, Cambridge University Press, Cambridge

Libois R M, Hallet-Libois C & Rosoux R 1987, 'Éléments pour l'identification des restes crâniens des poissons DulÇaquicoles de Belgiquie et du Nord de la France 1 – *Anguilliformes, Gastéiformes, Cyprinodontiformes et Perciformes*', *Fiches D'Ostéologie Animale Pour L'Archaéologie* 3, Centre de Recherches Archéologiques – CNRS, France

Libois R M & Hallet-Libois C 1988, 'Éléments pour l'identification des restes crâniens des poissons DulÇaquicoles de Belgiquie et du Nord de la France 2 – *Cypriniformes*', *Fiches D'Ostéologie Animale Pour L'Archaéologie* 4, Centre de Recherches Archéologiques – CNRS, France

Litten J 1991, *The English Way of Death*

Lilley K D 1994, 'Coventry's Topographical Development: the Impact of the Priory', in Demidowicz G (ed) 1994, *Coventry's First Cathedral*, Paul Watkins, Stamford, pp 72-96

Lilley K D 1998, 'Trading Places: Monastic Initiative and the Development of High Medieval Coventry', in Slater T & Rosser G (eds) 1998, *The Church in the Medieval Town*

Locker A 2001, *The Role of Stored Fish in England 900-1750 AD; the Evidence from Historical and Archaeological Data*, Ph.D. Thesis, University of Southampton (Archaeology Department), Publishing Group Limited, Sofia, Bulgaria.

Locock M 1995, *Medieval Tiles from St James's Priory, Dudley*, Swansea

Locock M 1999, 'Animal bones and the urban economy: 30 years of archaeozoology in Coventry', in S Anderson (ed) 1999, *Current and Recent Research in Osteoarchaeology* 2, Proceedings of the Fourth, Fifth & Sixth Meetings of the Osteoarchaeological Research Group, pp 12-16

Lovejoy C O, Meindl R S, Pryzbeck T R & Mensforth P 1985, 'Chronological Metamorphosis of the Articular Surface of the Ilium: a New Method for the Determination of Adult Skeletal Age', *American Journal of Physical Anthropology* 68, pp 15-28

Marks R 1993, *Stained Glass in England during the Middle Ages*, Routledge, London

Mayer J J & Brisbin I L 1988, 'Sex identification of *Sus scrofa* based on canine morphology', *Journal of Mammalogy* 69 (2), pp 408-412

Mayes P & Scott K 1984, *Pottery Kilns at Chilvers Coton, Nuneaton*, Society for Medieval Archaeology Monograph 10

Mays S 1991, *The Medieval Burials from The Blackfriars Friary, School Street, Ipswich, Suffolk (excavated 1983-85)*, Ancient Monuments Laboratory Report 16/91

Martin R 1928, *Lehrbuch der Anthropologie*, (2nd edn), Gustav Fischer, Jena

Moffett L 1991, 'The archaeobotanical evidence for free-threshing tetraploid wheat in Britain', in Hajnalová I E (ed) 1991, 'Palaeoethnobotany & Archaeology', *Acta Interdisciplinaria Archaeologica* 7, Nitra, pp 233-243

Moore M K, Stewart J H & McCormick W F 1988, 'Anomalies of the human chest plate area', *American Journal of Forensic Medicine and Pathology* 9, pp 348-354

Morris G 1990, 'Animal bone and shell', in Ward S W 1990, *Excavations at Chester – The lesser medieval religious houses*, Chester City Council Department of Leisure Services, pp 178-190

Morris R K 1992, 'An English Glossary of Medieval Mouldings', *Architectural History* 35, pp 11-15

Morris R K 1994, 'The Lost Cathedral Priory Church of St Mary, Coventry', in Demidowicz G 2000, *Coventry's First Cathedral*, Paul Watkins, Stamford, pp 17- 66

Morris R K (forthcoming), 'Hulton Abbey, Staffordshire: The Architecture and the Worked Stones', in Klemperer W D & Boothroyd N (eds), *Hulton Abbey, Staffordshire: Excavations 1987-1994*, Medieval Archaeology Monograph

Newdick J 1979, *The Complete Freshwater Fishes of the British Isles*, London, Adam & Charles Black

Noddle B 1986, 'Animal bone', in Bateman J & Redknap M 1986, *Coventry: Excavations on the town wall, 1976-8*, Coventry Museums Monograph 2, pp 100-119

Noppen J G 1932, 'The Westminster Apocalypse and its source', *The Burlington Magazine* 41, pp 146-59

North J J 1960, *English Hammered Coinage* 2, London

Oakey N & Andrews P 1998, 'Coventry, Cathedral Priory Church of St Mary', *Church Archaeology* 2, pp 61-63

O'Connell L 1999, *The Human Skeletal Remains from Coventry Cathedral*, Bournemouth University

Ogden M S (ed) 1971, *The Cyrurgie of Guy de Chauliac*, Early English Text Society 265, Oxford University Press

Page W (ed) 1965, *The Victoria History of the County of Warwick* 2, Dawsons, London

Pantin W A 1937, *Documents illustrating the activities of the general and provincial chapters of the English Black Monks 1215-1540* 3, Camden Society Third Series 54

Parsons F G 1916, 'On the Proportions and Characteristics of the Modern English Clavicle', *Journal of Anatomy* 48, pp 238-267

Payne S 1985, 'Morphological distinctions between mandibular teeth of young sheep (Ovis) and goat (Capra)', *Journal of Archaeological Science* 12, pp 139-147

Pearson K & Bell J 1919, 'A Study of the Long Bones of the English Skeleton. I The Femur', *Drapers Company Memoirs Biometrics Series* 10, pp 1-224

Perry J G (forthcoming), *Excavations on Derby Lane, Coventry, 1982-4*

Phenice T W 1969, 'A Newly Developed Method of Sexing the Os Pubis', *American Journal of Physical Anthropology* 30, pp 297-302

Pierce J E, Vince A G & Jenner M A 1985, 'Medieval Pottery: London-Type Ware', *London and Middlesex Archaeological Society* 1985

Poole B 1870, *The History and Antiquities of Coventry*

Pretty J N 1989, 'Sustainable Agriculture in the Middle Ages: The English Manor', *Agricultural History Review* 38, pp 1-19

Purves R K & Wedin P H 1950, 'Familial incidence of cervical ribs', *Journal of Thoracic Surgery* 19, pp 952-956

Reader W 1823, *New Coventry Guide*

Redknap M & Perry J G 1996, 'The pottery', in Rylatt M & Stokes M 1996, *The Excavations at Broadgate East, Coventry 1974-5*, Coventry Museums Monograph 5

Reilly L 1997, *An Architectural History of Peterborough Cathedral*

Resnick D & Niwayama G 1981, *Diagnosis of Bone and Joint Disorders*, W B Saunders, Philadelphia

Rigold S 1977, 'Romanesque Bases in and South East of the Limestone Belt', in Apted N *et al* (eds) 1977, *Ancient Monuments and their Interpretation*, London & Chichester, pp 99-138

Rogers J 2000, 'The Palaeopathology of Joint Disease', in Cox M & Mays S (eds) 2000, *Human Osteology in Archaeology and Forensic Science*, Greenwich Medical Media, London, pp 163-182

Rogers J, Watt I & Dieppe P 1981, 'Arthritis in Saxon and Medieval Skeletons', *British Medical Journal* 283, pp 1668-1670

Rowell R (forthcoming), 'An Archaeology of Hospitality: The Stoneleigh Abbey Gatehouse', in Bearman R (ed), *Stoneleigh Abbey*, Shakespeare Birthplace Trust and Stoneleigh Abbey Ltd

Rowling M 1968, *Everyday Life in Medieval Times*, Batsford Ltd, London

Rylatt M 1977, *City of Coventry: Archaeology and Development*, Coventry Museums Monograph 1

Rylatt M & Soden 1987, 'Excavations at St Mary's Cathedral, Coventry', *West Midlands Archaeology* 30, p 66

Rylatt M & Soden I 1990, 'Hay Lane Coventry', *West Midlands Archaeology* 33, pp 92-94

Rylatt M 1994, 'Revisiting the Archaeological Evidence for the Priory', in Demidowicz G (ed) 1994, *Coventry's First Cathedral*, Paul Watkins, Stamford, pp 67-71

Rylatt M & Stokes M E 1996, *The Excavations at Broadgate East, Coventry 1974-5*, Coventry Museums Monograph 5

Sandler L F 1986, *Gothic Manuscripts 1285-1385* (2 vols), A Survey of Manuscripts illuminated in the British Isles 5, Harvey Miller and OUP, Oxford

Scarisbrick J J 1994, 'The Dissolution of St Mary's Priory, Coventry', in Demidowicz G (ed) 1994, *Coventry's First Cathedral*, Paul Watkins, Stamford, pp 158-68

Shaw M 1996, 'The Green, Northampton', *Post- Medieval Archaeology* 30

Shelton J B 1935, 'Priory Pool and District', *Austins Monthly Magazine* 27/ 331

Silver I A 1971,'The ageing of domestic animals', in Brothwell D & Higgs E (eds) 1971, *Science in Archaeology: A Survey of Progress and Research*, London, Thames and Hudson, pp 283-302

Singh H K 1973, 'Incidence of Congenital Rib Anomalies', *Indian Journal of Chest Diseases* 15, pp 157-164

Smith F 1946, Coventry – Six hundred years of municipal life

Soden I 1995, Excavations at St Anne's Charterhouse, Coventry, 1968-87, Coventry Museums Monograph 4

Stace C 1997, *New Flora of the British Isles*, (2nd edn), Cambridge University Press

Steele D G 1976, 'The Estimation of Sex on the Bias of the Talus and Calcaneus', *American Journal of Physical Anthropology* 45, pp 581-588

Stephens W B 1969, *A History of the County of Warwick* 8, Oxford University Press, London

Stirland A 1996, 'Patterns of Trauma in a Unique Medieval Parish Cemetery', *International Journal of Osteoarchaeology* 6, pp 92-100

Stroud G 1993, 'The Human Bones', in Stroud G & Kemp R L 1993, *Cemeteries of the Church and Priory of St Andrew, Fishergate,* York Archaeological Trust 12/2, York, pp 160-241

Taylor H M & Taylor J 1965, *Anglo-Saxon Architecture* 1

Trotter M & Gleser G C 1958, 'A re-evaluation of estimation of stature based on measurements of stature taken during life and long bones after death', *American Journal of Physical Anthropology* 16, pp 79-123

Turner B 1985 'The patronage of John of Northampton. Further studies of the wall-paintings in Westminster Chapter House', *Journal of the British Archaeological Association* 138, pp 89-100

Ubelaker D H 1984, *Human Skeletal Remains, Excavation, Analysis and Interpretation*, Taraxacum, Washington

Waldron T 1987, 'DISH at Merton', in Capecchi V & Rabino Massa E (eds) 1987, *Proceedings of the 5th European Meeting of the Paleopathological Association, 1984*, Paleopathology Association, Siena, pp 373-378

Wall S M 1980, 'The animal bones from the excavation of the hospital of St Mary of Ospringe', *Archaeologia Cantiana* 96, pp 227-266

West B A 1982, 'Spur development: recognising caponised fowl in archaeological material', in Wilson B, Grigson C & Payne S (eds) 1982, *Ageing and Sexing Animal Bones from Archaeological Sites*, BAR British Series 109, pp 255-261

West B A 1985, 'Chicken legs revisited', *Circaea* 3/1, pp 11 – 14

Weston W J 1956, 'Genetically Determined Cervical Ribs: a Familial Study', British *Journal of Radiology* 29, pp 455-456

Wheeler A 1977, 'Fish bone', in Clarke H & Carter A 1977, *Excavations in King's Lynn 1963-1970*, Society for Medieval Archaeology Monograph Series 7, pp 403-408

Whitcomb N R 1956, *The Medieval Floor Tiles of Leicestershire,* Leicester Archaeological and Historical Society, Leicester

Wilson C 1998, 'The Stellar Vaults of Glasgow Cathedral's Inner Crypt and Villard de Honnecourt's Chapter-House Plan: A Conundrum Re-visited', in Fawcett R (ed) 1998, *Medieval Art and Architecture in the Diocese of Glasgow*, British Archaeological Association Conference Transactions 23, Leeds, pp 55-76

Woodfield C C 1981, 'Finds from the Free Grammar School at the Whitefriars, Coventry', *Post-Medieval Archaeology* 15, pp 81-159

Woodfield C C (forthcoming), *Excavations at Whitefriars, Coventry, 1963-78*

Wright A 1996, 'Animal Bone', in Rylatt M & Stokes M 1996, *The Excavations at Broadgate East, Coventry 1974-5*, Coventry Museums Monograph 5, pp 121-4

Wright S 1986, 'Much Park Street, Coventry: the development of a medieval street. Excavations 1970-74', *Transactions of the Birmingham and Warwickshire Archaeological Society* 92

4. Unpublished Secondary Sources

Anderson T, 'The Human Bones', in Chapman A (in prep), *Excavations at Brackmills*, Northamptonshire Archaeology Report

Armitage P L 1977, *The Mammalian Remains from the Tudor Site of Baynard's Castle, London: A Biometrical and Historical Analysis*, Ph.D. Thesis: Royal Holloway College & British Museum (Natural History)

Armitage P 2000, 'Faunal Remains', in Soden I 2000, *St Peter's Walk, Northampton: Archaeological excavations on Woolmonger Street 1994-7*, Northamptonshire Archaeology Report

Carruthers W 1997, 'Plant Remains' & 'Wood Identification', in Hawkes J W & Fasham P J 1997, *Excavations on Reading Waterfront Sites 1979-88*, Wessex Archaeology Report 5, pp 62-64 & 78-94

Carruthers W 2000, 'The mineralised plant remains', in Lawson A J & Gingell C J 2000, *Potterne 1982-5: animal husbandry in later prehistoric Wiltshire.* Wessex Archaeology Report 17, pp 72-84 & 91-95

Dickinson J E 1992, *Excavations at 114-115 Gosford Street, Coventry*, Coventry Museums Archaeological Unit Report

Flitcroft M 1997, *Coventry's Millennium Project: Initial Appraisal of Archaeological Implications*, Coventry Museums Archaeological Report 20

Hallam T 2000, *Excavations in the Frater Undercroft, St Mary's Benedictine Priory, Coventry*, Northamptonshire Archaeology Report

Lloyd R 2000, 'Mammal and bird bone', in Hallam, T 2000, *Excavations of the Frater Undercroft, St. Mary's, Coventry*, Northamptonshire Archaeology Report, pp 20-24

Lloyd R 2001, 'Mammal and Bird Bone' in Soden I 2001, *Excavations on St Mary's Cathedral Church, Coventry*, Northamptonshire Archaeology Report, pp 29-33

Locock M 1992, 'The Animal Bone', in Rylatt M, Soden I & Dickinson J E 1992, *Excavations at Cheylesmore Manor, Coventry*, Coventry Museums Archaeological Unit Report, pp 49-54

Rylatt M & Thompson P 1998, *An archaeological investigation of the north nave wall of St Mary's Cathedral Church, Coventry*, Coventry Museums Archaeological Unit Report

Soden I 1990, *Excavations at St Mary's Benedictine Priory 1989-90*, Coventry Museums Archaeological Unit Report

Soden I 1991, *The archaeological implications of major redevelopment of the old Standard Car Factory, Canley, Coventry*, Coventry Museums Archaeological Unit Report

Soden I 2001, *Excavations at the Cathedral Church of St Mary, Coventry 1999-2000 Summary Report*, Northamptonshire Archaeology

Thompson P & Lewis M 1999, *Excavation of GR5, Blue Coat School, Priory Row, Coventry*, Coventry Museums Archaeological Unit Report 99/43